Praise for *The Maverick Mountaineer*

Winner of *The Times* Biography of the Year Prize, Cross British Sports Book Awards 2017

'[A] compelling biography … As a study of a man whose greatness we would do well to remember and applaud, it sparkles.'
The Independent

'Wainwright has done a fine job of rescuing his protagonist from the footnotes of climbing history.'   *The Telegraph*

'Robert Wainwright has conjured up the rasp of crampons on sheet ice, the taste of peaches eaten from the tin, and the bitchiness endemic among the frozen-bearded tribe of climbers and explorers.'   *The Spectator*

'The best passages … are those that describe the battle of scientific progress against entrenched snobbery – a fight that may have cost Finch the chance to stand on top of the world, but ought to be remembered.'   *The Economist*

Praise for *Sheila*

'This splendid biography evokes the glamour of a vanished age.'
Mail on Sunday

'A marvellously entertaining story.'   *Daily Express*

'Sheila Chisholm's story is well worth disinterring, and it's undeniably enjoyable to read of all that glitter and gold.'
Selina Hastings, *The Spectator*

'The charm of Wainwright's biography is that he makes us see what an engaging, admirable and sometimes heroic quality it is to be a life-enhancer like Sheila.'   *Daily Mail*

MISS MURIEL MATTERS

The Fearless Suffragist who Fought for Equality

ROBERT WAINWRIGHT

ALLEN&UNWIN

First published in Australia by HarperCollins*Publishers* Australia Pty Ltd in 2017
First published in Great Britain in 2017 by Allen & Unwin

This paperback edition published in Great Britain in 2018 by Allen & Unwin

Allen & Unwin
c/o Atlantic Books
Ormond House
26–27 Boswell Street
London WC1N 3JZ

Phone: 020 7269 1610
Fax: 020 7430 0916

Email: UK@allenandunwin.com
Web: www.allenandunwin.com/uk

A CIP catalogue record of this book is available from the British Library.

Paperback ISBN 978 1 76063 268 7
E-book ISBN 978 1 92557 674 0

Typeset by Kirby Jones in Adobe Caslon Pro
Printed in Italy by Grafica Veneta

10 9 8 7 6 5 4 3 2 1

To my daughters Rosie and Allegra,
their generation and those to come

Contents

PROLOGUE

The woman in the thick green coat and jaunty driving cap stamped her feet and danced in circles. To the huddle of reporters and photographers watching nearby, it looked like some sort of crude flamenco, but Muriel Matters was simply cold, and probably a little nervous, and a little jig might just keep her warm.

It was just after 1.00 pm on February 16, 1909 and the temperature hovered around freezing by the banks of the Welsh Harp Reservoir near Hendon in north London. Despite the cold, the journalists and a clutch of onlookers had gathered to watch an historic moment in political campaigning and the fledgling world of aviation.

Although the area had been used on and off for fifty years by aeronautical companies for experimental flights, scientific journeys and even tethered balloon rides for picnickers, this would be the first time that a powered aircraft had taken off from the green expanse that would become integral to the city's wartime defences.

And a young woman whose feet had never left the ground was preparing to take to the skies. The plan to drop hundreds of 'Votes for Women' leaflets on the head of King Edward VII as he sat in his golden carriage trotting down The Mall to open the new session of parliament seemed crazy. But what a story!

Like many historic moments, opinion would be divided about its sanity. Was this lady naive, reckless and foolhardy or a brave crusader? In truth, Muriel Matters fell somewhere in between; the thrill of the ride and the sense that what she was doing was necessary and would make a difference to others was more powerful than the fear of physical harm.

It would be 5 degrees cooler once they were aloft, hence the layers of heavy clothes beneath Muriel's coat. Other than the cold, though, the weather was favourable: bright, clear skies with a forecast of light to moderate winds out of the north – hence the need to take off from this side of the Thames. It would have been impossible to take off south of the river and try to fly into the prevailing wind toward the city. Even Hendon wasn't perfect, lying slightly north-west of the city centre, but there were few possible launch sites, highlighting the nascent and precarious nature of aviation.

Muriel looked over toward the airship, stretched out like a cigar with what appeared to be the foresail of a yacht at the rear to act as a rudder. The balloon was adorned with the slogan *Votes for Women* in huge lettering, so it could be seen from the ground, and streamers in the Women's Freedom League colours of white, gold and green would trail behind.

The framework beneath the balloon was a different matter, a skeletal scaffold of wires, ashwood and bamboo with a wicker gondola slung in the middle barely big enough for two people to squeeze into. Comfort was not an option in a design for as little weight as possible.

She focused on the man scurrying around the airship. Henry Spencer, the pilot, looked a bundle of nerves checking the struts and ties and engine, which seemed tiny for its job of driving the airship in a series of yacht-like manoeuvres across the prevailing winds to position it over the Houses of Parliament as the King's procession made its approach.

As she watched and waited, Muriel might have reflected on her incredible life transformation. It seemed only yesterday that she was in the city of Adelaide on the other side of the world, enjoying the plaudits of critics as an aspiring actress, an elocutionist who could hold the attention of audiences for hours as she recited great dramatic verses. She had travelled across the world in pursuit of those dreams, had been welcomed in some of London's great entertainment venues but then decided she had a greater calling than footlight fame, a calling for which she was prepared to risk her life.

It was almost 1.30 pm, lift-off time if they were going to get south to Westminster and greet the King's carriage. Several men moved forward, loaded the bundle of pamphlets and then lifted Muriel into the basket while a dozen more clung onto ropes attached to the framework to steady the ship.

But there was a problem. The motor wouldn't start. All Muriel could do was busy herself, stacking the pile of pamphlets neatly and fastening her hat to her head with a scarf tied beneath her chin. She smiled and posed for the cameras, a megaphone clasped casually in gloved hands. In the background Henry Spencer looked on anxiously.

Finally, after furious minutes of tinkering, the engine spluttered into life and the giant ship lifted slowly into the air. Muriel Matters had taken flight.

1.

THE COW LADY OF BOWDEN

Mary Matters, a widow with four children and an ageing
mother, wrote asking permission to depasture her cow on
the parklands free of charge. Communications favourable to
the request were received from Mrs Gawler and Dr Whittell.
Referred to finance committee.

— South Australian Register, August 10, 1862

The request made of the Adelaide Municipal Council seemed
reasonable enough. Even a neighbour, a Mrs Gawler, and a
respected GP, Horatio Whittell, a man of 'high character, integrity
and ability', according to the same newspaper, felt compelled to
support Mrs Matters' case for recognition of hardship, but the men
of the council took a different view.

As trifling a matter as it appeared to be for a council in charge of
a growing city, the widow's request was shunted off to a committee
where it would be denied out of hand, the august body of gentlemen
deaf to the plea of an enterprising woman with no husband that she
be allowed to feed her only asset – a cow – on public land, even
though it would help keep the grass down.

It was a mean-spirited decision by the male political elders
of a colonial city supposedly rooted in a spirit of entrepreneurial

endeavour and equity. The travails and challenges of a widow seemed to have no bearing on their considerations. If anything, it annoyed them that a woman would seek to challenge laws enacted by men.

Adelaide, capital of the freely settled colony of South Australia, had been founded less than three decades before, designed by the Surveyor-General Colonel William Light in a grid pattern on either side of the Torrens River: broad avenues, narrower streets and public squares surrounded by great parklands filled with trees that would help keep the air clean, in contrast to the poor light and dank, polluted air that permeated most overcrowded European cities.

The genius of Light's design was matched by the utopian impulses fuelling both his garden city's construction and the settlement of the colony. Adelaide was not to be built on the back of convict labour, like the east coast capitals of Sydney and Melbourne, but as a free settlement, financed by selling investment parcels of land to the wealthy in faraway Britain. The proceeds from the sales (to largely absentee landlords) would fund the cost of shipping a ready-made working-class population from the United Kingdom to build the new city.

'The great experiment in the art of colonisation' was considered an immediate success. The initial land release sold quickly and a campaign was launched in London to lure settlers across the seas with promises of a paradise: a new society that championed civil liberties, tolerance and religious freedom, far from the human crush and crime-filled streets of the Mother Country. So bright was this beacon that no jail had been planned, let alone built, for the city named by William IV after his German wife.

Free passage was offered to men aged under forty-five, single or married, who were skilled farm labourers, shepherds or copper miners, interested in living and working in the rich agricultural regions opening up outside the city. There was also room for men good with their hands who could help build the city that was fast rising from the riverbanks – bricklayers, stonemasons, farriers, gardeners, sawyers, carpenters, mechanics, wheelwrights and the like, provided they were 'sober, industrious, of general good moral character ... free of all bodily and mental defects'.[1]

Women were welcome too, single or married, particularly those with experience as domestic servants, farm girls, plain cooks or nurses. A letter from the Bishop of Adelaide offering advice to emigrants to the colony painted a rosy picture: 'Wages are high and there is no fear of starvation,' he wrote. 'Respectable servant girls are sure to find employment.' There was even the enticement of land ownership, via a scheme under which a man could buy his own plot of land and put aside wages to pay it off.

In 1852, Mary Matters and her husband, Thomas, heeded the call, leaving a settled if crowded life in the port city of Plymouth to start afresh. Thomas was a 32-year-old stonemason with the ideal combination of youth and trade experience required in the fledgling community.

His wife, although six years older, fitted the criteria for 'acceptable' women. Mary was the eldest of twelve children of a struggling Devon farm worker. With little chance of an education, she had followed her mother into domestic service and helped raise her siblings, and was thirty-three before she found a husband.

The marriage certificate sheds no light on how Mary Adams met Thomas Matters. They lived in towns fifty kilometres apart and their families had no obvious connection. The only link appears to be religion, both families being devout followers of the Methodist philosophy of John Wesley. It would be a driving moral force for several future generations.

Mary had only stopped working after the birth of her third child, a daughter to follow two sons, which meant financial pressure was growing as much as the family's need for space, crammed as they were into three rooms of a five-room house near the city docks. A fresh start seemed a godsend and too good to refuse, even if it was on the other side of the world.

Mary wasn't the only member of her family to emigrate. A younger brother, John, had already left for South Australia, and three unwed sisters and her widowed mother would follow a few months later. Another brother would settle in New Zealand and a third in Victoria.

On August 24 Thomas and Mary packed their children – Charles, Thomas and baby Mary – along with a small bundle of clothing and personal effects and joined 339 other souls aboard the three-masted barque *Sea Park* to set sail for the unknown.[2] It was the seventy-ninth such government-funded ship to make the trip carrying the future citizens of Adelaide, whose population now stood at about 50,000. Most of the family's belongings had to be left behind, traded for a new beginning. They would never return.

* * *

Mary had turned forty by the time the family stepped ashore in Adelaide almost four months later. Port Adelaide, where the *Sea Park* lay at anchor, must have appeared a little like Plymouth, with its bustle and grime, but nothing else gave the family any sense of being in the soft environs and gentle light of England.

They had arrived in the early heat of an Australian summer, into a landscape they could not have imagined with its open spaces, wild glaring skies and remorseless sunshine. Here the roads were dry and dusty, the fine, pale sand blown by hot, swirling winds.

Men working outside hid beneath large straw hats to keep the baking sun from their faces and spoke with a strange 'independence of manners', a frankness that jarred British sensibilities.[3]

Yet it was clearly a place of prospect and plenty, the storehouses in the centre of the now bustling city stocked with an abundance of fruit and vegetables – grapes, tomatoes, plums, peaches, apples and more. The talk in the streets was of opportunity rather than hardship, and of mineral and grazing riches beyond the blue-grey hills that ringed the mangroves and the coastal plain on which the city had been so carefully placed.

It was also a blessed relief to be free of the squalid living conditions and putrid food aboard ship, for there was great sadness amid the excitement and anticipation of their arrival, a few weeks before Christmas. Mary's infant namesake daughter was among the fourteen babies and young children who had died from infection and illness at sea. By contrast there had been nine births.

And Mary was pregnant again, the conception almost certainly occurring on August 23, the night before the family sailed from Plymouth – a celebration of a new life ahead in so many ways.

The welcome was promising. In the first days after arrival, families like the Matters were housed in cottages along the harbour foreshore and the 'Stranger Friend Society' was on hand to relieve distress among the newly arrived. It all seemed too good to be true. Thomas secured work within days, and the family leased a house constructed of pisé, a form of rammed earth, with a dirt floor and tin roof, in the village of Bowden on the northern fringe of the city. The small outpost had been roughly cleared and chopped up into irregular lots set along nameless streets.

The lease came with the inducement of the prospect of securing a mortgage to buy the modest, four-room house, squeezed onto its tiny allotment, perhaps as small as one-sixteenth of an acre and sized to maximise profit for its developer rather than create amenity for the lessee. The Matters' neighbours were labourers and tradespeople: tanners, millers, lime-burners and bricklayers with skills but little money, grateful for the work and security that sprang from a city still largely under construction.

Few would make the change from lessee to landowner. A developer named Eckley owned 117 properties in Bowden and the rest were held by half a dozen individuals. Families made the homes their own by planting fruit trees and vines and digging tiny vegetable plots into the bushland, creating a little Europe amid the native wattles and gums, mallees, myrtles and quandongs. Pigs and goats wandered freely in the village that soon had five hotels, a dozen stores, a collection of brickworks and tanneries and even a modest schoolhouse.[4]

In May 1853 Mary gave birth to a third son, John Leonard, a renewal of sorts and an event that went some way to ease the pain of her baby daughter's death. But life was fragile and the fates cruel. In February 1857, barely four years after arriving in the colony, Thomas Matters was dead from gastric fever. He was just thirty-seven. The funeral notice would say it had been sudden, the stonemason passing away at home after a 'short illness'. A fortnight later his grieving widow gave birth to their fourth child – another son. The promise of a new, wondrous life had now turned to despair.

Although Mary had familial support, resources would not stretch to financial help because her sisters and mother were living hand to mouth. Nor could her brother John, who had his own family to feed, spare any money. At the age of forty-five, with four young children and no likely marriage prospects, Mary Matters was on her own in a city that wanted contributors, not passengers.

The cow therefore took on an extra significance, bought from the little money Mary could scrape together and symbolic of her resourcefulness and determination amid the setbacks of colonial life.

* * *

On a clear, bright summer morning in late 1865, a man climbed the rickety scaffolding around the almost completed Adelaide Town Hall. He carried a heavy bag and tripod, and on reaching the top braced himself, faced north and began to take photographs. For the next hour or so, Townsend Duryea, an American mining engineer turned photographer, carefully made his way around the tower in an anti-clockwise fashion to avoid the sun's sharp rays shining into his lens while he took fourteen photographs, creating the world's first photographic panorama.[5]

The result showed the precision and success of the Adelaide experiment. Each point of the compass was dominated by a wide avenue, splitting rows of modest housing and timber-framed shopfronts, grand sandstone public buildings and neat parks of carefully planted trees that would one day spread to cover the flat landscape to help the city 'breathe'.

But behind the innovative photography lay another, more complex story. The system of land title, so carefully plotted, had been rorted and botched in the early years of the colony and had stunted its development until the Real Property Act, which would revolutionise land ownership not only in Adelaide but around the world, was passed in the South Australian parliament.

In the distance, just beyond the range of Duryea's camera, lay the ring of villages that would one day merge to become suburbs all the way to the sea. Among them was Bowden, where the Matters family lived, and the village of Croydon where 'Mary Matters of Bowden' had recently applied to have four housing allotments registered in her name under the new Torrens title system.

Croydon had been carved out of the bush by two investors who named it, as so many did, after their home town in England, but the land remained largely unsold because of the confusion about land ownership. Mary had seen her chance to acquire land cheaply and build a future for her family. Significantly, hers was the only female name on the registry.

Aged fifty, she had also established a small business run from her home, hand sewing hessian sacks that she sold to farmers to hold their produce. The business prospered, if slowly. There was more than a single cow too, the profits from sack-making poured into increasing the herd. By the mid 1860s she was described as a 'cow-keeper' in official documents when her animals occasionally strayed onto public verges and caught the attention of the ranger and she was dragged before the courts to face a fine of a few shillings and a lecture from a pious magistrate.

The land purchase would be a turning point in her life, and turn adversity into triumph. Through the next three decades she would buy and sell land and cottages, mainly in and around Bowden, using some to house family members and others to provide an income – 'a good stone house of four rooms let at 10s per week', as one newspaper advertisement would note.[6]

Mary would only move from Bowden in the later years of her life, buying a large house at Semaphore, within sight of the beach where the *Sea Park* had arrived with her young family, full of hope, more than three decades before. She had survived and thrived in spite of circumstances and social attitudes and raised four sons.

* * *

The true legacy of Mary Matters did not lie in a bank balance or a row of houses, a cow or a pile of hessian sacks, but in her determination for self-improvement, a desire apparently embedded in the religious ethos of her upbringing and carried not only into her own life but into those of her children and grandchildren.

Her father, Leonard Adams, may have been a struggling farm worker, but he was also a man of God, a follower of the founder of the Methodist Church, John Wesley, who preached personal accountability, championed social issues such as prison reform, railed against slavery in the United States and believed in a greater role for women in the Church. Mary held the same philosophies, and despite having no formal schooling herself, decided that it was important for her own children to benefit from a good education, even though, economically, sending her boys out to work would have made more sense in the early years of her widowhood.

She chose Whinham College, a school that had sprung from modest beginnings. John Whinham was a self-taught 'educationist' who had fallen on hard times and emigrated from England with his family in 1852. His school had begun simply enough, with a single student in a room, and would grow to be one of the most respected in Australia. At the time the Matters boys attended, it was still a relatively modest school in Ward Street, North Adelaide.

Whinham had a broad notion of the benefits of education. On his retirement, he would say: 'In education I have two main objects in view: the first is to try to enlist the sympathies of my pupils on the side of everything that is good and noble, and the other being to enlarge and cultivate their minds in everything appertaining to political and every-day life, so that they might be enabled to discharge the duties of social and civil life faithfully and well.'[7]

The Matters boys would take their opportunity with both hands. The eldest, Charles, would find his way into a banking career before opening an auction house as the possibilities for land development grew. His brothers Thomas, John and Richard would join him as the business expanded.

Charles would also rise in Adelaide's social and political circles, and would later move to Melbourne where he also made a name for himself. He stood for parliament and travelled widely in Europe, America and Japan, where he helped form the Welcome Society of Japan (Kihin-Kai) to promote international tourism with the west. Like his maternal grandfather, he took religion seriously and chaired an association of Methodist preachers. He wrote expansive articles for newspapers about his experiences and his diverse interests, which included being a devotee of the famed American horticulturalist Luther Burbank.[8]

Charles and, to a lesser extent, Thomas would not only have influence in an economic sense but in the social development of the city and the rights of its citizens. He and his wife, Hester Ann Jessop, would become heavily involved in the temperance movement, a favoured cause of Wesleyan Methodists.

In 1891 the couple would travel to England via America to undertake a study of social problems, particularly those caused by liquor laws. British newspapers noted the visit of the Australian contingent, mentioning their attendance at the annual conference of the Rechabite movement, which believed in total abstinence. Mrs Matters was said to have made 'a very neat little speech' in which she noted that a number of South Australian clubs and organisations now accepted female members, describing it as 'another great step in the process of giving the woman equality with the man'.

During the trip, the Matters would also meet with Millicent Fawcett, a leading light of the British women's suffrage movement, who later noted of the discussion: 'It would almost seem that

Australia will lead the way in this reform. Be that as it may, the progress on your side of the world is most gratifying and encouraging to us over here in the old world.'[9]

There was another who would be greatly influenced by the social reforms of the far-flung colonial outpost the Matters clan had made their home – Muriel, the teenage niece of Charles and Hester and granddaughter to Mary, the stubborn cow lady of Bowden.

2.

ROLE MODELS AND INSPIRATIONS

Illiteracy gave Muriel Lilah Matters the memorable name that would accompany her deeds in life. She would have been born with the surname Metters but for a spelling error by the priest who baptised her paternal grandfather, Thomas, the stonemason who would emigrate to Australia with his bride, Mary.

The mistake had been long forgotten by the time Muriel was born on November 12, 1877, delivered in the family cottage at Bowden. Outside, the city of Adelaide was finally beginning to fulfil its utopian promise. The Overland Telegraph had linked communications from Australia to London and the telephone was on its way; the city's engineers had forded the Torrens River with a decent traffic bridge and horse-drawn tramways would soon dominate the city centre.

Public health was improving with the completion of new facilities, including a children's hospital and the nation's first sewerage system. The arts were flourishing and becoming a feature of the city's life, as was education, with two tertiary institutions, both of which accepted enrolments from women.

John Matters was working as a cabinetmaker when his daughter was born, yet to join the family firm that would establish his two older brothers as leading citizens. His apprenticeship had been marred by a court appearance in 1872 in which he admitted using insulting language to his master, a Mr James Gibbs. It was clearly considered a serious offence in a society that demanded civility and the magistrate not only fined him £1 but warned that if it was repeated then he would be jailed. 'Oh, all right,' was the reported response of the young man, aged nineteen and described as 'son of Mary Matters, widow' as if he were still a juvenile.[1]

It was not his first brush with the law. At the age of ten, John had been caught hurling stones and shattering windows at an empty building near the city centre. He was fined and warned, the incident brushed off as typical of 'lads in the habit of amusing themselves',[2] but it would be an indication of John Matters' attitude to life; he was a gambler who struggled to settle and tended to ride on the coat-tails of his older brothers, Charles and Thomas.

On another occasion he became embroiled in a rape case as a witness and companion of the alleged perpetrator, the newspaper coverage of the case revealing the young man's somewhat nomadic existence in which he frequently travelled to small towns outside Adelaide seeking work. Even after he married and had a family, John was known to leave home for months at a time chasing mining riches, including investing in a silver mine that, like all of his early ventures, came to little or nothing.

It was in stark contrast to the steady rise of his older brothers, not only Charles but also Thomas, who had gone into business after leaving Whinham College, forming a partnership with a friend and building and operating a chaff mill near Port Adelaide, a half day's ride north-west of the city centre, where they produced horse feed. He later moved into civic affairs, employed as a district clerk until 1878 when he was recruited by Charles to help expand his real estate business, opening a branch in the port area of the city. Thomas would marry twice and have eight children, each announced triumphantly in the newspapers.

In 1874 John Matters had married Emma Warburton, daughter of a Welsh immigrant family. If his young bride ever had ambitions beyond motherhood they were drowned in a sea of children – five in as many years, including one death, before her husband ceased his meanderings, at least for a time, and settled down to take a job with C.H. Matters and Co. They would eventually have ten children – five girls and five boys – over twenty years,[3] Emma, as resourceful as her mother-in-law, would be the stoic rock of the family, covering for her frequently absent husband whom she stood by despite his errant ways.

Although they lived barely a mile from the bustling centre of the growing city, the family's modest cottage might as well have been in the middle of the bush. Muriel's brother Leonard would give a sense of their childhood in the introduction to a book he would write about his own adventures as a traveller and journalist. He wrote of learning to tell the time by the passage of the sun across the sky, of wandering through 'trackless scrub' and climbing into the lower reaches of the Adelaide Hills, exploring ravines and caves and getting caught in landslides. His wanderings were not appreciated at home, his muddied, ragged appearance after a day of exploring alarming his 'fond but overly anxious' mother and enraging a father who was wont to wander himself.[4]

Muriel, four years older, would also have a fraught relationship with her father, an authoritarian man whose word was law, a man not to be crossed who enforced rigid rules such as excluding younger children from eating at the table until they learned Victorian manners. Unlike most of her brothers and sisters, Muriel was prepared to stand up to his anger more often than not. He would mellow with age.

In 1884 the family moved to Port Augusta, a town built on mangrove swamps and the flat, sandy plains at the top of the Spencer Gulf, three-hundred kilometres north of Adelaide. Its streets were filled with teams of camels, donkeys, bullocks and mules hauling anything from food and wool bales to rolls of wire that would be used to mark the boundaries of the great pastoral leases. Progress had been stunted by drought, but the town's natural harbour and the fervour created by the discovery of mineral riches had ensured its survival. The Overland Telegraph had been connected in 1872 and in 1882 the railway to Adelaide was completed.

Despite its progress, Port Augusta was still something of an overgrown village when John Matters and his family arrived, and he quickly found himself elected to the local council. He established a chaff mill and attempted to promote the Matters family business, but became embroiled in several court cases, one involving alleged larceny by an employee and another claiming that a friend had borrowed and then lost one of his horses. He was unsuccessful in both matters.

But for all his shortcomings, John Matters would follow his mother's example and ensure that his children went to school. Records show that the older children – Elsie, Muriel (then aged seven) and Harold – were enrolled at the local school in 1885 and 1886.

The school had small, stuffy rooms, poor lighting and featured a teaching style that was more about berating than instruction. Fragile funding and a rollercoaster economy meant there were frequent teacher shortages and senior students were often called upon to fill in. But it was a start, not only for Muriel and her siblings, but perhaps of her attempts many years later to ameliorate the hardships of early childhood for families with little or no money.

The family's stay in Port Augusta would last just three years, cut short, it would seem, because of controversy over John's questionable sale of land 'at low tide', the details of which were never fully explained. In 1887 they scurried back to Adelaide and the bosom of the Matters family.

* * *

In years to come Muriel would nominate a play written by the Norwegian Henrik Ibsen as a defining influence in her life. She was given a copy of *A Doll's House* to read at the tender age of fourteen, when most young ladies were probably more familiar with more dutiful literary heroines, like Charles Dickens' Amy Dorrit and Jane Austen's Anne Elliot.

Ibsen's play had a different message – one of independence and achievement outside marriage – and one that Muriel's literary sponsor considered her intelligent and curious enough to appreciate, even though she was too young to attend performances of the controversial work when its production divided Australian audiences (and audiences around the world) because of its apparent nod to the women's suffrage movement.

The three-act play tells the story of Nora, who leaves her husband and three children to discover her own identity: 'A woman cannot be herself in modern society,' Ibsen would explain in notes to the play, going on to say that it was 'an exclusively male society, with laws made by men and with prosecutors and judges who assess feminine conduct from a masculine standpoint'.

Ibsen would later insist that his play was a depiction of humanity and the right to be an individual rather than any specific endorsement of the women's suffrage campaign, which had begun to find voice in Australia. Regardless of the author's opinions, the play would be grabbed by the suffrage movement and placed at the heart of the social phenomenon involving the 'New Woman' – the growing discussion about the nature and role of women in society that would spawn dozens of books and plays over the next thirty years.

The arrival in Australia of *A Doll's House* in September 1889 had caused a storm of protest. Nora's character, interpreted as noble by supporters, was seen as villainous by opponents who viewed her search for self-worth as an abandonment of her family and, therefore, her responsibilities as a woman. 'Ibsenism is not likely to become the rage in Australia,' one predicted. How wrong he would prove to be.

The seeds had been sown, including in the mind of a teenage girl in Adelaide. Most likely, a copy of the play was given to her by her Uncle Charles and Aunt Hester, both stalwarts of the theatre, who would have been among the audience in August 1891 when it was staged at the Albert Hall, later the rallying point for women's suffrage meetings.

Muriel and her sisters were enrolled at the Parkside High School, which advertised, without further detail, 'particular attention is given to a sound English education, together with all modern accomplishments'. Parkside, one of a number of small private schools that had sprung up around the city, was run by sisters Olive and Maude Newman and had clearly been noticed by authorities. Senior government ministers often attended its annual prize-giving ceremonies – where Muriel won the occasional prize but more often was the star performer of the night's entertainment, singing, playing the piano and performing elocution: 'Several young ladies acquitted themselves with marked success, especially Miss Matters,' press coverage noted in 1891.[5] At the same presentation, the Minister for Education, while presenting prizes, pointedly referred to changing social attitudes to women: 'Ladies in the future, I am glad to say, will take a more prominent part in public affairs and I would encourage you to fit yourselves for the positions women are to occupy.'

Exposure to such messages, ideas and powerful rhetoric would leave a lasting impression on Muriel who, as the second eldest, would have been forced to be resourceful, helping her mother run a big household from an early age. Not only did it run counter to her mother's lot in life, which she could not fail to notice, but it also came during a significant moment in history when the women's movement was beginning to gain traction in her home city: 'I will never forget my joy in finding that the sentiments I had always vaguely but keenly felt had been put into words, forcible, majestic, dignified,' she would reflect in an interview.[6]

In fact, South Australian women who owned property had been given the right to vote three decades earlier, although only at local government level and without the right to stand for election.

There had been howls of dismay around the colony at the time, with some newspaper editors in Queensland and New South Wales at first refusing to believe that 'women have voted' in an election for the Port Adelaide mayoralty in 1863. 'It is difficult to us in the nineteenth century to believe in the truth of such a statement as that telegraphed,' wrote one Brisbane editor who, fearing that a woman had actually been elected to lead the council, conjured images of female riots and 'Adelaide insurrectionists electing one of their number by force of arms'.[7]

The following year, women in the neighbouring state of Victoria were inadvertently given the right to vote at a state election when electoral laws granted the vote to 'all persons' on municipal rolls. A number of women took the opportunity, as numerous papers reported: 'At one of the polling booths ... a novel sight was witnessed. A coach filled with ladies drove up, and the fair occupants alighted and recorded their votes to a man, for a bachelor candidate.'[8]

But it only served to highlight the challenge that lay ahead. Rather than enshrine the 'mistake' in law post-election, the Victorian parliament quickly closed the loophole. It would be another two decades before women began to organise themselves politically and form the first suffrage societies, initially in Melbourne and then South Australia, just as John Matters and his family were returning to Adelaide from Port Augusta.

It was a time of significant social reform. The Women's Suffrage League of South Australia had emerged from the Social Purity Society, a movement aimed at righting the 'social evil' of prostitution and the mistreatment of women. The Society's campaign was successful in part, raising the age of consent for girls to sixteen to assist authorities in keeping girls from prostitution. The members then pledged 'to advance and support the cause of women suffrage in this colony'.

Likewise, the temperance movement in South Australia emerged from the Christian desire to address social ills. Charles Matters was among the most vocal members of the Independent Order of Rechabites and relished taking to the stage at meetings where, as chairman, he had a reputation as a 'forcible' speaker. He made his views known loudly and often, as he did at church meetings where his niece was often in the audience.

Muriel's aunt Hester was a member of the Woman's Christian Temperance Union which had been formed in Adelaide in 1886 with 57 members. At first, the group, made up largely of members of the Wesleyan, Baptist and Congregationalist Churches, targeted alcohol use and domestic violence, but its causes grew quickly as membership swelled to include the poor treatment of Aborigines, factory workers and prisoners and the promotion of women's rights.

In 1891, just as Muriel was being entranced by Henrik Ibsen, the WCTU joined forces with the Suffrage League, headed by the anthropologist Edward Stirling, a university professor and former member of parliament who in 1885 had introduced a bill in which he proposed voting rights for women, including widows and single women, even quoting the philosopher Plato. The plea had fallen on deaf ears as would the next seven attempts.

The women's suffrage cause would not only be opposed by indignant men, who cruelly cast the female proponents as the 'shrieking sisterhood and gimlet-eyed', but also by equally indignant women who argued that women's duties in the home had been divinely ordered and could not be relieved by men, and that political equality would deprive women of unspecified 'special privilege'.

There were also powerful opposing voices from Britain, most notably that of Eliza Lynn Linton, ironically the first female salaried journalist in Britain, a vehement anti-feminist who in the same year as the women of Adelaide began their push for suffrage would publish an essay titled 'Wild Women as Politicians', parts of which found their way into Adelaide newspapers:

> This question of woman's political power is from beginning to
> end a question of sex, and all that depends on sex – its moral
> and intellectual limitations; its emotional excesses, its personal
> disabilities, its social conditions. It is a question of science,
> as purely as the best hygienic conditions or the accurate
> understanding of physiology. And science is dead against it.
> Science knows that to admit women – that is, mothers – into
> the heated arena of political life would be as destructive to
> the physical well-being of the future generation as it would be
> disastrous to the good conduct of affairs in the present.

But the most prominent critic of all was the woman the suffragists needed most – Queen Victoria – who wrote:

> I am most anxious to enlist everyone who can speak or write to join in checking this mad, wicked folly of 'Women's Rights', with all its attendant horrors, on which her poor feeble sex is bent, forgetting every sense of womanly feelings and propriety. Feminists ought to get a good whipping. Were women to 'unsex' themselves by claiming equality with men, they would become the most hateful, heathen and disgusting of beings and would surely perish without male protection.[9]

If female suffrage were ever to be made law, the monarch would have to sign her name to it.

3.

'THE WOMAN QUESTION'

Ladies poured into the cushioned benches to the left of the
Speaker and relentlessly usurped the seats of gentlemen
who had been seated there before. They filled the aisles and
overflowed into the gallery on the right, while some of the
bolder spirits climbed the stairs and invaded the rougher
forms behind the clock. So there was a wall of beauty at the
southern end of the building.

— *The Advertiser*

On the morning of December 18, 1894, the lamb-chopped
members of the South Australian Legislative Assembly voted 31–
14 to grant women aged twenty-one and over the right not only
to vote but to stand for election. It was a momentous occasion
in a chamber normally the preserve of quiet nodding, reported
one observer: 'The Ayes were sonorous and cheery; the Noes
despondent like muffled bells.'[1]

The previous year New Zealand had given women voting rights,
but South Australia had become the first parliament to confirm the
twin rights of an electoral voice and parliamentary representation.
The battle had taken nine years and eight parliamentary petitions,
which in the moment of triumph seemed to have been a marathon,

but in context of what was to come would be a positively swift campaign.

In truth, the argument had been turned in women's favour by economic circumstances and political expediency rather than a wholesale change in social attitude. Australia had been plunged into an economic depression which had helped to shuffle in a new era of politics and aided the election of a progressive South Australian government in 1893, the result of a coalition between the Liberal Party and the newly formed United Labor Party.

Still, the incoming premier, the Liberal Charles Kingston, was anti-suffrage and it was only when he was persuaded that the addition of women to the electoral roll would give him an advantage in city electorates that he agreed, somewhat tentatively, to ease the passage of the suffrage bill.

It had been a painful process.

Women by the dozen had watched the debate 'in groups of silk and muslin', filling not only the ladies' gallery where, until now, they had been confined, but also spilling into benches usually reserved for men. The debate had rolled on for several days, first at committee level and then in the house proper where the speeches of suffrage opponents were filled with stonewalling invective, predicting political chaos, belittling the intellect of the female gender, raising spurious obstacles such as guessing a woman's age and hence her eligibility to vote and lamenting the degeneracy of the human race.

There was also a stream of amendments designed not to improve the fairness of the legislation but introduced as a cynical tactical manoeuvre. Opponents had hoped that broadening the bill to allow women to be eligible to stand for office as well as vote would make it unpalatable enough to force waverers, such as Premier Kingston, and even supporters to abandon the bill altogether. Ultimately, the tactic hadn't worked. The vote was overwhelming and the news was greeted by newspaper editors, most of whom had once campaigned against the changes, as inevitable.

Between parliamentary sessions, the women had met upstairs at Mrs Aish's Café de Paris in Rundle Street around the corner, the modest timber rooms in stark contrast to the granite and marble edifice to politics where their relevance was being decided.

It was here that they cheered their heroes, women like Mary Lee, the vibrant and at times abrasive mouthpiece of the Suffrage League who delighted the crowd with her appraisal of their political enemies: 'Those who had the least to say took the longest time to say it,'[2] she said, exhorting her sisters to return to the parliament if only to maintain a visual presence that would make it difficult for their male supporters to abandon them. There were more than two hundred women in the gallery when the vote was taken.

'How can men represent women?' Lee argued. 'Men cannot think for women because they cannot think as women; they cannot think as women because they are not women. Is progressive civilisation for man only? Can woman be dispensed with in this progress? If not, how can she be allowed to fall behind? Surely it is due to the race, nay, an absolute necessity to it, that she should keep step with its advance. Masculine and feminine influence must be wedded.'

Another was Catherine Helen Spence, a preacher, reformer, governess, journalist, founder of kindergartens and girls' secondary schools and Australia's first woman novelist, who in 1854 was forced to publish *Clara Morison: A Tale of South Australia during the Gold Fever* anonymously rather than use a male pen name.

Spence would stand as the country's first female political candidate in an 1897 poll to elect the ten South Australian representatives to the Federal Convention, the committee convened to draft the Australian Constitution and the rules required to form a national parliament.

Her candidacy was controversial, evoking 'sincere applause and audible smiles' among supporters while opponents insisted that she withdraw because of legal questions about her right, as a woman, to take her place on the committee. Spence laughed it off: 'Lawyers always differ. It is their business,' she quipped, before adding, 'I have the strongest desire to give the results of a lifetime of reading and thought, of experience and travel, towards the work of laying the foundations of a great nation on the secure basis of righteousness and peace.'[3]

She would later recount how her name was included on a poster list of 'Ten Best Men' by a campaign organisation. When the list was taken to the printery owned by a former member of parliament, he objected to the heading and suggested her name be dropped as inaccurate, and a man's put in its place. The organiser responded with incredulity: 'Not say she's one of the ten best men? Why she's the best man of the lot.'[4]

Spence would finish twenty-second of the thirty-three candidates, her chances cruelled by the controversy, although the result was less important than exercising her right to stand. It would be another six decades, the late 1950s, before this most progressive of communities would elect its first female politician.

Elizabeth Nicholls was the daughter of a grocer, a 'lucid and forceful public speaker' and president of the Women's Christian Temperance Union. She was also a councilor of the Women's Suffrage League and the main organiser of the great petition of 11,600 names that had helped persuade Charles Kingston and the parliament to finally take seriously the issue of women's suffrage.

Among her many roles, Nicholls was a prominent member of the North Adelaide Wesleyan Church, the congregation where the

Matters family worshipped, including John and Emma and their children. Charles and Thomas Matters and their wives, Hester and Jane, became heavily involved in the Women's Suffrage League and served on a committee headed by Elizabeth Nicholls.

At a joyous public meeting held after the suffrage bill received royal approval, Charles not only attended but made a speech, which was reported in *The Register*: 'Mr C.H. Matters announced that the Women's Suffrage League proposed to form a Women's Liberal Federation on the lines of the English association, of which the Countess of Carlisle was president. The members would meet to discuss questions and to find guidance thereon. Members would consist of women only, but there would be a council of advice consisting of four gentlemen. Lady Colton and Mrs Lee had the matter in hand. The motion was carried with acclamation.'[5]

* * *

Ibsen's words and her family's involvement in social issues were significant influences for Muriel, who had just turned seventeen when women were granted the vote. As she would later write: 'There is not the slightest doubt I was born a suffragette. I cannot remember a time when I was not interested in the woman question. Then, when quite a girl, I was reciting from Ibsen … I used to do a piece from *A Doll's House*, when Nora is told that home and children are her first duty she says: "No, my first duty is to myself." I used to begin with a little explanatory interlude telling what had led up to this. People used to say how dreadful it was to hear such a young girl giving utterance to such sentiments.'[6]

The shapes and influences emerging in Muriel's life were a strange mix of religious and social conservatism, daily prayer and abstinence of declared vices like alcohol wrapped up in the Wesleyan philosophy of public service to acknowledge faith but also a belief in individual freedom and artistic creativity. From the age of ten (and probably earlier) she was singing, and playing the piano, interests she probably picked up from her mother's side of the family, and was performing recitals at festivals and meetings organised by the various church and temperance groups overseen by her uncles.

There seemed to be events several times a week in all parts of the city and towns beyond, in front of rapt audiences – like-minded believers there not to critique but to applaud and encourage. At first, Muriel and other children were put forward as sideline entertainment, delightful warm-ups to the main business of the evening. Muriel shone, a tiny figure with striking features that resembled her mother's fine-boned countenance more than the paternal line, and with a voice that belied her physical stature.

By her early teens the stage held no fears for Muriel, as she discovered the power of her own voice and its natural place in the art of elocution, the skill of dramatic recitation of poetry and prose – public speaking on steroids.

Like everything else in her life, elocution seemed to spring from the community of the Church. Unlike the United Kingdom where the art of oration first emerged as drawing room entertainment for the privileged, the broader popularity of the art grew in the United States under the influence of the Methodist Church as families sought to improve themselves, mostly by attending organised activities in church camps, halls and lyceums.

And yet, Muriel's passion for the arts was not matched by any of her siblings. Younger sister Mary was said to be artistic though she took a more conventional course in life and brother Charles would become a veterinary surgeon while Len would become a well-known journalist and supporter as her career as an agitator for social change blossomed on the other side of the world.

She would later recall: 'I did dream, even in my really young youth, of reforming many things, but Art was to be my magic weapon – the power of beauty – beauty of thought, beautifully expressed.'[7]

Rather than the inspiration of a single moment, such as the discovery of Ibsen, Muriel's path in life seemed to be the result of a series of events and a collection of discoveries. She read Ibsen not in rebellion but rather in affirmation of her family's belief system. Likewise, she learned the art of public speaking not merely to entertain at school and church concerts, but as a means to convey a powerful message of good.

Muriel would say later that she had been inspired to take up elocution not just because of Ibsen but because of two other writers, the English poet and playwright Robert Browning and the American humanist poet and essayist Walt Whitman: 'I felt sure that all I had to do was to take all their beautiful, inspiring messages and everyone would be straightaway uplifted and reformed. So I determined to be an elocutionist, and I started studying at once, and by the time I was seventeen, I was lecturing at the high school.'[8]

One of the most important influences in Muriel's development as an elocutionist would be a man named Edward Reeves, who had arrived in Adelaide the year Muriel was born and would make a name for himself not only as a performer able to recite from memory Dickens' *A Christmas Carol* and Byron's *The Siege of Corinth*, but as a teacher at Whinham College where the Matters brothers had studied.

He also taught Muriel Matters the art of public speaking in private lessons that began around the age of fifteen. Reeves regarded her as one of his best pupils, clearly proud of her success when interviewed for a newspaper several years later during which he also made clear his distaste for Australia's 'faulty colonial accent', painful to the ear, he winced, when an 'a' was pronounced as an 'i', an 'e' became an 'a', and an 'i' sounded like 'oi'.[9]

He despised the level of parliamentary debate and believed that the study of oration improved the quality of a student's reading and, therefore, their education. Most importantly, he argued that the most successful men were powerful public speakers. Muriel Matters was one of his first female students at a time when it was rare to see a woman on the stage as a speaker. That situation was about to change.

* * *

Samuel Langhorne Clemens, travelling under his famous pseudonym Mark Twain, steamed into Adelaide aboard a train from Melbourne in mid October 1895. The American author and humorist was at the height of his fame and on a journey around the world, arranged ostensibly to raise funds and clear personal debts amassed by an unhealthy love of speculation through a series of paid lectures, one hundred and fifty in all, conducted in town halls and theatres before adoring crowds who paid up to five shillings for the privilege.

Clemens would write generously of the city and its people; he was beguiled not only by Adelaide's design, courtesy of Colonel Light, but also the city's liberal social attitudes and innovation. He praised its religious tolerance – 'she is a hospitable home for every alien who chooses to come' – and, to prove his point, produced a list of sixty-four religions represented among the city's 320,000 citizens. (Wesleyans numbered almost 50,000, second only to Anglicans.)

He recounted with delight, conversations with old-timers who spoke of Aborigines as 'intelligent and clever' rather than as savages and praised support for the working class: 'The working man is a great force everywhere in Australia, but South Australia is his paradise. He has had a hard time in this world, and has earned a paradise. I am glad he has found it.'[10]

Clemens was also a man whose attitude toward women's rights had changed markedly: he had been decidedly anti-suffrage in his letter to the *Missouri Democrat* in 1867: 'Women, go your ways! Seek not to beguile us of our imperial privileges. Content yourself with your little feminine trifles – your babies, your benevolent societies and your knitting – and let your natural bosses do the voting. Stand back – you will be wanting to go to war next. We will let you teach school as much as you want to, and we will pay you half wages for it, too, but beware! We don't want you to crowd us too much.'

But by 1895, after visiting South Australia and New Zealand during his travels, he had changed his mind, undoubtedly influenced by his wife, Olivia, who was a vocal supporter of feminism and women's suffrage and who accompanied him on his travels, Clemens would scrawl in his notebook: 'We easily perceive that the peoples furthest from civilisation are the ones where equality between man and woman are furthest apart – and we consider this one of the signs of savagery. But we are so stupid that we can't see that we thus plainly admit that no civilisation can be perfect until exact equality between man and woman is included.'

While in Adelaide, Clemens would play to packed audiences at the Theatre Royal in Hindley Street, the crowds enthralled by his magnetic presence and laconic style. By chance, his whistle-stop visit would coincide with the public arrival of another original performer. On October 29, a few days after Clemens had been cheered off at the city railway station following his final monologue, Edward Reeves presented his students onstage at the nearby Victoria Hall. Recently turned eighteen, Muriel Matters was among the star performers, her name prominent in the newspaper advertisements that promised a 'grand, elocutionary, dramatic and musical entertainment'.[11]

Until now, Muriel's performances had been in front of smaller, niche audiences: school plays, church outings, temperance society meetings, literary clubs, fetes and the like where she was noticed and warmly applauded but not judged, at least not in any meaningful way. This night marked a significant step toward her future and ignited her determination to become a performing reformer – performing not only in front of a paying audience but one that almost certainly contained professional critics.

The response was heartening. The *Register* concluded: 'Miss Muriel Matters, who had evidently gauged the acoustic capacity of the hall to a nicety, gave "Karl the Martyr" in a clear, sympathetic voice and with appropriate action.'[12] The *Express and Telegraph* was equally effusive: 'Miss Muriel Matters ... gave a decidedly clever interpretation of "Karl the Martyr", in which she displayed no little dramatic force.'[13]

The poem Muriel had chosen was written in the style of an epic and told the story of a blacksmith, a man of iron frame and tender heart who tackled bare-handedly a werewolf creature to save his children and village and then chained himself to his anvil to ensure that, poisoned himself, he could not harm those he loved as he changed.

Not only did it give the young elocutionist the chance to show off her capacity for the dramatic, but it was also a performance of some portent as the poem had been written by the grandmother of Robert Brough, one of Australia's leading dramatic actors and promoters of the day – and a potential future employer of Miss Muriel Matters.

4.

THE STAGE BECKONS

FULLARTON LITERARY AND MUSICAL SOCIETY
Members of the above society are requested to meet at
Kindermann's Café, Rundle Street, at ten o'clock tomorrow
morning to bid bon voyage to Miss Muriel Matters, who is
leaving for Sydney — Walter Cross, Hon. Sec.

The Advertiser, November 27, 1897

Kindermann's stood in the heart of the city's commercial district, the cherished business of the late Gustav Kindermann, now run by his sons. The old man had abandoned his trade as a confectioner in a small German town to seek his fortune in the Australian gold rush, arriving in 1852, the same year that Thomas and Mary Matters stepped ashore in Adelaide to begin their new life. When he realised his folly, Gustav decided to remain and parlay the funds he had left into a restaurant where he could ply his former trade. Kindermann's would become an institution, a place for the famous and the ordinary alike, and a testimony to the migrant soul of the city.

Outside its doors on the morning that Muriel's friends gathered, the city appeared to have shrugged off the economic gloom that had haunted the colony for most of the decade. The first electric street lighting had been installed, ornate shopfronts gleamed in late spring sunshine and an arcade boasted a glass-panelled ceiling for its fifty shops. Brightly painted signs jostled for prominence above neatly paved footpaths and horse-drawn trams had right of way down the middle of wide streets lined with photographic studios, dentists, drapers, jewellers, cabinet-makers and a clutch of hotels.

It was two years since Muriel's debut at the Victoria Hall, and now aged twenty she had decided it was time to seek her fortune beyond her colonial home. Adelaide's wooded surrounds, beautiful and reassuring, were also its boundary and, therefore, its limitation for a young woman who harboured dreams beyond marriage.

Inside the café, Mr Stockman, chairman of the St John's Dramatic Society, presented her with 'an exceedingly choice purse'[1] while suggesting that other cities might not be as welcoming. Likewise, Mr Plint, president of the Fullarton Literary and Music Society, spoke grandly about Muriel's natural flair, but, as he handed her a 'handsome travelling case', left open the chance that she may not choose 'that avocation' but would choose the more traditional route of marriage and children.

It was clear she would be missed by those who valued her energy and enthusiasm as much as her talent. Clustered inside the café, they wished her the best, but hoped she would soon hurry back.

Muriel had taken her time in deciding to pursue a career on the stage. University had come first: she studied music for two years, according to family recollections, courtesy of a scholarship to the Elder Conservatorium at the Adelaide University. 'The Con' has few records of its earliest students, and no record of Muriel's academic performance, although there is evidence of her involvement in public performances staged by the university.

At the same time, her public performances had continued, as had her growing interest in society and politics; she starred in fund-raisers for church groups, aged homes and distressed farmers and became involved in the Australian Natives' Association,[2] a mutual society created to encourage the political movement toward Australia becoming a federation. Then still a teenager, Muriel was too young to play an active part in political affairs of the day but was clearly engaged in the ideals of federalism and impact on social policy.

She revelled in stage roles as heroic women and underdogs – a factory girl whose pure heart and actions win the love of a gentleman, an heiress who chooses an artist over a villainous nobleman – but it was her dramatic elocution recitals that drew most attention: stories of grand heroics and sacrifice like the tale of a slave who saved a southern American church from a fireball and won his freedom, and ode to a teenage girl who saved a rebel colonel from British redcoat dragoons by riding ahead of them, Paul Revere-like, to warn the soldier in question. The poem asked: 'Why should men do all the deeds?'

Newspaper reviews of Muriel's performances with various dramatic and musical societies were frequent, and her reputation had grown steadily. Critics seemed to be universally impressed by her range and applied a balance of adjectives to her performances that would become a hallmark of her reputation – not only was she 'powerful', she could also be 'pretty and coquettish'.[3]

Muriel had been too young to register and vote in the 1896 South Australian election but would have watched, inspired by the impact the women's vote would have on the outcome, as she expressed in later interviews. There was no intent by the suffrage organisations to rock the boat and nominate women candidates, but more than 60,000 women registered in time to vote and the organisations ran mock elections to ensure their ballots would not be informal.[4] Although Conservatives had opposed the women's suffrage bill, they now encouraged registration as 'fashionable'.

Interstate observers would head home to implore their colonial parliaments in New South Wales, Victoria and Queensland to follow the South Australian example, dismissing concerns that voting 'degraded or unsexed refined and sensitive women'. In fact, women had tended to have a calming effect on previously rowdy political gatherings.

Contrary to dire predictions, women voted in slightly higher percentages than men (66.4 to 66.3 per cent), and across all classes of voters, although their manner of voting differed noticeably. Women tended to vote at different hours to men and didn't want to be badgered by party officials at polling stations or to display party colours. 'Ladies of wealth and leisure' voted early; 'the poorer and more hard-working' later. Many mothers carried their babies.

While men tended to stand around talking outside polling booths, women chose to sign in, get their papers and vote swiftly, 'walking out with the same businesslike despatch as though they were buying a ticket at a railway station', as one observer noted.[5]

Women were expected by polite society to vote as their fathers, husbands and brothers instructed them, but the predictions did not always hold true, as officials witnessed a man 'of obvious conservative proclivities' demand that his three daughters vote for his favoured candidate. They refused and voted for the Labor candidate instead. Another man, a well-known lawyer, accompanied his wife into the booth and was heard telling her how to vote. He was ordered out by officials and his wife 'went on and quietly voted for the candidate she fancied'.[6] Another man tried to sack a servant girl when she disobeyed his voting order.

On election day – April 25 – a number of newspapers carried a poem, a rallying cry written by the philanthropist and reformer Caroline Emily Clark, which opened:

Australian sisters, young and old,
The time is drawing near
When we must stand up manfully
For all we hold most dear
And choose men wise and capable
The good ship state to steer.

We may be young in politics,
But women's wit is keen,
To scent out knaves and hypocrites,
To scorn the base and mean
And recognise true-hearted men
Where'er they may be seen.[7]

Muriel, still eighteen years old, was too young to vote in the historic poll but she would exercise her right seven years later when women were permitted to vote in a Federal election for the first time.

* * *

Sydney welcomed Muriel Matters with open arms on a rain-sodden night in October 1898. It was almost a year since her send off at Kindermann's Café, indicating it had been a struggle to gain attention in the bigger city, limited to low-key appearances in drawing rooms and salons of Sydney's wealthy, surviving on modest payments and travelling to and from Adelaide where she had continued appearing.

But October 20 was her big break, heralded by newspaper advertising and articles as a debutant of note for her appearance in the elaborately decorated YMCA building near the corner of Pitt and Bathurst Streets, its coloured leadlights and stone carvings lending it dramatic prominence. She would be accompanied by the flautist and composer John Lemmone who had won international acclaim as a soloist and for appearances with the opera diva Dame Nellie Melba. The hall was filled despite the weather, the applause and calls for encores drowning out the torrent outside, as the *Sydney Morning Herald* reported the next day:

> Miss Muriel Warburton Matters was rewarded for her enterprise in arranging such an excellent entertainment of recitations and music by a numerous attendance. Miss Matters, who is youthful and fair-headed with an open expression of countenance which wins her audience from the first, is really a bright example of an Australian girl, for she never faltered in her task as an entertainer and recited her pieces with unexpected judgment in the use of voice with the apt addition of gesture. Miss Matters made her chief success in 'Poor Little Joe', the story of a street Arab who brings flowers to the bedside of a dying brother. The reciter evidently possesses a special talent for depiction of boyish character. The dialogue was cleverly assumed, and the touch of tragedy at the close had a natural ring. Miss Matters then delivered archly 'Sister Edith Helps Things Along' with 'The Country Squire' in response to an enthusiastic encore. The fair Adelaidean declined the wished-for encore after 'Ladybird's Race' at the close of which she was presented with beautiful flowers from Sir Langdon Bonython. Miss Matters also encored for 'The Ballad of Splendid Silence' to which she added touches of sly humour which delighted the audience.

The review, stodgy prose and all, revealed much about Muriel and the immediate warmth with which the young woman, about to turn twenty-one, was received by audiences and critics, although why she had borrowed her mother's maiden name – Warburton – must be left to assumption. It might have been simply because it added gravitas to her stage presence or, perhaps more likely, that it was a nod to her maternal line.

That would certainly have fitted with her liberated views about the role of women. She was now on a path far different than her mother's; Emma was already a wife and mother at this stage in her life. So much had changed for women in a single generation, from places at universities becoming available to the seizing of the right to a voice in the process of democracy and the acceptance that there were professional roles to which women might aspire.

It was the last of these that Muriel Warburton Matters (she would drop Warburton after a year or so) intended to pursue, well aware as she was of the risk of failure. One of her teachers, at least briefly, was an English actress named Amy Roselle, who had arrived in Australia with her husband, Arthur Dacre, in 1895, seeking to turn around their mixed fortunes on the stage in London. Amy had been well known but her husband, a physician turned actor who had an overly inflated opinion of his own talents, had struggled.

Arthur had insisted that they be hired together, but he turned off promoters and audiences alike and their work dwindled. The folly was repeated in Australia during a fateful nine months in which they travelled to Melbourne then Adelaide, where Amy met and taught a teenage Muriel Matters before the couple sought the lights of Sydney.

But instead of fame they found infamy, the desperate couple dying in a bloody suicide pact in their hotel room. Arthur shot his wife and then, realising he had run out of bullets, slashed his own throat with a razor. He was still alive, gurgling and crying for help, when terrified staff burst into the room. It was too late and he died on the floor in a pool of his own blood.

Their deaths were as unnecessary as they were macabre, coming as audiences began to respond to their critical success. Arthur left three short letters in which he told of their despair: 'Be anything – a butcher, a baker, or a candlestick maker – but get work as anything but an actor.'; 'We are broken hearted. We have simply tried to live pluckily in the life and at the business we both have loved. We have failed and I have had a rough time of it lately.'[8]

Their deaths shocked the city, hundreds lining the funeral procession route to Waverley Cemetery. The incident shone a light on the precarious nature of the stage and the battle actors and actresses faced. But to a young woman like Muriel, imbued with the words of Ibsen, it also spoke of the misogyny of marriage and how the ego and dominance of an unhappy man cruelly crushed the potential of his talented wife and then brutally took her life.

Muriel's own fortunes seemed very much rosier as offers began pouring in. She also enjoyed society support from the outset which ensured an audience. Langdon Bonython, for example, the man who presented her with flowers the evening of her debut,[9] was no ordinary member of the audience. He too was from Adelaide, the proprietor of the *Advertiser* newspaper, where Muriel's younger brother, Leonard, now worked as a cadet journalist.

Bonython, one of the country's most generous philanthropists, was also a prominent member of the Wesleyan community in Adelaide and would become a member of the first Australian federation parliament. The son of an English carpenter, he and his family had migrated not long after Thomas and Mary Matters arrived in South Australia. Given their closeness in age and involvement with the Church, it is highly likely that Bonython knew Charles and Thomas Matters. The success of their niece Muriel that night would have been personal. She was on her way.

The plaudits would continue, Muriel's performances across the city now advertised not as those of a young amateur but the offerings of a performer of promise and note. At a time when an elocutionist was as sought after as a singer or a pianist, she was quickly embraced as among the city's best: 'a student of the dramatic', eloquent and clear with the versatility to tell stories of suffering and anger, of bravery and pathos, and the wit and sparkle required for comic and playful pieces.

Although diminutive, Muriel seemed to dominate the stage with her presence. She was fair and graceful in her full skirts with their narrow waists and gathered sleeves, her thick hair piled high beneath wide-brimmed hats. Then there was her voice: 'Miss Matters never failed to secure merited approval.'[10]

Suddenly, the young girl from Adelaide was invited as a guest rather than a performer to society events, her deportment assessed, her clothing noticed and commented upon as she mingled with 'musical and theatrical celebrities' of the city. Two months after her debut she announced that she had decided to 'adopt the stage as a profession', signing on with a company for a one-off tour of New Zealand.

When Muriel went home to Adelaide in September 1899 she was celebrated as a returning success story, headlining a charity event at a packed Victoria Hall where she dazzled in an Empire line gown of white cashmere – but no gloves. It was a sign of the times, a modern woman making a bold fashion statement – her 'pretty hands guiltless of kid coverings', as one critic noted.[11] But any social audacity was snuffed out by her equally emboldened performance:

To a pleasing personality Miss Matters unites the power of engaging the sympathetic interest of her hearers, whatever her chosen subject may be. Gifted with a full, clear voice, which she has learned to moderate so as to express the most varied emotions, she has also at command the delicate play-by-play and change of facial expressions, which give life to the art of the elocutionist, and to these essential qualifications she adds a natural charm of manner which, at once, places her on excellent terms with the audience. The talented young artist was … in quite another class.[12]

* * *

In the later years of the nineteenth century, Robert Brough was the most famous theatre promoter in Australia, so much so that when he died in 1906 he would be described as a national loss in his adopted home. He and his wife, Florence, had arrived from London as performers in 1885 initially for a six-month season, but then, realising the huge demand for live performance, they decided to stay and start their own troupe.

Brough went back to London, hired a clutch of aging but acceptable talent and returned to the colonies with the intention of shaking up the theatre scene in Sydney and Melbourne. Within months he had taken leases at theatres in both cities and his troupe was being acclaimed by critics and audiences. For nine years he ran his programs from the Bijou Theatre in Melbourne and the Criterion in Sydney, his players a combination of experienced actors shipped in from Europe and Australian actors hoping to make their mark in Europe.

The Broughs were not only popular performers but had a canny knack of reading the changing mood of Australian audiences, which had been fed a diet of comedies, farces, classic tragedies and melodramas, but by the 1890s were searching for scripts and issues with a little more meat on the bones. 'The sex question',[13] as Brough would describe gender politics, was one direction audiences were ready to explore, and he eagerly embraced productions that featured strong female identities, such as the plays of Oscar Wilde, whose infamy would only enhance the public appetite for his work.

The first, *Lady Windermere's Fan*, was produced in 1894 in Adelaide. Brough was keen to capture what he perceived, rightly, to be the flavour of the day – heroines with 'a past', so-called 'bad women' who were yet capable of self-sacrifice and nobility while others supposedly trod the path of virtue. Mrs Erlynne, who would rather sacrifice her own social position than betray her daughter, the virtuous Lady Windermere, was one such character.

Similarly, Brough's favourite production was the Arthur Wing Pinero classic, *The Second Mrs Tanqueray*, in which Florence Brough often played the lead role of Paula Jarman, a woman of low birth who marries into society and then sacrifices her life for her step-daughter.

Brough was probably not aware of Muriel's 1895 performance of his grandmother's poem 'Karl the Martyr', although it was almost certainly the first recitation in Australia by a woman. But four years later the promoter had begun to pay attention to the young woman from Adelaide. In September 1899 he attended one of her Sydney performances. The next day he offered her a job.[14]

Muriel's first performance was back in Adelaide just three weeks later as 'Lizzie, the vicarage servant' in a play called *The Physician*. But by November her roles had improved, and in playbills her name was featured just below those of Mr and Mrs Brough, who headlined most productions. More importantly, she was attracting media attention, as the *Advertiser* noted: 'Already she has won press encomiums by her stage performance. She is a clever, vivacious and unaffected little lady'.[15] Muriel Matters was on her way to becoming a stage star.

5.

FIRST LOVE, FIRST VOTE

Brooding. It seemed to be the favoured countenance of Bryceson Treharne as he strode around the music rooms and lecture halls of the Elder Conservatorium at Adelaide University. The city's music critics could sense it too, in his gifted but unadorned style at the keyboard, free of the 'showy effects and manual gymnastics'[1] of many professionals of his era, yet with an emotional complexity that matched his demeanour.

A studio portrait of the 21-year-old Welshman, taken not long after he arrived in Adelaide in the first months of 1900 to become the second teacher appointed to the 'Con', shows a man who seemed to view the world as one giant puzzle. Not overly tall but thin as a rake with a long face and matching fingers, he was not ruggedly handsome but somehow intriguing, Oscar Wilde-esque even, with his dark, soulful eyes beneath heavy eyebrows and a wild thatch of hair.

Class photographs taken over the next decade, as he stamped himself as one of the city's leading arts figures, echo that same dark, professorial mien in a sea of smiling, innocent student faces. He even seems out of place among his peers in staff photos. While others pose, stiffly Victorian, in top hats, bowlers and handlebar moustaches, a clean-shaven Treharne sports a broad brim, his head cocked at an angle as if to hurry the cameraman so he can rush back to his beloved piano.

He had beaten twenty-six other applicants in a series of musical tests held in London to be appointed professor of the pianoforte. A former student of the Royal College of Music in London and conservatoriums in Paris and Munich, Treharne had chosen the artistic outpost of Adelaide rather than the safe haven of Europe where he was already well known and admired.

Treharne was greeted in South Australia as a star, the expectation surrounding his appointment enhanced by the news that three of his compositions had been bought in a recent copyright sale in London – akin to having three singles concurrently in a 21st-century Top 40 hit parade. In their excitement, university officials even installed a piano at the Torrens Island quarantine station where he and fellow ship passengers spent a fortnight on their arrival because of concerns about smallpox.

Treharne's first public performance in Adelaide had critics in raptures: 'An artist to his fingertips,' gushed the *Chronicle*. 'One of the finest pianists who has visited us. South Australians should congratulate themselves upon the acquisition of such a talented instrumentalist.'[2]

And yet for all his seriousness, the young man was not without a sense of humour. Asked by a reporter why he was not married, Treharne laughed, remarking that he had noticed the word *bachelor* had been underlined by immigration authorities when he stepped ashore: 'No, I am not married, nor am I engaged, but for goodness sake do not say that or the ladies will think I am throwing myself at them.'[3]

The range of courses offered by the Con was still in its infancy, among them theory and history of music, ensemble and orchestra playing, singing and musical composition. There was one other course, which would bring the intriguing Welshman into contact with Muriel Matters – the art of elocution.

* * *

Muriel's professional aspirations had been shaken since joining Robert and Florence Brough's operation. There was kudos in being hired as a member of the high-profile and popular theatre company, and her new stage name of 'Muriel Mathers' was prominent enough in the bill to suggest that the young actor was destined for more, but life on the road would prove a confronting experience for a young woman used to the decorum and earnestness of the tight Wesleyan community which would have provided her with domestic sanctuary not only in Adelaide but when performing in Sydney.

It wasn't that her performances had let her down, although she had largely abandoned her greatest skill – elocution – to be a comedic actress in a series of plays staged up and down the east coast from Brisbane to Hobart. That was almost certainly the reason for her name change – to distinguish the elocutionist from the actress. They were very different worlds: the former occupying a glamorous, controlled stage where the spotlight was firmly on her and her ability to capture and hold the attention of a well-to-do audience. By contrast, her life on the road was feverish in pace, moving from city to town and back again every few days, and sharing the stage as part of a team of players, often in secondary roles or even as male characters – 'hiding her delicate womanhood figure' – and unable to make the best use of her extraordinary presence and voice.

But it wasn't the lack of attention that bothered Miss Mathers; rather, it was the living conditions for her fellow female performers. Varying audience numbers and tight profit margins squeezed budgets, which inevitably affected troupe members – hectic schedules, reduced wages and cut-price accommodation became the norm. Transport, particularly to rural areas, could be rough and audience behaviour varied. Muriel's worries had reached a crescendo by the time she returned from a four-week tour of New Zealand in November 1899. As she later explained, rather than argue and push for improvement, Muriel decided little could be done and chose to resign and accept a position as 'second lady' with a rival firm, Rignold and Co.[4]

George Rignold, like Robert Brough, was an English-born actor of some renown who had branched out into theatre management and become a successful promoter. He had long held the lease on Her Majesty's Theatre in the heart of Sydney but also organised theatre troupes. While Brough preferred a circuit that went north to Brisbane, through rural New South Wales and then across the Tasman to New Zealand, George Rignold usually went south through New South Wales to Victoria and then Tasmania.

If Muriel was looking for a solution to her concerns she would be disappointed. George Rignold had the handsome face and cultured image of a leading man, but his visage concealed an ugly reputation as a demanding and impatient man. He was sixty-one years old and at the end of a sparkling stage career that had taken him to the West End of London and on several trips through the United States. He wanted an end and it couldn't come quickly enough. A tour of Tasmania in January 1901 with a troupe of twenty-five 'specially selected' actors would be his farewell to Australia before he returned to England and retirement.

Rignold's final curtain call would be at the Theatre Royal in Hobart on January 21. It would also be the final appearance of Muriel Mathers, in a five-act play called *Man to Man* that cast her as a male lead, a character named Ned Doyle.[5] Despite her performance being hailed as 'bright and versatile', Muriel's career was at the crossroads as she headed back to Adelaide where she would resume her former identity as Muriel Matters, elocutionist:

'I found the conditions of stage life for women so repugnant that I returned to my old work of teaching elocution,' she would say later in a newspaper interview. In another she went further: 'I left the stage at a day's notice, indignant at certain abuses that affected other, less protected girls far more than they affected me.'[6]

The cause of Muriel's return to her home was masked by the announcement that she had cancelled engagements to 'bid adieu' to her younger brother, Leonard, who was sailing with the 5th South Australian Imperial Bushmen's Contingent to fight as a trooper in the Boer War.[7] Muriel and Leonard were close as siblings, both opinionated and adventurous – as would become evident in the years to come. Leonard would not only survive the experience of war but it would spark a wanderlust that would be a hallmark of his life.

While her brother was fighting overseas, one of among 1531 soldiers from South Australia (including the controversial Harry 'Breaker' Morant), Muriel would become a prominent figure in the committee raising funds for a war memorial, featuring a bronze figure on horseback, which would remain a dominant feature of the city. That experience and the death during the Great War of another brother, Charles, would fuel an anti-war campaign later in her life.

Despite her misgivings, the stage had brought Muriel local fame; she was a celebrity, though in a world that was yet to embrace the cult that would dominate society a century later. Newspaper columns had begun to mention her, not only in critiques of her performances but as a glamorous woman frequenting society events – at the Morphettville races in 'a clinging frock of blue voile, cream serge Eton coat and smart toque of pale-blue glace and sapphire blue velvet',[8] at the Mayoress' reception 'in white muslin [and] forget-me-not wreathed hat'[9] and at the YWCA 'in a neat navy skirt and black crinoline hat'.[10]

Her image was in demand, her photograph surreptitiously positioned beneath display advertisements for beauty products under the heading 'All the elite use'. There was Pearl's lavender water with musk – 'A delicious and lasting perfume, the best Best' – and Marion's violet powder – 'Ladies who use this are delighted with its softness, fragrance and cooling qualities.'[11]

Muriel was probably not even aware of the rather deliberate use of her image, much less endorse any perfume, but the attention was, nonetheless, not only heady but useful for a young woman who recognised the entrepreneurial opportunity as she launched a series of her own newspaper advertisements:

> Miss Muriel Matters
>   Late of Brough Comedy Company and Geo Rignold's
> Dramatic Company is prepared to receive pupils in the art of
> elocution. 'Elsinore', Hurtle Square East.[12]

A few months later, buoyed by the response, she rented rooms in the city and advertised private lessons in the 'Delsarte system of voice production and dramatic expression' two days a week, as well as taking a teaching post at the School of Mines and Industry in North Terrace where students were charged ten shillings a term. 'The class should be popular,' the registrar warned.

Not that her public performances had stopped or even slowed. If anything, Muriel was in more demand than ever, although the stages on which she performed had changed, from the city's grand theatres to the more intimate realms of arts societies, clubs and private salons – the Cowandilla Salon and Mrs Quesnel's music rooms among them – which had sprung up around the city as interest in the arts flourished.

It was inevitable, in such an environment, that Muriel Matters would meet Bryceson Treharne.

* * *

Australia became a Federation on the morning of January 1, 1901 when its six self-governing colonies united to form the Commonwealth of Australia. It had been an unnecessarily protracted tussle, the way forward resisted by selfish men determined to hang on to their power bases. But the best argument and strongest men had finally triumphed.

New Year's Eve had been a night celebrated with street parties, fireworks and grand balls across the country, from dry bone rural towns battling midsummer drought to cities polished bright by oceans, green parks and grand boulevards.

In Hobart, where Muriel Mathers rehearsed for the Rignold troupe's final few performances, the weather had been dull all day, and rain threatened to spoil the night-time celebrations. But as the afternoon wore on into evening, the ominous purple cleared and the sky brightened. Bunting came out, streets were strung with lights and citizens dressed in their finery for the unique occasion, keen to welcome a future they hoped would be great.

Edmund Barton, leader of the Protectionist Party, had been caretaker prime minister and would win the first election to confirm his position two months after the New Year declaration. Women did not vote but the right to do so and to stand for election would be confirmed a year later, although begrudgingly and accompanied by the ridicule of large portions of the media.

An editorial in the Sydney newspaper, *The Evening News*, was typical, insisting that the majority of women were against getting the vote and supportive men were merely reconciling their consciences rather than believing it to be right. It referred to a Biblical parable that told of a judge worn down by a widow's nagging so that he gave in to her argument: 'It is the parable of the importunate widow over again. Or this maybe is rather hard on widows: perhaps one should say importunate old maids.' It was a perverse interpretation of a parable that Christians believe teaches the importance of persistence in prayer and never giving up – a hallmark of the suffrage movement.

More than thirty organisations were by then represented by the United Council for Woman Suffrage, led by thirty-year-old Vida Goldstein, a relative latecomer to the women's movement who would prove one of its most potent figures. Tall, striking and considered, she was the antithesis of the cruel image opponents had cultured of feminists as bitter, ugly women with no hope of marriage.

Typical of the media poison was this newspaper column, published just as the new federal parliament was debating the legislation: 'Miss Goldstein is altogether too attractive to be leagued with the cross-grained ladies who are crying out in shrill voices for the suffrage. In her more youthful days, Miss Goldstein was belle of the university, a champion tennis player and other nice things. She suddenly took up Woman's Suffrage as a fad, pursued it for the fun of the thing and finally made a profession of it.'[13]

Although women had voted in three South Australian elections to great applause, only one other state – Western Australia – had embraced (in 1899) female suffrage. The federal parliament now did so and the remaining states fell into line, albeit reluctantly – New South Wales in 1902, Tasmania in 1903, Queensland in 1905 and, stubbornly, Victoria in 1908. The right to stand for election would be even slower – Queensland conferred the honour in 1915, New South Wales in 1918, Western Australia in 1920, Tasmania in 1921 and finally Victoria in 1923.

In 1903, Vida Goldstein, with three others, would be one of the first women in the British Empire to stand for election to a national parliament. She stood as an independent, with the support of the newly formed Women's Federal Political Association, but would fall short of a seat in the Senate.

Muriel Matters, who was voting for the first time in a federal election having been eligible to vote in the 1899 and 1902 South Australian elections, would have been aware of the outspoken woman from Victoria and admired her oratorical flair. Little did she know that the two would become colleagues and close friends in the years to come.

6.

LONDON BOUND

Girls are gaining little under modern conditions. Both men
and women are ceasing to marry young. Seeing so much of
each other without any definite end in view, they postpone
all serious thoughts of matrimony until their youth is gone.
Then it is the men who look among the younger girls for
partners, if they look at all, and leave the girls who grew up
with them to wither away into hopeless spinsterhood.

The Catholic Press, February 9, 1905

The lament was loud among those who longed for the past. Perhaps
it was coincidence, but the death in January 1901 of Queen Victoria
marked not only the end of the most enduring reign by an English
monarch but ushered in a new attitude to life and love, or at least its
management.

No longer did men ask to be introduced to single women or sit
politely in drawing rooms sipping tea and talking of their financial
and social prospects. Friendships were more easily and openly made
in public, at least in Australia's middle classes.

Although glaring divisions between the sexes remained, such as
the automatic transfer of a woman's financial assets upon marriage
to the ownership of her husband, the beginning of the twentieth

century heralded a re-evaluation of family life and marriage. Where once young women were courted, betrothed and hitched by the time they ended their teenage years, it was now common for women to wait until their late twenties. Wooers had become acquaintances, betrothal had slipped to camaraderie, engagements were occasional and marriages seemingly rare, as one columnist moaned in an article with the sub-heading 'Where girls are to blame':

> A very small percentage of Australians are marrying, but a huge proportion are company-keeping, or sweet-hearting. Company-keeping has no responsibilities. It may be merely a friendship; it may be nothing more than a flirtation. It is not taken seriously either by the parents or the principals. People keep company for years without ever mentioning marriage. It is in most cases no serious link – more a matter of amusement than a real affair of the heart – a sort of extended flirtation that has a certain amount of recognition from relatives, yet which need not necessarily ripen into anything definite.[1]

Now approaching twenty-five years of age, Muriel epitomised the New Woman, as the phenomenon would be described, by supporters in adulation and opponents with derision. She was diminutive, standing about 160cm tall, but somehow seemed larger thanks to her personality; not simply pretty, sweet or appealing, though she was often described that way, but 'natural and convincing', 'artistic and powerful', 'commanding and articulate'. Her repertoire was evolving as was her business – and it was still rare for a young woman to set up on her own. She had branched out beyond rehearsed poems to not only join debates on political issues, but to offer a series of lectures on her literary heroes.

A recital on the life of Elizabeth Barrett Browning prompted this glowing assessment: 'Miss Matters is much more than an elocutionist. She has perfected herself in the dramatic side of her art, but her power lies deeper than this. She is an artist in the real sense of the word. The gift of swift sympathy, insight into the changeful moods of human nature, and the power of interpreting vividly and convincingly are possessed by Miss Matters to a degree which would secure her reputation anywhere.'[2]

And there was a man on her arm, or at least in her thrall. The first public evidence of the budding relationship between Bryceson Treharne and Muriel Matters came in May 1901 when Muriel and her Aunt Jane attended a music program at the Elder Conservatorium.

The event was reported by a columnist writing for *Quiz* newspaper, a short-lived satirical, society and sporting journal, which praised Treharne's performance – 'The audience knew they were being treated to the touch of master hands' – before noting that Miss Muriel Matters was among those listening.

Treharne appeared to return the favour a month later when Muriel performed at a private salon and 'sent thrills of appreciation through the audience', according to a newspaper report that went on to note that 'a musical professor listened critically to her selections and applauded'.[3] When that same music professor and Muriel sat together in the audience at another Elder Conservatorium event in July it seemed to show that the brooding Welsh music maestro had been entranced by the feisty Australian orator. Later events certainly confirmed this.

But was it a romance or merely an intellectual and musical kinship? Treharne was a complex man and polarising figure. He had initially been embraced by Adelaide as a musical genius, but after penning a series of newspaper columns about music and the critical capabilities of local audiences, he found himself accused of being an elitist in a city that prided itself on its egalitarianism. In part, he wrote: 'The public likes inferior productions; as a rule prefers it because it understands it more easily; and this preference may irritate the artist in a burst of wrath.'[4]

The rebuke was swift, his musings dismissed as high-sounding nonsense and the young professor labelled something of an eccentric: 'In the street, in the train, in the tram and even at meals he wades through books,' one columnist noted.[5] 'The curly-haired Bryceson writes largely, but there is always a sense that his pen is over-paced by his soul.' Another wrote: 'Evidently Mr Treharne is feeling very sore over the letters which wanted to know whether his contributions are pure art or pure drivel.'[6]

But if Bryceson Treharne was bothered by the response he was not about to show it, his self-confidence clear as he continued to beguile the city with concerts which drew large audiences and accolades.

It was just a matter of time before Muriel, whom he had probably met at the university when she agreed to do some elocution lectures, would feature in his program of events. In October 1902, Treharne announced a typically audacious concert at the Elder Hall, headlined by Muriel who would narrate the poem 'Enoch Arden', a tragic epic written by Alfred, Lord Tennyson.

The poem told the story of a fisherman named Enoch Arden, lost at sea for more than a decade during which time his wife, believing him drowned, remarried. But Enoch had survived, and by the time he returned, not only had his wife remarried but one of his three daughters had died. Rather than disturbing the lives of the women he loved Enoch chose to remain hidden, unable to reveal himself. He died, alone, of a broken heart.

The poem had been put to music by the famed German composer Richard Strauss who performed it publicly just a few months before at the Queen's Hall in London alongside one of Europe's best known actors of the era, Ernst von Possart. Now Treharne wanted to bring the challenging rendition to Adelaide.

Elder Hall was filled to capacity by seven hundred people as Muriel took the stage shortly after 7.00 pm. It would take ninety minutes to recite the poem, interrupted by the musical interludes composed by Strauss and played by Treharne. The *Advertiser* would review the performance two days later:

> The success of Mr Bryceson Treharne's concert on Thursday evening was mainly due to Miss Muriel Matters, who touched the hearts of her audience by her recital of the pitiful story of Enoch Arden. The pathos and sadness of the poem were beautifully expressed by Miss Matters. Mr Treharne played Strauss' piano accompaniment to the poem. At the conclusion of her recital Miss Matters was presented with three choice bouquets.

Her delight, however, would be short-lived.

* * *

The Matters family had gone their separate ways in the mid 1890s. Time, opportunity and different interests had combined to break apart the family bond that had helped transform the fragile lives of colonial settlers into years of fortune and stability.

Muriel's mentor and oldest uncle, Charles, and his wife, Hester, had moved to Melbourne in 1892, their interests by then firmly in travel and writing, although Charles would recraft himself as a leading businessman in the larger city. The Adelaide partnership was formally broken up in 1895,[7] with Thomas carrying on the property business in his own name with the help of three of his sons.

Muriel's father, John, had long since left the firm and resumed his wandering ways. Land Titles Office records reveal his continuing interests, frustrations and ultimately losses in mining; he bought into a silver lead mine in the desert beyond Port Augusta which was profitable for a period but closed in 1903, the year his wife, Emma, decided that she'd had enough of her errant husband and moved the family to Perth in Western Australia.

The move was at the suggestion of her 22-year-old son, Len, a young man unafraid of adventure, as his later exploits would reveal, who had landed a job as a reporter on the city's afternoon paper, the *Daily News*. Friends who saw them off at the Port Adelaide docks expressed concern at the family's leap into 'a land of sand, sin and sorrow'.

But Emma was determined not to rely on a man she could no longer trust. With eight of her children, from 26-year-old Elsie to eight-year-old Keith, she would settle in a large house in Mount Hawthorn, one of the new suburbs just north of the city centre, where she earned a living by renting rooms to some of Leonard's workmates.

Among the children was ten-year-old Isabel who would later marry and have three children, including a daughter, Jocelyn, now aged ninety-four, who recalls family stories about her grandfather. Young Jocelyn heard tales of John Matters prospecting at Broken Hill, winning and losing money on the stock market and being obsessed with gold, so much so that on a subsequent ocean journey to Europe he spent most of the voyage leaning over the side of the steamer trying to sift gold from sea water.[8]

John Matters eventually followed his wife to Perth. She accepted him back and he finally settled down, working as a carpenter making furniture for a department store.

John may have mellowed, but just as he had fallen out with his brothers, he alienated his own children; he was a father who demanded obedience despite his own waywardness. In his memoirs Len recalled a tyrannical figure full of rage while another brother, a promising artist named Harold, ran away from home and was never heard of again after sending a letter from Darwin to his mother, letting her know he was all right.

Muriel, too, had a poor relationship with her father, but insisted on making her own life choices, pursuing her acting career against his wishes.[9] She had not gone to Perth with her mother and siblings, choosing to remain in Adelaide for the time being at least, buoyed by the success of her elocution business and, it seems, her relationship. But the romance would not last, one of the factors almost certainly being her beau's loudly proclaimed views which struck at the heart of her beliefs – equality for women.

Bryceson Treharne had published a series of long and meandering columns in the *Register* newspaper entitled 'Musings of a Musician'. The fifth instalment, devoted to 'Woman and Music', described the New Woman as a 'barbaric creation', quoting not only a nineteenth-century view that women's brains were inferior to men's but that they were 'deficient in tactile sensibility' and, as musicians, misguidedly interested in playing the 'emotional' compositions of the Polish virtuoso Frédéric Chopin:

> I declare that most women only succeed in playing his
> [Chopin's] music – abominably. This is entirely due to a lack of
> true soul-force – that force which, as Cicero states, makes us
> 'break forth into singing when our heart is moved by great and
> sudden emotion in the wail of grief, in the exaltation of joy,
> in the sigh of melancholy longing'. Girls are naturally buoyant
> and self-reliant, and should be full of healthy sentiment. Why

then, should they seek to interpret the subjoined utterances
of a wounded, moody soul, the soul of a sorrowful, subdued
race? To be quite frank, I consider Chopin's music very lovely
but also very morbid music. If women desire to play, let them
choose Bach and Beethoven as the bread and butter of their
musical menu. Gentle ladies play Bach! Play Beethoven! Yea
Brahms if you like – but not in public.[10]

Even his compliments were back-handed: 'Women know how
to give their words a peculiar saintliness,' he wrote, quoting a
nineteenth-century novel by Balzac, *The Secrets of the Princesse de
Cadignan*. 'They communicate in a vibration I know not what,
which extends the sense of their ideas and lends them profundity;
if later their charmed auditor no longer recalls what they have said,
the object has been completely attained which is the proper quality
of eloquence.'

They may have been kindred souls, dramatically and even
intellectually, but Muriel's relationship with Bryceson Treharne was
doomed, the fabulous response to their 'Enoch Arden' partnership
forgotten as she disappeared from the Elder Conservatorium
programs, instead taking an interest in fundraisers for nurses
and the blind, giving speeches on curriculum at the Teachers
Association and offering recitals at the Literary Association where
she performed with her family friend Lionel Logue, another of
Edward Reeves' pupils who would become famous for his work
helping 'Bertie', King George VI, overcome his stutter.

But by March 1904 she'd become restless, unsettled by the
collapse of her relationship with Treharne, who would continue to
pursue her and even propose marriage. She was still advertising for
students and appearing at salon events but it seemed that the city
was too claustrophobic and she decided to follow her family west. A

small item in the *Daily News*, the newspaper on which her brother Leonard had found work as a journalist, announced her arrival in Perth aboard the steamer SS *Kyarra* in the first days of April.

Muriel's reputation was enough to draw a crowd of city dignitaries a month later to a performance of 'Enoch Arden' that garnered rave reviews. The city's arts community was ecstatic to adopt such a well-known performer as its own. It would also have pleased Muriel, given Treharne's dismissal of women pianists, that her accompanist was a young woman named Annette Scammell.

'Both the young artists, Miss Muriel Matters and Miss Scammell, are to be congratulated on the rare gifts they possess in interpreting two master minds such as Lord Tennyson and Richard Strauss,' gushed the *Daily News* reviewer. 'Miss Matters has a fascinating personality, and as she stood on the raised platform at one end of the room in her pale heliotrope draperies, the charm of her appearance added to that of her voice.'[11]

The *West Australian* went further: 'It is no small tribute to Miss Matters' powers to say that she brought home more vividly than ever the poet's marvellous quality as a story teller and vivid word-painter of human life in its infinitely varied and touching phrases of love and sorrow. But perhaps the characteristic in Miss Matters and which raises her talent so greatly above that of the ordinary reciter is her utter freedom from affected mannerism, the staginess of action which so often distracts the listener's attention from the poem.'[12]

Nevertheless, it was clear that her opportunities would be limited as she searched for roles on the local stage and advertised once more for students. If Adelaide was small professionally, then Perth was minuscule, isolated from the east coast and with half the population of her home town. Something greater beckoned that could not be fulfilled in Australia.

The opportunity and inspiration came, as it often does, from coincidence and chance rather than design and planning. Among the promising musicians struggling for work in Perth was a young baritone named Frank Robertson, an insurance salesman by day and singer by night. He and Muriel had known each other since childhood, growing up on the same North Adelaide streets and competing and performing in junior musical events.

Like Muriel, Robertson was longing for something more and announced that he was going to London to pursue his passion, leaving amid great fanfare and promise as the autumn of 1905 faded. Three months later Muriel announced she too was leaving, aiming to follow in the footsteps of another young Australian, Alice Crawford, who 'has risen from wearing white pinnies at ANA competitions to a walking part of five pounds a week in a first-rate English company'.[13]

On August 22, a few hours after a farewell recital described as 'a fitting climax to the many similar successes she has achieved during her sixteen months in this city,' Muriel boarded the SS *Persic* for the two-month voyage with letters of introduction and vague plans to pursue a career on the stage – 'earning my living by means of such dramatic power as lay in me', as she would later reflect.[14]

The reality would be vastly different.

7.

ART AND LIFE

Muriel arrived in London in the first days of October 1905, thrilled at the possibility of a stage career in the world's metropolis but wary of the potential for disappointment concealed beneath the grease paint and footlights.

Her caution would have been fed by the regrets of her first romance. Bryceson Treharne had left a mark that would not easily be erased. She had lost herself to a man who appeared capable of great thought and action, but was not what he initially seemed. Treharne's views on women in particular were confronting and if marriage had been discussed, the revelation of his beliefs would have shattered the fragile perceptions of wedded security and bliss for a young woman already questioning their relevance in a life full of independent possibilities.

The break-up had forced a retreat, creatively and personally, and undoubtedly had been the catalyst for Muriel's move to Perth where she could shelter in the family bosom. But it had been a momentary pause, her passion rekindled and enthused by those around her, including Frank Robertson, the young baritone who would meet her on the Southampton docks and escort her to London.

Robertson had departed amid fanfare, but six months later his bloated hopes had been pricked by reality, the hype of Perth and

Adelaide firmly placed in context when he was confronted by the biggest stage of all. In a nutshell, the young man had failed; a harsh judgment in some ways but accurate in the sense that he would sail for Perth barely a year after arriving, 'having neither the voice nor presence enough for the noise-making profession in that city of champion noisers', although his career in Australia would thrive.[1]

Robertson's story was all too common. Dozens of aspiring performers each year paid the £19 for a below-decks steerage cabin for the six-week voyage aboard a White Star steamer. It was only when they arrived that reality struck. The city was clogged with aspirants. Few succeeded as they would have hoped. Most failed and sought other work, if that is the right way to describe their brave misfortune, staying because they didn't want to return without a level of success. They camped together in boarding-house rooms across the city, in suburbs like Maida Vale in the north where a room without heating cost 13 shillings and 6 pence per week and the bus fare into the city each day cost 2d. One young poet would recall that the winter of 1906 was so cold that his hair oil froze in its bottle.

By contrast Muriel would have a charmed entry to London, perhaps because of her reputation but more likely because of her contacts. She was greeted in the city by an actor named Fred Permain and his wife, Florence, who had toured Australia the previous year with a comedy company. The Permains took Muriel under their wing, keen to offer not only short-term sanctuary but the all-important introductions in a world that offered little sympathy to newcomers.

She was given a room in the couple's Russell Square apartment in Bloomsbury, at the heart of the city's literary set and just a mile from the theatre district, as she would write excitedly a few weeks later:

I went to Wyndham's Theatre to see *Leah Kleschna*, Lena
Ashwell and Charles Warner playing lead. It was good.
Saturday evening the Permains got seats for Forbes-Robertson
in *The Conqueror*. He is magnificent. J.T. Grein received my
letter on Monday and by five o'clock in the afternoon was
down at my lodgings to look me up. He is a great man here,
and told me his pockets were full of letters from professional
folk, asking for a 'push on'. He has promised to do all he
can for me. Am to be introduced by him to Bernard Shaw
and William Archer very shortly. He is going to take me to
meetings, in the afternoon and evening of October 24, of the
Shakespeare League, at which Henry Arthur Jones, Arthur
Bourchier, Bernard Shaw, Grein and others will speak.[2]

The names she mentioned were among the city's best known and
most influential – the theatre impresario Jacob Thomas Grein,
the critic and writer William Archer, the playwright and future
Nobel Prize and Academy Award winner George Bernard Shaw,
the author and dramatist Henry James and the actor and theatre
manager Arthur Bourchier. It seemed that a combination of luck,
an engaging personality and a niche skill had given her immediate
entry into London's 'Theatreland'.

Within a month Muriel had found her way onto the stage. Her
first engagement was in the West End where she appeared as an
elocutionist with the pianist Adela Verne, considered one of the
finest women pianists of her era, who had toured with Australia's diva
Dame Nellie Melba. Newspaper reviews of Muriel's performance
were not only positive but offered the possibility of greater work:
'Miss Matters is hopeful of securing another engagement shortly
through the instrumentality of George Bernard Shaw at the Royal
Court Theatre in the forthcoming Ibsen productions.'[3]

A few weeks later she had an agent who persuaded her to concentrate on breaking into the London theatre scene rather than making a planned tour as an elocutionist through Scotland and Ireland or accepting an offer to appear in Amsterdam. Patience and persistence were the only ways to succeed in London, she was told.

There was also a warning about revealing her background as an Australian – not because Australians were disliked, but because, as she would recount, 'too many Australians have come here to England and thought they only had to arrive to capture the market'.

Perhaps recalling Frank Robertson's experience, she added: 'If he excels and gets a start he will receive absolutely fair play and consideration, but he must not look for a start over the Englishman. If he does expect it, he is a fool. Success in England confers the highest hallmark of merit and it is only to be won by the really capable man or woman by waiting.'[4]

The opportunities kept coming, including recitals at Bechstein Hall (later Wigmore Hall), opened four years before as the city's premier chamber music venue: 'To no small extent Miss Matters may be said to have earned the compliments which fell to her,' crowed the *Daily News*.[5]

There were invitations to shooting weekends on country estates, in stark contrast to her own, now modest accommodation after leaving the Permains' house, selective 'at homes' in the mansions and clubs of Sloane Square and Mayfair and requests to do voice coaching with leading actors and actresses performing in Shakespeare productions at the Garrick Theatre. She was in demand at the Austral Club to deliver lectures on Robert Browning and when there was a gap in her city appearances she went north to Tyneside and south to Eastbourne where she gave elocution performances.

If she had any concerns about her background, they were dismissed when a *Times* reviewer expressed surprise that she was Australian. A correspondent for *The Age* reported:

> It was suggested that she might have passed for a cultivated
> English artist. This struck her as odd and, as an Australian, she
> was somewhat inclined to question the implied comparison. It
> was natural enough, however. The writer of the criticism had
> no doubt listened at the same hall to other Australian reciters
> and to Australian vocalists whose business agents are constantly
> telling them that they must get rid of the handicap of their
> 'colonial accent'. Miss Matters happens to be an exception. By
> careful training and the exercise of a good ear she has managed
> to acquire a habit of expression indistinguishable from that of
> the most cultivated class of English people. It was that which
> the *Times* critic found so agreeable.[6]

The unnamed *Times* critic showered her with praise. 'Her voice is round and soft, her air is gentle, even a little deprecatory,' he wrote, praising her 'pleasant touch of modesty and shy humour' and concluded: 'Anyone can achieve elocution; the important and difficult thing is intelligence and the dramatic sense, and these Miss Matters possesses.'

Perhaps the greatest compliment was the night she was introduced to the composer Richard Strauss backstage after his performance of *Don Quixote* at the Queen's Hall. He promptly offered to accompany her in a production of 'Enoch Arden' if she was available.

She politely declined, insisting she had not enough time to prepare for such an occasion, but it would turn out to be an opportunity gone forever.[7]

* * *

The audience adulation and critical reviews were gratifying, but in spite of her immediate success, life remained fragile financially, her dreams of the weekly wage enjoyed by her compatriot Alice Crawford remained simply that – a dream. Instead Muriel would resort once more to teaching elocution and performing in private houses, as she had done in Adelaide, to supplement her earnings as an elocutionist and actress. And it was through her business ingenuity that she met a man who would become integral to her life.

Peter Kropotkin was a Russian prince, born into a powerful aristocratic family, although he had eschewed his title as a twelve-year-old, ashamed that his father 'owned' 1200 serfs who managed and worked his large tracts of land. Kropotkin, who was known and admired in London's literary circles, would variously be described as an activist, anarchistic, communist, writer, scientist and philosopher. He had been imprisoned and then expelled from Russia for his pronouncements as a revolutionary socialist and found his way to London where he would live for more than two decades until the Russian Revolution of 1917.

Muriel would meet him when she was engaged to perform at an event in front of Kropotkin's family and friends at his home in Bromley in the city's south-east. Years later she would recall the impact he would have on her. She had finished reciting a poem, but Kropotkin, an imposing wizard-like figure, offered no verbal response. He simply looked at the young woman who was seeking his approval. To the others in the room it must have appeared an awkward silence, but to Muriel his stare was magnetic and challenging. She recalled the incident in an interview in 1910:

I turned for some recognition from this great artist.
His influence was silent, his interrogation unspoken but
unmistakably this – 'To what end? To what end?' And in the
silence my answer went – 'A personal career. A name in the
world of art!' The wise man's eyes compassionately retorted,
'What folly! What a waste! The futility of such an ambition.
Art is not the end of life but a means. It points but the way –
it is the handmaid of religion.' And still the silence. But the
wonder was worked. It proved to be the lifetime in a moment
lived, my entire mental outlook was changed. I went my way.[8]

Muriel's 'way' would continue on the stage, at least for the time
being. There would be more recitals at the acoustic haven of
Bechstein Hall, which seemed the natural home for her art, as
well as at private salons and 'at homes', but as she passed the first
anniversary of her arrival in London her attentions were beginning
to shift.

The change was caused partly by disillusionment, not with the
struggle to succeed that had convinced others like Frank Robertson
to head home, but by yet more evidence that young actresses and
female stage crew were being abused at the hands of unscrupulous
men, some even lured into prostitution.

Just as she had walked away from success in the Brough and
Rignold companies more than a decade before, Muriel decided
that she could not simply ignore the way her current colleagues
were being cheated and abused. She organised the League of
Light, a group of like-minded women to support vulnerable young
women: 'The object of the league was to go quietly among the
girls – chiefly girls of the stage and studios – and let them know
where friends were to be had if they wanted them,' she would
remark some years later. 'We wanted to try and prevent immorality

being forced on women and girls through the exigencies of their having to earn a living.'[9]

In particular, she was enraged by the treatment of a young actress who had been injured when a stage curtain suddenly dropped. It was a clear issue of poor management and yet the young woman was denied help. Muriel took up her cause and, on the advice of Peter Kropotkin, approached the influential newspaper editor William Stead.

Stead, credited with being the father of investigative journalism, was famed for his campaigning on behalf of the underprivileged, particularly a crusade against child prostitution for which he would be jailed after 'buying' the thirteen-year-old daughter of an East London chimney sweep to demonstrate how easy it was to do so. The story, told in *The Maiden Tribute of Modern Babylon*, and the child, Eliza Armstrong, would be the inspiration behind Shaw's play *Pygmalion* and the lead character Eliza Doolittle.

'We knew each other at sight,' Muriel would later write of Stead, who immediately agreed to help fight the actress' case. 'He hailed me as a fighter, too, for which I was very proud. He was my friend. No application was ever made to him in vain. He had the secret of "making time".'[10]

The actress won her case in court but the victory was a hollow one, the judge refusing to issue any orders against the company. Furious, Muriel took the case to the Home Secretary, Viscount Gladstone, asking that the government begin registering agents so the abuse could be curtailed. He refused.[11]

It was the final straw:

My chances of success on the stage seemed assured and yet daily the conviction grew that it was not for this that I had been drawn 16,000 miles from home and friends. I became

aware of the meaning of that clash and conflict which had
characterised my short career on the Australian stage. I
realised why I had been 'up against' conventional pillars of
society throughout my life. I was a born agitator – a shocking
fact it may seem to some, but true.

I don't expect to make people moral by legislature, but
we can remove stumbling blocks which lie across the path of
women and grant them facility of development denied them
today by their economic dependence on men.[12]

Muriel had peeked behind the curtains, the applause and the
bouquets of Covent Garden, and the heady intellectual discussions
in the salons of Bloomsbury, to find a city of damp cold, gathering
winter shadows, poverty and inequality that were impossible for her
to ignore.

The squalor was brought to life in a feature article published next
to one of her Bechstein Hall recital reviews in the *Daily Chronicle*.
The writer described a building in the east of the city where a dozen
women sat sewing in a darkened room off a paintless corridor,
the windows nailed shut, for tuppence an hour, minus cotton and
needles. Across the hallway a family of six lived in a single room
that doubled as the father's boot-making workshop. A rotting
staircase led to more rooms upstairs, where an aging couple lived
without natural light and sanitation. The pattern was repeated time
and again in nearby streets: greasy walls, darkened, airless rooms
and minimal sanitation. They were scenes of utter social desolation.

'These people have absolutely no incentive to live decently,' the
writer concluded: 'There is no hope or joy for them at all, and they
fly to drink to enable them for a little while to forget. Who can
blame them? Assuredly not those who know anything about their
life. What hope is there for the children? Brought up under these

conditions they have no opportunity of learning anything good from the cruel, sordid existence of their parents. There is nothing more infinitely pathetic than the great temples these poor people have erected to the god Alcohol in the midst of their poverty-stricken homes.'[13]

The imagery did not pass by unnoticed and the issues – working conditions, decent accommodation, health, help for mothers in poverty and childhood education – would become Muriel's obsessions in years to come. Coupled with encouragement from men like Shaw, Stead and the silent Kropotkin, it hastened her decision to quit the stage:

> Believing ... that the present social and industrial structure was inimical to the well-being and development of the masses of people, it was but natural that I should be taking part in the women's agitation for political freedom. This was but a phase in the greater movement, evolutionary and spiritual, stirring civilised people. I had to cross the line to discover myself as an active agitator in this movement.
>
> Everything in this country conspired towards this discovery. The chill November days of mist and fog; the sordid general environment for the masses of people, with extreme wealth and luxury on one hand and bitter black poverty on the other; those rows of awful lodging houses sampled by all new-comers, presided over by dejected landladies who, according to their own tales, had each and all 'seen better days'; the squalor of their basements, inhabited by the typical lodging house slavery and moth-eaten, half-starved cats; the incessant grind from street organs invariably wailing out hymns of petition; the raucous voices of street singers and the endless beggars meeting one's gaze and tugging at one's heart strings from the

corner of every street. These and other things, too numerous
and too dreadful to be mentioned, work mightily on the spirit
for all who, having eyes to see and hearts that feel, enter this
capital of the world.[14]

By November 1906, as she celebrated her twenty-ninth birthday,
Muriel was reporting back by letter to friends in Australia of
'the great disturbance' of women's suffrage and of eleven women
who had been sent to prison for storming parliament, five of
them married, as if to make the point that the perception of the
suffragette as a bitter single woman was wrong: 'All of them are of
good families and occupy prominent positions in society,' she wrote.
'The husband of one of them has promised £10 per day to the cause
for every day his wife is in jail, so that as she is doing two months
he will have to pay £600.'

For months she had been attending meetings at Caxton Hall,
a red-brick and pink-sandstone building in Westminster which
would become the headquarters of the women's suffrage campaign.
For the most part she had been a silent observer – 'drinking in
rebellious sentiments, longing with all my heart to be with you',
as she would later write – but as the demands grew louder and the
street protests more raucous, Muriel Matters was ready to add her
own voice to the campaign.

8.

THE PANKHURST FACTOR

The figure of Emmeline Pankhurst looms large over the story of the suffrage movement in Britain, her force of will and personality both inspiring and divisive. Although there were many women who played significant roles in the long struggle for electoral equality, it is the Pankhurst name that casts the biggest shadow.

She was born into political activism, the daughter of a master cotton spinner and bleacher named Robert Goulden, who had campaigned against slavery, and a mother, Jane, who reared ten children but doted on her eldest daughter whom she began taking to suffrage meetings as a fourteen-year-old in the 1870s. Emmeline was not given the same educational opportunities as two brothers, instead inspired by reading, in particular *The French Revolution: A History* by the Scottish historian Thomas Carlyle which had similarly stirred Charles Dickens while writing *A Tale of Two Cities* and Mark Twain, who was reading it when he died in 1910.[1]

She married, at the age of twenty, a barrister, Richard Pankhurst, a friend of her father and more than twice her age who encouraged her to continue her political activities even as she had five children of her own.

Richard Pankhurst was a champion of freedom of speech and of education reform and became involved in the suffrage cause in 1889 when he and Emmeline formed the Women's Franchise League which was credited with helping women secure the vote in local council elections.

When the group fell away, as so many did, Mrs Pankhurst found herself part of the National Union of Women's Suffrage Societies (NUWSS) which was formed in 1897 by the indomitable suffragist Millicent Fawcett in an attempt to draw together the aims and resources of more than five hundred individual suffrage groups across the country. When Richard Pankhurst died the following year, Emmeline threw herself into politics and work, becoming a Poor Law guardian, distributing aid and overseeing conditions in workhouses. The experience struck her deeply:

> The first time I went into the place I was horrified to see little
> girls seven and eight years old on their knees scrubbing the
> cold stones of the long corridors ... bronchitis was epidemic
> among them most of the time ... I found that there were
> pregnant women in that workhouse, scrubbing floors, doing
> the hardest kind of work, almost until their babies came into
> the world ... Of course the babies are very badly protected ...
> These poor, unprotected mothers and their babies I am sure
> were potent factors in my education as a militant.[2]

By 1903 and now living back in Manchester, Mrs Pankhurst was frustrated by the NUWSS's lack of progress in achieving the vote for women, as she would later write: 'The movement had sunk into an almost moribund coma of hopelessness.' She and her three daughters – Christabel aged twenty-three; Sylvia, twenty-one; and Adela, eighteen – founded a more radical group, which they called the Women's Social and Political Union (WSPU). Their motto – *Deeds Not Words* – hinted at their frustration and their desire to abandon peaceful means and introduce a more militant approach to the campaign for women's suffrage.

Newspapers had begun to lose interest in the fray, the news coverage sparse and Letters to the Editor by leading suffragists often ignored, so the WSPU's focus, at least initially, was on political persuasion rather than militant action – petitions and speeches – aimed mostly at members of the Liberal Party who were expected to win the looming 1906 general election. The challenge was to elicit some sort of commitment that a new government would include women's suffrage in its manifesto.

But that would all change on the night of October 13, 1905, just as Muriel Matters arrived in London and settled into Fred and Florence Permain's flat in Russell Square. Christabel Pankhurst and a young textile worker named Annie Kenney, who had only just joined the WSPU, attended a meeting at the Free Trade Hall in Manchester to hear a speech by Sir Edward Grey, a future senior minister in the soon-to-be-elected government of Sir Henry Campbell-Bannerman. Alongside Sir Edward sat a young Winston Churchill, hoping to be elected as the member for Manchester North West.

The women had planned to position themselves in the upstairs gallery and unfurl a large banner emblazoned with the words *Will the Liberal Party Give Votes for Women,* but their plans were foiled because the seats were taken, so a smaller banner was hurriedly prepared with the three-word inscription *Votes for Women* – a phrase born from chance that would become the standard slogan of the movement.

According to an account by Sylvia Pankhurst in her 1931 book *The Suffragette Movement, an intimate account of persons and ideals,* Christabel and Annie sat toward the back of the packed room and waited patiently until the speeches were finished and questions had begun, allowing several to pass before Annie Kenney rose to her feet to ask, 'If a Liberal government is returned to power, will they take steps to give votes for women?' Beside her, but seated, Christabel held up the new banner.

On the stage, Sir Edward ignored the question as Annie was forced to her seat by surrounding men, one of whom tried to cover her face with her hat. When anger died down Christabel tried to pose the question again, to no avail, while the crowd, mostly men, howled in anger. A police constable then offered to take the question in writing to the politicians. They sat and watched the note being passed between the men onstage. Sir Edward smiled as he passed it to Winston Churchill, but said nothing.

Annie tried a third time, this time standing on her chair, which prompted stewards and plain-clothed police in the crowd to wrestle her down and drag the pair out of the hall, past the platform and into a nearby anteroom. It was there that Christabel exploded in rage, spitting at two officers as they tried to pin her arms and then throwing a punch at one, hitting him in the mouth, as they were thrown out of the building. Outside, the women attempted to stage an impromptu meeting and engage with the crowd as they filed out of the hall, only to be arrested for blocking the street and marched to the cells.

In court the next day they refused to apologise and were fined – Christabel, ten shillings and sixpence and Annie, five shillings. Christabel remained defiant:

I have nothing against the police. They were carrying out their duty, no doubt, as far as they saw it. The assault was meant to be made against some member of the party responsible for that meeting. It was not delivered, unfortunately, against the right and responsible people; never-the-less I don't regret it.

My conduct in the Free Trade Hall and outside was meant as a protest against the legal position of women today. We cannot make any orderly protest because we have not the means whereby citizens may do such a thing; we have not a vote; and so long as we have not votes we must be disorderly. There is no other way whereby we can put forward our claims to political justice. When we have that you will not see us at the police courts; but so long as we have not votes this will happen.[3]

In a final act of defiance, the two women refused to pay their fines and were jailed, Christabel for seven days and Annie for three – the first time women had been jailed for suffrage protests. A planned peaceful protest, in the passion and fury of the moment, had created the catalyst for an unthinkable response – violence in the name of justice. It would change the course of the campaign, as Emmeline would write in her autobiography:

This was the beginning of a campaign the like of which was never known in England, or, for that matter, in any other country. Our heckling campaign made women's suffrage a matter of news – it had never been that before. Now the newspapers were full of us. For another thing, we woke up the old suffrage associations. During the general election various groups of non-militant suffragists came back to life.

There would be a new name too, one that would still resonate a century later. A journalist named Charles Hands, writing for the *Daily Mail*, referred to the Pankhursts and their colleagues as *suffragettes*, intending it to sound derogatory in comparison with the more traditional *suffragists*. Instead, it became a badge of honour, and was pronounced by the Pankhursts and the WSPU with a hard 'g' to proclaim that they intended to *get* the vote.

* * *

In a single evening, two young women had woken up the suffrage movement, dusted off its polite and ponderous manner and announced that they were a political and social force to be reckoned with. The mood and style had changed, the modus operandi hardened, as the revitalised band of 'Suffragettes' made the newspapers sit up and take notice. The media derision had not lessened – jokes were still made about their dress and intellect, and sly digs at sexual preferences abounded – but voting rights for women was again a matter to be acknowledged.

It was time for the suffragettes to make their presence felt in London and in March 1906, a few weeks after the Liberal Party had swept into power with a landslide general election victory, Emmeline Pankhurst sent her second daughter, Sylvia, and Annie Kenney to begin organising and finding members. Within weeks they had rented Caxton Hall and begun organising a rally and march on the Houses of Parliament. Emmeline was astonished by their success and rushed down to the city from Manchester in time to lead the procession of more than four hundred women:

'Those women – poor working women from the East End, for the most part, leading the way – had followed me to the House of Commons,' she recalled in her autobiography. 'They had defied the police. They were awake at last, they were prepared to do something that women had never done before – fight for themselves. Women had always fought for men, and for their children. Now they were ready to fight for their own human rights. Our militant movement was established.'[4]

In May, a group of thirty women tried to enter the Downing Street home of the new prime minister, Henry Campbell-Bannerman, but were ejected by a footman. Three women were arrested, but the prosecutions were dropped. The stunt succeeded, though, in pressuring Campbell-Bannerman to see a WSPU delegation, but they walked away with no commitment and a plea for patience which only served to harden Mrs Pankhurst's determination.

A month later, the Chancellor of the Exchequer, Herbert Asquith, was confronted by an angry mob at a meeting in Northampton and then at his Kensington home, finally escaping in a car from the back of the property. Four women were arrested, including Annie Kenney and Teresa Billington-Greig, who refused to pay her fine and would be the first suffragette to be sent to the notorious Holloway Prison.

The campaign of heckling also continued as senior politicians were targeted at public meetings, women rising to their feet and unfurling their banners to ask the same question – if they would give women the vote – only to be thrown out by police, arrested, charged, fined and jailed. Some events turned violent as police moved from a policy of ushering and cajoling protesters from the meetings to physical bullying, with some women being punched and choked.

If the Pankhursts were achieving their aim of being noticed, their efforts were still largely scorned – 'those wild women can never turn a vote'[5] – until August when they intervened in a by-election for the seat of Cockermouth, in Cumberland, where a cousin of Winston Churchill was standing for the Liberal Party, which had won the seat comfortably in the general election six months before. Their campaign to encourage Liberal voters to turn their back on the party candidate helped turn that win into a loss, and although party officials tried to play down its significance, it was clear that the arguments of the suffragettes were having an impact.

The pattern of disturbance continued into the autumn when Mrs Pankhurst led a delegation to the Houses of Parliament, this time succeeding in getting a group of twenty women as far as the Strangers' Lobby where a message was sent to Campbell-Bannerman asking if he, as a proclaimed supporter of the suffrage movement, 'held out any hope' of presenting legislation for the session.

When the reply 'No, Mrs Pankhurst, the Prime Minister does not' came back, Emmeline called a protest meeting. One of the women stood on a settee and began to speak, only to be pulled down by parliamentary staff. Another stood and was again pulled down, and so it went on. Mrs Pankhurst, by then aged forty-eight, was thrown to the floor in the melee. She quickly regained her feet and led the women outside where the protest grew in number, intensity and sound. Eleven women would be arrested and imprisoned for two months, Annie Kenney yet again among them.

Watching from the sidelines and attending meetings at their main meeting place, Caxton Hall, was Muriel Matters,[6] still pursuing her stage career but with an eye on a social and political battle she had seen before, albeit with a degree of violence and despair that were never a part of the campaign in Australia, where only the state of Victoria continued to deny women the vote.

* * *

Charlotte Despard was born in 1844 to wealth and position but was still a child when everything important in life was lost: her father, a famous naval commander named John French, was dead before her eleventh birthday and her mother, Margaret, was declared insane and carted off to a sanatorium a year later. Raised by relatives, she married, at twenty-six, a successful businessman, Maximilian Despard, who had made his fortune in the Far East. He bought his new wife a grand estate on the outskirts of London, with fifteen acres of rolling woodlands overlooking the Surrey countryside and a dozen servants to keep it dazzling.

But the wealth and splendour never made up for a twenty-year marriage affected by her husband's recurring kidney problems, and when he died at sea and left her childless, Charlotte decided not to dwell in sorrow but to devote the rest of her life to the poor. At the age of forty-six she moved out of the large, empty home and into the inner city where she tended to the destitute of Lambeth, opening a soup kitchen, a youth club and a welfare shop above which she lived in contented simplicity – a personal crusade against draconian 'Poor Laws' that forced those who needed help to go to a workhouse.

'Intellectually, I was affected in two ways by the Poor Law,' she would later write. 'The hopelessness of the whole business and the ocean of misery through which I was compelled to wade made me search desperately for some remedy. Party politics held out no hope. I saw the terrible problem of the people's necessities played with. I heard promises made to them which I knew would not be fulfilled. The other was a deeper love, and, no doubt, a fuller understanding of my sister women – those who, in discouragement, nay, sometimes in despair, are struggling … I knocked my head against a law to which neither my sisters nor I had consented, and which, though we were bound to obey it we had no chance of getting altered. The thought of all this nearly made me wild.'[7]

In 1906, inspired by Emmeline Pankhurst and her band of unruly suffragettes – 'the dashing courage of this little band … that revolutionary movement for which all my life long I have been waiting' – Charlotte Despard joined the WSPU.

The two women were both driven by outrage, and admired as strong personalities, engaging and natural leaders, who had come from relative privilege and responded selflessly when challenged by adversity. There were clear differences between them too: Charlotte childless and Emmeline a mother of five; Emmeline almost regal in aspect – tall, striking and graceful with thick flowing dark hair – while Charlotte was more than a decade older – thin, her white hair pulled back severely emphasising her almost skeletal features, and with piercing blue eyes.

But it was attitude that counted most, and Charlotte's gravitas and stern demeanour immediately identified her as a leader with a level head and a sharp speaker, and made her a readily recognisable figure at the front of WSPU marches, leading the chorus of 'Glory, Hallelujah'. Inevitably, she would be arrested, but, much to her annoyance, she would not be charged – because of her age but more so because she was the 'sister of General French', her younger brother John having followed his father into a glittering military career.

Charlotte would finally break from her brother's protective shadow in February 1907 when she led eight hundred suffragettes in a march on the Palace of Westminster to interrupt the King's speech, marking the opening of the parliamentary year, only to be met by a phalanx of mounted police who rode down several women.

More than a dozen protesters forced their way inside the Houses of Parliament before they were carried away, among them 'their leader Mrs Despard', who was fined forty shillings, but, like the others, refused to pay and was jailed for three weeks. A suffrage bill was introduced to the Commons the same day. Although four hundred of the six hundred and seventy members privately supported the move, it would languish without debate or vote and eventually be extinguished.

The WSPU campaign would continue through the English spring and summer, a mixture of rousing WSPU meetings – more than three thousand in five months – aggressive interference at political meetings and repeated marches on parliament where the same scenario would be played out: women were met by police lines and horses; there would be buffeting and bruising and eventually breakouts, arrests and imprisonment. The suffragettes often took the opportunity to lecture the sentencing magistrates on the validity of their cause; in their eyes, it merely added to the honour of being jailed.

The persistence was being noticed. Even newspapers began to give grudging respect, such as the *Tribune*, the official organ of the Liberal Party, which noted: 'Their staying power, judging them by the standards of men, is extraordinary. By taking afternoon as well as evening meetings, they have worked twice as hard as the men. They are up earlier, they retire just as late. Women against men, they are better speakers, more logical, better informed, better phrased, with a surer insight for the telling argument.'

But inside the WSPU there was change coming on three crucial fronts. More aggressive action had been successful to the extent that membership was rising and media interest had been renewed, but the suffragettes seemed no closer to success. Bigger and more violent protests were in store.

More immediately concerning, though, was the reappearance in London of Christabel Pankhurst who had been absent while she finished a law degree. As a woman, she was not permitted to practise as a barrister, so she rejoined the London operation where, unhappy at the membership slant toward working-class women, she orchestrated a move away from the fight for universal suffrage to a battle for suffrage on equal grounds with men, limiting the potential women's vote to property owners and the moneyed.

The motto on the WSPU stationery told the unequivocal tale; changed from 'We demand the parliamentary vote for women on the same terms as it is or may be granted to men' to 'Taxpaying women are entitled to the parliamentary vote'. In essence, the WSPU was abandoning the majority of women, most notably the hundreds of East End workers who had led their first march on parliament the previous year.

The move would cause immediate disquiet, particularly from members in the northern reaches of England who began referring to the WSPU, tongue in cheek, as the Society Women's Political Union. As unrest grew, one delegate reported the London headquarters to be 'full of fashionable ladies in silks and satins.'[8] Christabel did not apologise for what she insisted was a pragmatic decision: 'It was evident that the House of Commons, and even its Labour members, were more impressed by the demonstrations of the feminine bourgeoisie than of the feminine proletariat,' she would write.

The third, also controversial, change was the decision by Christabel and her mother to disassociate the WSPU from political parties in order to attract more of the middle-class women they now targeted. Not only would the tactic upset many members who had affiliations with one or more political parties, but it would make it harder to win parliamentary support from political parties with their own multi-faceted agendas.

The Labour Party, which was emerging as a political force, had adopted a manifesto focused on suffrage for working-class men; the governing Liberal Party was generally supportive of women's suffrage, but its leaders, like Campbell-Bannerman and Herbert Asquith (who would soon take over as prime minister), were worried that suffrage would hand an extra swathe of votes to the Conservatives; the Conservative Party was anti-suffrage. The issue was mired in fears and clashing theory, and unlikely to change despite Emmeline's belief, revealed in a letter to her daughter Sylvia, that 'it won't be long before the Tories too will be forced to take the question up in a practical way'. Christabel would secretly instigate discussions with the Tory leader Arthur Balfour, seeking a pledge that he would support suffrage legislation if he formed a Conservative government. Balfour refused.

To compound matters, Christabel and Emmeline were worried that a group of committee members led by Charlotte Despard and Teresa Billington-Greig, the teacher and union official who had drafted a constitution that rested ultimate authority with branch delegates, was preparing a coup to oust Emmeline as leader. The tensions bubbled to the surface at a WSPU meeting in September.

Emmeline demanded fealty, cancelling the forthcoming annual conference and annulling the draft constitution. The WSPU committee would be appointed by her, she declared. The membership would simply have to go along with her decisions. Democracy, apparently, had no place in the WSPU – a body created to demand equitable democracy. Emmeline did not recognise the hypocrisy in her demand, arguing instead that the WSPU was a military force under her command:

If at any time a member, or a group of members, loses faith in our policy; if any one begins to suggest that some other policy ought to be substituted, or if she tries to confuse the issue by adding other policies, she ceases at once to be a member. Autocratic? Quite so. But, you may object, a suffrage organisation ought to be democratic. Well, the members of the WSPU do not agree with you. We do not believe in the effectiveness of the ordinary suffrage organisation. The WSPU is not hampered by a complexity of rules. We have no

constitution and by-laws; nothing to be amended or tinkered
with or quarrelled over at an annual meeting. The WSPU is
simply a suffrage army in the field.[9]

Emmeline Pethick-Lawrence, a supporter of Emmeline and
Christabel, described the scene:

> She [Mrs Pankhurst] called upon those who had faith in her
> leadership to follow her, and to devote themselves to the sole
> end of winning the vote. This announcement was met with
> a dignified protest from Mrs Despard. These two notable
> women presented a great contrast, the one aflame with a
> single idea that had taken complete possession of her, the
> other upheld by a principle that had actuated a long life spent
> in the service of the people. Mrs Despard calmly affirmed
> her belief in democratic equality and was convinced that
> it must be maintained at all costs. Mrs Pankhurst claimed
> that there was only one meaning to democracy, and that was
> equal citizenship in a state, which could only be attained by
> inspired leadership. She challenged all who did not accept
> the leadership of herself and her daughter to resign from the
> Union that she had founded, and to form an organisation of
> their own.[10]

The press sniggered: 'The women suffragists are quarrelling fiercely
among themselves, and thereby giving admirable proof of their
peculiar fitness to rule mankind,' one journalist noted. 'It is a pretty
little quarrel, and is being urged as fiercely as if the parties to the
struggle were "mere men".'[11]

Emmeline's demand would cause a schism not only in the
women's movement but in the Pankhurst family. Christabel chose

to stay with her mother, but Sylvia and Adela would eventually fall out with their older sister and mother. Sylvia refused to sign a pledge demanded by them and watched as the organisation morphed into a volunteer army 'at war', in which unquestioning assent was demanded and campaigns were steeped in pageantry, colour and symbolism, one leader even riding at the head of processions in an officer's cap and epaulettes. Sylvia also saw the sadness in her mother as Christabel, 'the apple of her eye was aloof from her, absorbed in her work ... The mother was lonely and jealous for the companionship of her daughter.'[12]

Charlotte Despard and Teresa Billington-Greig led the walkout precipitated by Emmeline Pankhurst, followed by seventy members. A month later, on the night of the cancelled WSPU conference, they agreed to create a new body with democracy at its heart and non-violent militancy as its creed. The Women's Freedom League was born.

9.

A WONDERFUL, MAGICAL VOICE

Buckingham Street in central London runs south from near the Strand downhill to the Thames River at the back of the Embankment Gardens, a short stretch of cobblestones lined with Restoration period buildings erected in the second half of the seventeenth century, when the city was rebuilt after the twin catastrophes of the Great Plague and the Great Fire.

But it is not the buildings that have made the street one of the more famous in the city's maze of thoroughfares; rather it is the list of historical celebrities who bought, lodged or stayed over the centuries, some covertly. 'Quality Street', quips a London cabbie website that schools its drivers in the street's history and describes the famous residents – politicians, artists, actors, engineers, scientists, warmongers, inventors and literary figures among them.

The diarist and politician Samuel Pepys lived at no.12 and then next door at no.14 in the late seventeenth century, the Swiss philosopher Jean-Jacques Rousseau rented no.10, novelist Charles Dickens lived at no.15 in 1834 while working as a parliamentary reporter and used it as a lodging house for his beloved character David Copperfield in his famed 1850 novel, and the poet Samuel Taylor Coleridge moved into no.21 soon after publishing 'The Rime of the Ancient Mariner' in 1798. The Russian czar Peter the Great was said to have stayed at no.15, although specifics have been lost, as have the details of Napoleon Bonaparte's supposed lodging in another house in the street.

By the beginning of the twentieth century Buckingham Street had changed, at least behind its gracious facades, as spacious rooms were chopped up, partitioned and turned over to commercial purposes. In the lead-up to the winter of 1907 there were rooms to let behind the fluted Corinthian pillars of no.18, already home to the Strand Liberal and Radical Club and the Billiards Association. Alerted by Teresa Billington-Greig's husband, who worked for a billiard table manufacturer, Charlotte Despard and her breakaway rebels snapped up the rooms, paused for breath and formulated their plans.

At first, they would try to hold on to the WSPU name, hopeful that the membership would prefer their democratic approach over the Pankhurst autocracy, but it was soon clear that they would have to start afresh, with a new name, new motto and revamped tactics. There was a niche to be explored, somewhere between the confronting militancy of the WSPU suffragettes and the steadfast plodding of the NUWSS suffragists led by Millicent Fawcett. They, or the press, would eventually settle on the logical compromise 'militant suffragists'.

As Charlotte Despard would write: 'We are in a unique and peculiarly difficult position, but a useful one … in the middle of two opposing principles. Militancy to the WFL is an elastic weapon. We can use it or we can refrain. When we use militancy we put forward the logic behind it.'[1] Mrs Despard had been elected president of the league, while Teresa Billington-Greig and Edith How-Martyn, who had been jailed the previous year for trying to make a speech in the House of Commons, shared the secretarial roles.

In the days before Christmas 1907 the Women's Freedom League revealed its first campaign strategy – members would refuse to pay income or property taxes until they got the vote. The manifesto was grand and heroic, with history as its shield: 'If taxes are levied upon unrepresented people it becomes evil, unjustifiable and unprincipled. This has been recognised for centuries. Wat Tyler's rebellion against the poll tax, and Hampden's denunciation and resistance of ship money have left their mark upon English history and character. British women have inherited the spirit engendered by these struggles for liberty, and recognise that the taxes levied upon them while they are vote-less come under the head of illegal and tyrannical exactions.'

Protesters were instructed to scrawl across their tax notices: *I cannot conscientiously consent to taxation without representation*. This, they hoped, would trigger an attempt by authorities to confiscate household goods to pay the tax bill, at which time 'doors can be locked and a siege begun'. When the goods were finally seized – as was inevitable – a friend would buy the lot when they were put up for public sale, hopefully for less money than the initial tax bill. The WFL would step in and help if there was any financial hardship.

The campaign would go on for several years, and Charlotte Despard was stripped of her furniture on at least two occasions. It was a clever although complicated scheme that relied on protesters being willing to risk losing their household furniture and goods.

The WFL was now an effective third suffrage force on the streets of London and from the first weeks of January 1908 it would make its presence felt, lining the parade route with banners and petitioners as King Edward VII rode in his golden carriage along the Mall to open the year's first sitting of parliament. One eager protester tried to rush the royal coach, only to be hustled away by police. Although no arrests were made, the angry crowd tore the WFL's banners to shreds and mobbed a male supporter.

The WFL was keen to win supporters and create branches outside London. In Scotland, Teresa Billington-Greig marshalled members to stand up during police court proceedings against women and protest that they were being tried under laws over which they had no control. It was unjust, she cried in Glasgow one morning in February, prompting the magistrate to observe, 'You have entered your protest; that's all you can do. You can go away.'[2] By the end of 1908 there would be thirteen branches across London and another dozen in the regions.

Visibility was the key as a dozen women wedged into 'Votes for Women' sandwich boards marched through Piccadilly Circus and Trafalgar Square, handing out leaflets emblazoned with the WFL's slogan, *Dare to be Free*, rendered in the league's colours of green, white and gold – to distinguish themselves from the Pankhursts' tricolour of green, white and purple.

The league's objective reached much further into society's ills than the WSPU's, making clear that suffrage was merely the first stage of equality: 'To secure for women the parliamentary vote as it is or may be granted to men; to use the power thus obtained to establish equality of rights and opportunities between the sexes, and to promote the social and industrial well-being of the community.'[3]

By her own account, Muriel Matters had been attending WSPU meetings and lectures in Caxton Hall ever since Emmeline Pankhurst had sent Christabel and Annie Kenney to London in early 1906. Yet her involvement seemed to go no further than as a member of the audience as she concentrated on her promising stage career.

In late 1907, as she celebrated her thirtieth birthday with friends at the seafront in Eastbourne, Muriel decided it was time to act on the silent message conveyed by Peter Kropotkin. After a series of lectures on Robert Browning and another recital at Bechstein Hall, both greeted with generous reviews, she gave one of her last public performances as an elocutionist at the Empress Rooms in Kensington Gardens on December 6, 1907, reciting, 'Love's Protest' – 'a poem written under clairaudient conditions, of mystic character concerned with reincarnation'.[4]

An Australian journalist in London encountered Muriel in the street amid the Browning lectures: 'Saw Muriel Matters the other day looking very jolly, although she was in the throes of a series of lectures on Browning. Ugh! Fancy anyone being jolly under such circumstances. She lectures remarkably well, too, according to an authority.'[5]

Muriel's 'jolliness' was about to be tested in another way, as she swapped the relative gentility of her artistic life for the stark world of the battling reformer.

* * *

She made her first speech at one of the 'At Homes' held then in the offices at Buckingham Street and I remember how eagerly we discussed her afterwards. Who was she? She had told us in her speech that she was an Australian, but for the rest we knew nothing. Then in the usual cold-blooded fashion of NEC members [the national executive of the WFL] we debated how best we could use her gifts – her enthusiasm, her eloquence, her wonderful, magical voice – for the cause.[6]

The memoir reflections of Marion Holmes, another of the WFL leaders, show clearly the immediate impact that Muriel Matters would have on the suffrage movement. Here was a fresh face and more particularly a voice of imagination and authority that could be harnessed for the cause. She had come from nowhere, or so it seemed, not only geographically but in terms of background and purpose, not driven by the inequity of her own experience so much as by what she witnessed around her.

A woman like Muriel Matters was a godsend. It is not known whether any of the executive had seen her on the stage, but even so it was easy to recognise the potential of such a speaker, whatever the content of her speech that night. All the skills she had developed and honed professionally – clarity, volume, dramatic effect, powerful story-telling and eloquence – had a place at the lectern of protest. Not only was she unafraid of an audience, but Muriel embraced it – and the challenge of sweeping listeners away on a journey of discovery.

By mid February, 'Miss Muriel Matters' (occasionally rendered as Miss Muriel Mathers), previously unknown in suffrage circles, was being billed alongside Teresa Billington-Greig as a speaker of note, although her abilities would not be tested in the tiny rooms of Buckingham Street, which would soon be left behind as membership of the WFL swelled. Muriel responded to the executive's enthusiasm by launching herself into the league's work.

She was thrown into the fray in mid March when the WFL opened a branch in Peckham, a working-class suburb in south-east London. It coincided with a by-election caused by the death of a Liberal MP, which would prove fertile ground for local disenchantment. WFL member Mrs Manson reported back to the membership:

On Saturday morning the man in the street had already
begun to take us seriously. Letters, callers, reporters and
helpers now came thick and fast. We made two sallies as

sandwiches [carrying sandwich boards] and formed three
Indian-file processions with flags. Each one of us carried a
different handbill, and these the passers-by readily accepted
and read. At three in the afternoon we started for Peckham
Rye to hold our first open-air meeting, flags flying and a bell
ringing. We borrowed a chair and as a big crowd had followed
us we had an audience ready to hand. The speakers were given
a most attentive hearing. Miss Muriel Matters gave a brilliant
speech, illustrating her points by allusions to the effects of the
Women's Vote in Australia.[7]

Muriel spoke again at a meeting in the Peckham town hall that
night: 'We had been warned that we should not get an audience of
twenty, and that there would probably be a disturbance by the mob
who accompanied us from the committee rooms. However, the
small hall was packed; the audience behaved admirably and four
dozen copies of [WFL bulletin] *Women's Franchise* were quickly
sold. A large overflow meeting, numbering about six hundred, was
afterwards held outside the hall.'

There would be an occasional private elocution recital, but
Muriel's stage career was now a thing of the past, her future path
set, as she would tell Australian newspaper correspondents in
London when news broke of her career change that paid only a
small stipend offered by the WFL as an organiser: 'I knew that we
must concentrate on the vote for the pressure women would bring
to bear on a matter like this would ensure its redress. Womanhood
suffrage was not just an asking for the vote. The movement was
an awakening of women – their demand for light. In order that
they may have light there must be social, economic and political
equality for the sexes; in order that there may be social, economic
and political equality women must have the vote. The movement for

womanhood suffrage is not ephemeral and local, but universal and gathering strength.'[8]

It was a telling assessment of the political culture that would develop within the WFL as a feminist organisation rather than merely a suffrage protest group. The split with the WSPU had been blamed on a clash of personalities and decision-making, but in truth it was more about desires and outcomes, captured in the four names that had been suggested for the new organisation – Women Emancipators, Women's Enfranchisement League, Women's Association for Rights and the Women's Freedom League – which all avoided the word *suffrage*. The committee had favoured Women Emancipators, but the membership, who decided by referendum, had responded most strongly to the notion of Freedom.

Muriel, too, could see far beyond having the vote. In her mind, it was just a beginning. The greater question was equality and rights, which would drive her involvement in one of the most provocative protests seen in London since the famed match girls' strike of 1888 when workers at the Bryant and May factory in Bow went on strike over appalling pay and working conditions.

* * *

The Cabin Restaurant off Piccadilly Circus was among the biggest in the West End, a favourite for theatre-goers attending either matinee or evening sessions and so busy that it employed forty waitresses, each working twelve-hour shifts, six days a week, for just six shillings and ninepence plus tips, although the menus specifically advised diners that there were 'no gratuities'.

The restaurant was packed on the first Saturday in April, five hundred patrons dressed in their finery for an early meal before catching an evening performance – perhaps *The Merchant of Venice* at His Majesty's; a piano recital at the Queen's Hall; or the water extravaganza titled *Ladies of the Lake* at the Hippodrome – all unaware they were about to witness a spectacular performance of a very different kind.

At 5.00 pm exactly, the white-bonneted waitresses, en masse, put down whatever they were carrying, removed their aprons and marched upstairs to the manager's office, leaving a hot water tap running and mouths agape. Their grievance was the recent unfair sacking of a colleague, and the manager, a Mr Frankenberg, quickly agreed to reinstate the woman and offer secure employment, scrawling the agreement in pencil on the back of a paper bag. Satisfied, the waitresses went back to work, the evening rescued. The customers who had remained in their chairs cheered when the women returned, triumphant.[9]

But the dispute had only just begun. Several days later, when Mr Frankenberg refused to formalise his agreement, the women staged another protest, this time with the help of the Women's Freedom League and its newest member, Muriel Matters, who had realised, having read about the disturbance, that the waitresses had no industrial representation.

The protest was in the same vein, although held during the matinee lunch rush. At 1.30 pm, the waitresses stopped work, only this time – at the suggestion of Muriel, who saw strength in numbers – they were joined by the kitchen staff, bar staff and even band members, while crowds, who had heard whispers of some excitement, milled around in the street outside.

Mr Frankenberg, who arrived at the restaurant soon afterward, would not yield when one of the waitresses, who identified herself as 'Ken', thrust a typed sheet of paper in front of him for him to sign.

'Will you work?' the red-faced manager demanded.

'Not unless you sign,' the waitress shot back.

'Then you are dismissed,' he said.

The answer was expected. The response by the others was now critical.

'Then we will all go,' another waitress shouted in solidarity to cheers from the ranks and most of the customers, watching in a mix of horror and delight.[10]

'Ken' now clambered onto a table and began a speech, cheered with every sentence:

> We don't want notoriety. We can't afford to be out of work but
> we believe … that we have real grievances, and we are going
> to work quietly under them no longer. We have had to depend
> largely upon the gratuitous of the public in the past, and we
> believe they will sympathise with us when they know our
> story.[11]

Mr Frankenberg held firm, as did the waitresses; the remaining patrons were shown the door and the restaurant shut. Picketers appeared the next morning, among them colleagues from other Cabin restaurants around the city. There were just eighteen diners at midday, but outside the protesters had drawn a crowd and were raising donations. It was clear the public was onside with the waitresses.

Muriel's involvement, albeit with the misspelled surname of Mathers, was noted in the newspaper coverage the next day: 'It is often asserted, to the discredit of the suffragette movement, that the participators in it never offer any practical help to the working women of this country,' one paper reported. 'The assertion may have some foundation in fact, but Mrs Despard and Miss Mathers, who are very prominent members of the Women's Freedom League, have offered their assistance to the waitresses in Piccadilly who are at present on strike.'[12]

The WFL had recognised that the strike was an important test case for raising public awareness about the issue of the economic status of women. Muriel, 'very prominent in organising and helping the "Ken" waitresses', railed against the restaurant management's stance that although waitresses were paid pitifully, the 'attractive girls' could prop up their wages with customers' tips: 'It is putting attractiveness before careful and good work, a system that must be broken down,' she raged.[13]

As the strike continued, the WFL organised protests at Trafalgar Square, one attended by a crowd of more than two thousand, which ended in a shower of brass and silver coins. Donations to a strike fund poured in – a waitress handed in a £5 cheque given to her by a regular customer, a 'quiet little stranger' gave twenty sovereigns and offered to find lodgings for the waitresses in need. A businessman donated rooms for a campaign office in Golden Square; a theatre owner offered £60 if six of the girls would appear onstage; another offered the proceeds from a matinee performance. By the end of the week, Muriel had collected the equivalent of £20,000 in today's terms and the figure would double within a fortnight.

Then Lady Holland, a wealthy property owner, offered to provide the waitresses, rent-free, with a shop that could be turned into their own tea rooms: 'I was not a Cabin customer but I could not help feeling deep sympathy with the girls,' she told the astounded media, as she also offered £25 toward the capital cost of converting the shop, opposite Harrods department store, as well as donating £10 to the fighting fund.

When 'Ken's Cabin' (named after the waitress who had made the restaurant speech) opened in Brompton Road, Knightsbridge, across the road from Harrods department store a few days later, more than one thousand customers turned up and service spilled out onto the pavement. Milk and flowers were donated, a band played for free, a well-known perfumery distributed free scent bottles for women customers and shaving soap for men. A photographer produced 'Ken' postcards, and men wearing sandwich boards bearing the slogan 'Help the Cabin girls support themselves'. It was a carnival, even supported by a strike newspaper – *The Tea Shop Girls* – which hit the streets that evening.[14]

But the success was short-lived. When Lady Holland realised the restaurant's potential, she reverted to type and decided she wanted to control the enterprise. The waitresses, understandably, objected and the dispute ended up in court, with Muriel Matters an advocate for the waitresses.

A settlement was agreed and by early May a second, 200-seat restaurant, run by the staff as a co-operative, was opened in Leicester Square, sporting a sign over its door which read *The only Might is their Right*.

A strike over the sacking of a single waitress had turned not only into a comic opera but a major boost for the suffrage campaign and the broader subject of women's rights: 'Thus ends one of the shortest, pluckiest and most successful strikes on record,' the *Western Daily* concluded.

10.

AN AGITATOR IS BORN

Herbert Asquith became British prime minister on April 5, 1908. His elevation was as sudden as it was devastating for the suffrage movement, forced by the ill-health and subsequent death of Henry Campbell-Bannerman, under whose leadership there seemed at least some hope that a bill might be passed to give women the vote.

That hope all but disappeared the day Asquith travelled to Biarritz to be anointed by King Edward VII (kissing his hand as protocol demanded) who, despite the political crisis at home, had refused to return to London from the elegant French seaside town where he was on holiday.

The 56-year-old Asquith was a hostile roadblock to women's suffrage, happy to watch a bill that had passed the House of Commons by an overwhelming vote of 271–92 in February 1908 be effectively killed off by being referred to a government-controlled committee. It was the fourth time since 1870 that a suffrage bill had been approved by the majority of MPs only to be scuttled by the government of the day.

Asquith's opposition was difficult to comprehend, and seemingly at odds with his record as a left-of-centre social reformer; he was the architect of the 'People's Budget', and introduced social welfare and child protection laws. But he was immovable on the suffrage question and even angry at times, once describing women as 'hopelessly ignorant of politics' and 'flickering with gusts of sentiment'. He insisted that the vast bulk of women did not want the vote, or 'watched with languid and imperturbable indifference the struggle for their own emancipation'. Not only did the new prime minister want to be convinced of women's desire to vote, he also was not persuaded that it would 'be advantageous to their sex and the community at large'.

If he was serious about the latter point he only needed to look as far as Australia for contrary evidence. In the decade since South Australia had enfranchised women there had been at least sixteen pieces of legislation passed that benefited women and society, including laws for the protection of married women and their property rights, laws to contain gaming, indecent advertising and opium, laws improving access to workers' compensation and laws protecting children, including state wards. In Western Australia, which had given women the vote in 1899, there had been thirty new pieces of legislation, including laws to create better conditions for female factory workers, to protect women under the age of seventeen and to deal with drunkards and slander.

But Herbert Asquith did not want to be convinced, and providing evidence that women generally wanted the vote seemed fruitless. He would reject public protests and militancy as the actions of a few, and ignored several mass protests, the most prominent of which was in Hyde Park where more than 250,000 suffragettes and supporters congregated in the biggest public gathering in the city's history. Yet the prime minister refused to even discuss the issue or give his reasons for his continued opposition, infuriating suffrage leaders like Christabel Pankhurst, who, in a portent of the violence that lay ahead, concluded that peaceful agitation was useless.

From afar, *The Age* newspaper in Melbourne looked on in amazement at Asquith's pig-headedness, predicting correctly that it would lead to even greater lawlessness by frustrated suffragettes and turn their jailed heroines into martyrs. *The Age* had a vested interest, of course, given that Victoria remained the only state in Australia that had not yet given women the vote.

The leaders' intransigence prompted this indictment by the newspaper's editors: 'Mr Asquith and [Victorian premier] Sir Thomas Bent now share the dubious distinction of being the only two political leaders in the British speaking world who, after being repeatedly urged to do justice to the sex of their mothers, reply with a blank negation which relegates the white women of England and Victoria to a lower plane than that to which the American nation has deliberately elevated its negroid population.'[1]

Victoria would finally pass legislation to give women the vote on November 24, 1908, but it would be another decade, a world war and a change of prime minister before the cradle of democracy would finally yield to the notion of political equality.

* * *

The entry of Muriel Matters into the suffrage movement had been spectacular, even if much of her input had been behind the scenes. Not only had she presented as a brilliant public speaker but she had also showed tenacity as an organiser, first at the Peckham by-election and then again during the Cabin waitress strike.

In late April 1908 she would be thrown into the centre of the public fray when she travelled to Manchester as part of the WFL protest against the re-election of Winston Churchill, a man hounded by suffrage protesters because of his prominent position in the government and his stubborn opposition to granting women the vote.

Churchill's attitudes to marriage and household arrangements were distinctly Victorian: he believed that men and women had different roles – and politics was the business of menfolk. When challenged at a meeting by a banner-waving female protester, he is said to have replied: 'Nothing would induce me to vote for giving women the franchise. I am not going to be henpecked into a question of such importance.' He refused to waver even after he married Clementine Hozier, who would defy her husband to support women's suffrage and even attend a suffragette trial, declaring once that she was 'ardently in favour of votes for women'.

Churchill had entered parliament in 1900 as a Conservative, but switched parties four years later to join the Liberal Party after growing disagreements over trade barriers and won the seat of Manchester North West in the landslide election of 1906. But two years later, because of a quirk that meant newly appointed Cabinet ministers (he'd been appointed President of the Board of Trade) had to submit to re-election, Churchill was facing a by-election. The WFL and the WSPU pounced, flooding the electorate with protesters intent not only on heckling but ruining Churchill's campaign: 'Keep the Liberal out', was their rally cry. They would rather have a Conservative MP than Churchill.

Muriel Matters would take the protest one step further when she and two other WFL members arrived at the Manchester Town Hall just as nominations were being closed. One of Muriel's companions approached the desk and asked Lord Mayor Edward Holt how many candidates were standing and if their papers were in order. There were three nominations and, yes, their papers were in order, Alderman Holt replied. The Conservative candidate, Mr William Joynson-Hicks, who had lost to Winston Churchill two years before, had been nominated by thirty-four people; Mr

Churchill had been nominated by twelve; and Mr Dan Irving of the Social Democratic Federation had three backers.

Several reporters were standing nearby when another young protester stepped forward and asked loudly: 'Will you receive the nomination of a woman candidate if the papers are filled in and handed to you?'

The hubbub in the room died down at the question and the appearance of the petite but bold figure in the broad-brimmed hat. Muriel Matters stood waiting for Alderman Holt's reply: 'The deputy town clerk will answer for you,' he eventually stammered, flummoxed by the question and its audacity.

Muriel turned to the clerk sitting next to the mayor and waited expectantly. The man could only shake his head.

Emboldened by the insipid response, Muriel persisted: 'Would you be so good, Mr Mayor, to state your reasons.'

The room was now totally silent. No woman had ever asked such a question, let alone with such authority.

'I never give my reasons,' Alderman Holt replied without conviction.

The matter would not end there as Alderman Holt, eager to quell any public disturbance, suggested a private meeting. Muriel and her two companions agreed and waited patiently until nominations closed.

The journalists waited as well, including the *Manchester Courier* representative who collared the women as they left: 'The Lord Mayor was charming,' Muriel assured the reporter. 'He told us the reason he didn't give a reason for his decision was that he is a man of peace. But he was in favour of granting the vote to qualified women.'

The coverage the next morning was in contrast to the usual outrage at suffragette activity. *Ladies Interview the Lord Mayor*, the headline read above an account of the protest and its surprising ending: 'The cordial reception also given them by Mr Joynson-Hicks and Mr Dan Irving contrasted favourably with the attitude of Mr Winston Churchill who took no notice of them.'[2]

The *Courier* would follow the women over the next fortnight as they continued to heckle Churchill at every opportunity. And the WFL was not the only suffrage group in town. Christabel Pankhurst led a group of forty WSPU protesters who door-knocked the electorate, while the NUWSS held a series of 'educational meetings', but, typically, refrained from protesting publicly. There was also a cluster of smaller groups which made their presence felt, such as the Barmaids' Political Defence League, the Manchester and Salford Women's Trades Council and the Women's Liberal Federation.

But it was the Women's Freedom League, led by Muriel Matters (identified as a New Zealander) as the chief speaker, which attracted most attention, calling out Winston Churchill as a hypocrite when he changed his stance on the suffrage issue for political expediency. Churchill had put his position first, his party second and his principles third, she told the crowd at one meeting: 'We want politicians who put their principles first. Before this election, Mr Churchill had been opposed to giving votes to women but now he finds it expedient to say he is in favour of the movement. I hope Manchester electors will not be gulled by this death-bed repentance.'[3]

The *Courier* reporter was impressed:

Like the Women's Social and Political Union, the other society, which goes by the name of the Women's Freedom League, are proud of their feats of derring-do during the week in making Mr Churchill realise the gravity of his 'death-bed repentance'. They are supposed to be the anti-militant section of the movement, but it seems they have belied their

reputation. They are intensely proud of the fact that they have
put Mr Winston Churchill into one or two awkward corners
at his meetings. Since Mrs Despard, their leader, arrived
on the scene two days ago, they have been showing signs of
renewed activity which will be manifest until all the polling
booths have been closed ... Their program yesterday consisted
of three meetings, addressed by Mrs Despard, Mrs Manson
and Miss Muriel Matters. At the first meeting, however, at
one o'clock, partisan feeling ran high and the meeting broke
up in confusion. It seems, said one of the members of this
organisation, that many of the male section had 'come for a
lark'. As soon as the meeting had begun cheers and counter-
cheers were raised for Mr Joynson-Hicks, confusion reigned,
women screamed, furniture was broken, policemen were called
in and the meeting broke up in pandemonium. At the other
meetings, however, the arm of the law guarded the doorway
and order prevailed. Their program today is to continue their
propaganda work against the government to the last.[4]

And they did. On election day, the WFL staked out every polling
booth, button-holing electors and handing out leaflets that
damned Churchill. Anguished Liberal Party officials pleaded
unsuccessfully with police to remove the protesters, claiming they
were intimidating voters in breach of the Corrupt Practices Act.
Four WFL protesters commandeered a coach and drove it around
the city, blowing a horn.

By 9.00 pm the fate of Winston Churchill was sealed. His loss
to Joynson-Hicks would be attributed largely to a free-trade protest,
but the suffragette campaign clearly had an influence as the WFL
and WSPU protesters forgot their differences to celebrate together
the 'defeat of the wobbler'.

Charlotte Despard was triumphant, reporting that 'helpers from London', including Muriel, led marches and made speeches until they were hoarse: 'What days they were!' she exclaimed. 'Four and sometimes five times a day our great hall was filled. We spoke, in turn, always to attentive audiences ... one of the most vivid impressions was the delight in their faces. One could imagine that they saw a new world – one in which they could find the self-expression now denied to women – opening out before them.'[5]

Churchill would be too important to be lost to the government benches. Within a week he had been installed as the party candidate for the seat of Dundee, which was also facing a by-election after the sitting member was elevated to the peerage. Some WFL and WSPU members followed him north to campaign, but this time could not prevent their nemesis from being returned to Westminster, despite the success of one protester who followed Churchill around the hustings, ringing a bell every time he attempted to speak. Churchill gave up in disgust.

11.

MISS MATTERS
GOES VANNING

At its peak, Millicent Fawcett's NUWSS would have a membership of 50,000, made up from dozens of smaller suffrage, trade union, academic and arts organisations around the country. By comparison, Emmeline Pankhurst's WSPU was built not so much on membership numbers as the financial capacity and generosity of its five thousand mostly middle-class supporters.

The Women's Freedom League had neither members nor money. By May 1908, six months after its creation, they had gathered only a few hundred supporters and opened a dozen or so new branches, mostly in London. The WFL had colours, motto, manifesto and a campaign strategy, but what it desperately needed were supporters and funds, and cake stalls, raffles and sales of its propaganda didn't bring in nearly enough.

While it was relatively easy to create new branches in central London, such as Peckham, the regional areas provided more of a challenge. The cities and towns to the north such as Manchester, Liverpool and Leeds and the regions stretching into Scotland had long been strongholds for the established suffrage groups, but the market towns, villages and seaside resorts south of the capital offered new pickings.

More than two million people lived in the counties of Kent, Surrey and Sussex where the suffrage message should resonate. It was just a matter of getting to them and delivering the message. The train line linking London to the larger cities had been built in the 1850s, but travelling by rail would limit any membership drive to the larger towns along the route, missing dozens of town halls where addressing small, attentive crowds might bear fruit.

It was then that the idea of a horse-drawn wagon was floated, a gypsy-like van that could be manned by at least two suffragists who could stay on the road for weeks, perhaps months, at a time, driving from town to town. But the plan had certain dangers, not the least of which was the safety of the women who would not have the comfort and protection of others, but be isolated in an environment that was largely unexplored and unknown.

The WFL needed someone who was not only prepared to take the physical risk of the journey but was skilled enough to deliver a message that would be heard and accepted.

The choice seemed clear – Muriel Matters, the vibrant new face and voice in their midst, particularly after her successful appearances at the Peckham and Manchester North West by-elections where she showed not only her abilities as a speaker but her boldness as an agitator. By contrast, her travelling partner, Mrs Lilian Hicks, was aged fifty-five and a veteran suffrage campaigner who in the 1880s had fought to win the vote for agricultural labourers. It was clear that Mrs Hicks provided the credibility of age, as well as the skills to organise the roster of participants.

On the morning of May 16 the van set off from Charlotte Despard's home, a cottage that occupied one corner of the vast estate in which she had lived with her husband on the edge of the Oxshott Woods. The wooden van, painted bright green and emblazoned with the white slogans *Women's Freedom League*, *Votes for Women* and *Women's Suffrage*, was spartan inside: two camp beds, a writing table and small stove, and a tiny bookshelf stuffed with guides and maps.

But this was not about comfort. There was a message of hope and optimism to be delivered, friends to be found and brought into the fold. Personal sacrifice was a necessary part of the journey. Problems had to be confronted and solved, starting with the gate which had to be lifted off its hinges to allow the van to pass through. A report in the WFL's newsletter made light of the issue. The horse chosen to drag the van around the English countryside had been nicknamed Asquith, 'so naturally he would feel a reluctance to advance the cause of women's suffrage. May we soon lift off its hinges the gate which bars the progress of women.'

There was a procession of support carts and horses, and even cyclists joined the throng, as the van made its way down the King's Highway to Leatherhead, an Anglo-Saxon town a dozen kilometres south of Esher, where the escorting party would get a taste of the reception the women could expect over the next three months. They attempted to stage an open-air meeting in front of a crowd of five hundred who had gathered outside the Bull Inn: 'The Liberal elite of the district were ready for us with bells, whistles, trumpets, drums, rattles and other babies' toys and succeeded in creating such a pandemonium that we wished our heads to be made of leather also,' Lilian Hicks reported back to members, making light of the incident that clearly had serious overtones.

The women moved to a hall for a second meeting a few hours later where the crowd could be controlled, inside at least, as half a dozen police controlled the entry. But the crowd outside built up in size and tension, blocking the high street and occasionally making rushes toward the door in the hope of getting past the police. Eggs were pelted and a rock was thrown through a window. The police seemed to have lost control when a young man climbed onto the roof and tried to get inside through a skylight.

The commotion could be heard inside like a rising storm, but the speeches went ahead, the first from Charlotte Despard who spoke about the treachery of the Liberal Party which had accepted support from suffragists to be elected to power only to abandon their promises. She was interrupted several times by men in the crowd, including a Mr Fullex, who shouted: 'On your marriage day you promised to honour and obey.'

Then Muriel Matters stepped up on the podium. She began by relating the Australian experience and the impact suffrage had had on the federation and the states: social and economic improvements, not only for the good of women but the good of the whole nation had ensued: 'I believe it will be the same for England if women had the vote,' she said to rousing applause that momentarily drowned out the opposition outside.

> We are not fighting for the vote because we want to fight and we are not asking for the vote simply for the satisfaction of going to the voting booth. We want all that lies at the back of the vote, to realise the relationship of the vote to the social and economic conditions of the day. That's why we are making ourselves objectionable. Our cause is succeeding, and every day we are enlisting in our ranks a great number of men and women who are anxious to help us carry it through. If you want to be on the right side then come over and join us.[1]

The noise outside had reached a crescendo as the police signalled that they couldn't hold back the mob too much longer. One officer had already been injured and it was a risk to ignore the danger. The meeting, under way for an hour, should be shut down.

The decision seemed to satisfy the men outside and the angry shouts died down, although a menacing throng insisted on surrounding and following the suffragists as they made their way to the railway station for the journey back to London. Police eventually cleared the platform and ensured the Despard party, shaken by the experience, got aboard safely. They were jeered as the train pulled out. Muriel Matters, Lilian Hicks and Asquith, the horse, were now alone.

* * *

They left the next morning on a winding route that would take the van 'a-gypsying', as Muriel would call it, hugging the wooded escarpment of the Surrey Hills, lush and green and sprinkled with late spring blooms, through half a dozen villages, like Great Bookham where the novelists Jane Austen and C.S. Lewis, among others, had, or would, draw inspiration. They were headed for Guildford on the banks of the River Wey, twenty-five kilometres west, a much larger town than Leatherhead, where possibly the first game of cricket – recorded as *kreckett* – was played in 1550.

Instead of cricket balls, though, the small boys of the town threw apple cores and orange peels at the wagon. A photograph would show half a dozen of them, dressed neatly in woollen breeches and black caps standing innocently behind the wagon while Muriel perched in the window, smiling as if she didn't have a care in the world.

But there was nothing innocent about these boys' actions, imitating the outrage of their fathers that these witches had come to town. The crowd that formed that evening was large and troublesome. Police moved in to quell the trouble-makers who threatened to storm the stage. Muriel, broad-brimmed hat strapped beneath her chin, stood on the wagon step so she would be above the crowd to speak, but struggled to maintain control as things grew ugly. Defiantly, she faced the hostile mob and declared: 'We are free and independent women. I have been in the midst of a seething mob before, and I am ready to give up my life.'[2] Her bravery took the troublemakers by surprise. They had expected her to run, or at least hide, but she did the opposite. The crowd calmed and the night ended peacefully, but it was clear there was considerable risk.

At Godalming, a market town gifted by the Wessex king Alfred the Great to his nephew in 899, Muriel was drowned out during an event at the Masonic Hall and gave up speaking. Likewise the next day in Haslemere, another sleepy market town along the River Wey, where it seemed that the whole population turned out for an open-air meeting. Despite 'perfect police supervision', the meeting was abandoned because of the now inevitable tactics of men blowing whistles and ringing bells. The offending men were warned off while the women in the audience were taken back to the van where Muriel could speak.

Despite the mixed response, Muriel remained hopeful as she expressed in an update to the membership in the publication *Women's Franchise*: 'We hope that this van is but the forerunner of others, the pioneer of the movement for awakening in country districts an interest in votes for women, and spreading the knowledge of what women want and why they want it.'

The residents of Grayshott could not recall a bigger turnout when more than five hundred greeted the van as it rumbled over a hill and settled in a field on the outskirts of town. It had been a twenty-kilometre uphill trail, rising almost two hundred metres from the valley floor of Godalming, but the climb was worth it as Muriel and Lilian Hicks were greeted as heroines, the local hall crammed full and the senior ladies of the town insisting on rounds of thanks and applause although they still had to contend with bells and someone releasing a powerful-smelling chemical at the back of the room. While others expressed concern at the behaviour, Muriel dismissed it as minor trouble, particularly as her audience seemed to ignore the interruption.[3]

It was on the road to Petersfield two days later, after they had crossed from Surrey into Sussex, that police intervened. The local superintendent had been told by letter of their arrival and met the intrepid duo on the road to assure them they would be protected from thuggish men, although it didn't prevent eggs being thrown from the back of the room that night: 'Fortunately, they missed their desired course,' Muriel would joke.

The police escort continued to Midhurst, on the fringe of the South Downs, where the two women had been told they would find apathy. Instead, Muriel reported in her now weekly update in *Women's Franchise* that the town was 'one of the brightest and most likely spots for seed to take root', suggesting that an organiser be despatched from London: 'A keen spirit prevailed and the speakers were delighted at their reception. Women's suffrage was the topic that kept the men talking at their social clubs till Saturday night and even on the Sunday one heard "votes for women" in the mouth of all the townsfolk.'

Likewise in Petworth, a nearby market town where the crowd was enthusiastic and generous, one man even offering to help take the van south twenty kilometres to their next stop.

Chichester, a cathedral city of nine thousand people, was about to get its first electric streetlights, but the response of sections of the populace to the suffrage message would be anything but enlightened. Even before the open-air meeting in the market square had begun, Muriel found herself negotiating with a group of young men who planned to release cages of mice and rats through the audience to scare the women: 'I went to the youths, asked to see their tiny creatures and persuaded the owners to let me hold and stroke their pets. This had the desired effect. The boys, seeing that we had no fear, did not let their pets loose.'[4] The peace didn't last long as 'hostile roughs' disrupted the speeches, forcing Muriel to abandon the meeting with police having to steer the women from the scene and back to their van.

They tried again the next night but could not hire a hall, turned away by landlords fearing violence. Finally, they were given the use of the Corn Exchange where farmers and grain merchants had bartered cereals for more than half a century. The cavernous room was filled, and this time the crowd listened in silence as Muriel and Lilian spoke: 'Our doubtful reputation at first made us the victims of hostility, then our stolid respectability made us victims to the spirit of apathy,' Muriel would write. 'This is speaking broadly. Many converts were made, and enthusiasm roused amongst individuals, and we left Chichester feeling that we had conquered some but not all.'[5]

They had travelled more than one hundred and fifty kilometres in three weeks and it was clear already that life on the road would be tough, living hand to mouth on donations and relying on supporters for the occasional meal and essentials such as washing. They were now headed for the coastal towns of Bognor Regis and Littlehampton where the reception would continue to be mixed: big crowds, generous donations and promises of memberships and branches coupled with hostile men whose behaviour ranged from leering and catcalls to bells and arsenals of eggs and flour. By the time they reached Yapton, a small town with an 'enlightened vicar', they had resorted to meetings limited to women and 'guaranteed men'.

Muriel remained buoyant: 'We asked for a show of hands in favour of votes for women and there was not one against, although many had come to the meeting undecided. A member of the audience described the meeting and the atmosphere thereof as "like a beautiful Cathedral service".[6]

The next day she and Lilian Hicks left the van in a field outside Littlehampton and took the train back to London to join the first of two mass suffrage rallies through the city. The first, organised by the NUWSS, would see ten thousand women march under seventy-six banners of suffrage groups, professional women, working-class societies and political groupings. There were academics and medical staff, businesswomen, writers, musicians and actresses. Behind them came gardeners, farmers and home-makers, then the co-operative guilds and ethical societies as well as members of the main political parties who supported the cause.

They were followed by fifteen marching bands as, six abreast, the women made their way from the Embankment, past Westminster, Trafalgar Square and up to the Albert Hall opposite Hyde Park: 'They have recreated the beauty of blown silk and tossed embroidery,' a journalist from the *Morning Leader* wrote, admiringly. 'The procession was like a medieval festival, vivid with simple grandeur, alive with an ancient dignity.'[7]

Among the sea of banners was a painted standard depicting Australia as a young woman imploring an indignant Mother England: 'Trust the women, Mother, as I have done.' The scene would be played out in real life two years later with Muriel Matters taking a central role, but on this stage she marched toward the rear, alongside Charlotte Despard, who led members of the Women's Freedom League, clearly identifying themselves as suffragists rather than suffragettes.

Newspaper coverage was overwhelmingly supportive, led by the *Daily Express*: 'Unless we find a new meaning for the word democracy, it is difficult to discover an effective argument for

Hammer]   MISS MURIEL MATTERS,   [Photo.
A Gifted Adelaide Elocutionist.

Muriel Matters' growing fame as an elocutionist and a society beauty in the late 1890s made her the ideal candidate for newspaper columns sponsored by beauty products.
Muriel Matters Society

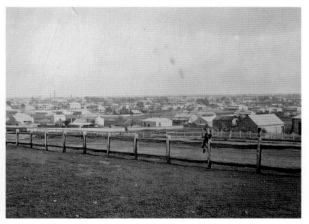

The village of Bowden (looking north-west) shortly before Muriel's birth in 1877. The bushland, so dominant when her grandparents arrived 25 years before, had given way to cottages and workshops, as the population of Adelaide expanded.
State Library of South Australia

Muriel's onstage costumes in London were as extravagant as her dramatic renditions. This photo was taken in 1908 at one of her last performances before she joined the women's suffrage movement.
Muriel Matters Society

Leonard Matters, Muriel's younger brother, served during the Boer War before becoming a journalist, world traveller and author. He supported his sister in her 1924 bid to become one of the first women elected to the British Parliament before becoming an MP himself in 1929.
Muriel Matters Society

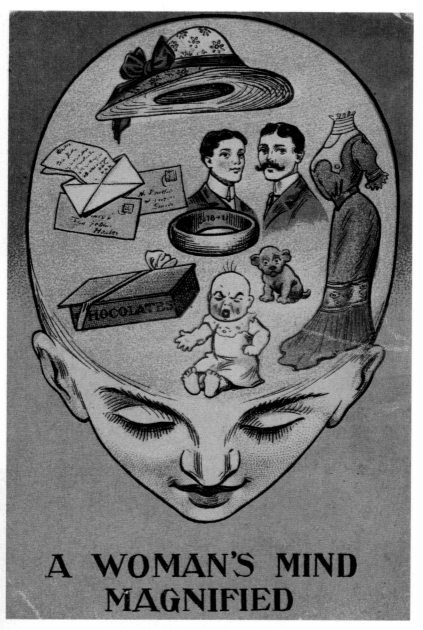

A WOMAN'S MIND MAGNIFIED

This 1906 postcard was typical of the mindset against woman in the early years of the twentieth century – the notion that they were incapable of mixing domestic life with politics. *Alamy*

A SUFFRAGETTE'S HOME

VOTES FOR WOMEN!

AFTER A HARD DAY'S WORK!
Published by the Campaign Committee, National League for Opposing Woman Suffrage, Caxton House, Westminster. JOIN!

This poster was produced by the National League for Opposing Woman Suffrage around 1910. A number of anti-suffrage organisations arose in response to the growing suffragist support base spurred by membership drives such as the caravan tour led by Muriel.
Muriel Matters Society

The Women's Freedom League badge in its colours of green, white and gold.
Wikimedia Commons/LSE Library

VOTES FOR WOMEN.

MISS MURIEL MATTERS.
WOMEN'S FREEDOM LEAGUE,
1 ROBERT STREET, ADELPHI, LONDON, W.C.

Muriel Matters, with her trained voice and engaging presence, quickly became one of the best-known faces of the suffrage movement. She appears here in a promotional postcard produced by the WFL. *Muriel Matters Society*

The WFL caravan arrives in Tunbridge Wells in Kent. It was here that Muriel met her closest friend, Violet Tillard. *Getty Images*

The House of Commons chamber with the Ladies' Gallery visible above the Speaker's chair. Muriel launched her protest from one of the central Grille panels, which had to be removed. Ironically, the panels were the only part of the chamber to survive a German bombing raid during World War II. *Public domain*

A belt of the type used by Muriel to chain herself to the Grille. Such belts were adapted from leather restraints that were widely used in psychiatric institutions. *Museum of London*

British media responded mostly positively to Muriel's Grille protest, painting her as a heroine of the women's movement. This dramatic full-page illustration of the protest appeared in *The London Illustrated News* a few days later. *Alamy*

Muriel – prisoner No.36 in Second Division – in her prison garb.
Muriel Matters Society

The commemorative badge presented to Muriel upon her release from Holloway Prison. Her initials and dates of her incarceration are on the reverse.
Muriel Matters Society

denying her the Suffrage.' The *Daily Mail* equally insisted that the women had cause: 'The numbers of the throng impressed even the most prejudiced that the desire of women for the Suffrage is no mere fashion statement of the moment, but a demand that must be taken seriously.'

Even *The Times* was impressed: 'The quiet, dignified earnestness of the demonstration, the number of notable and distinguished ladies who had place in the ranks, and last, but not least, that imposing legion of lady graduates in cap and gown whose passing even the most insensible spectator could scarce forbear to cheer.'

But one man remained unconvinced – the prime minister, Herbert Asquith.

12.

TILLIE

Muriel would have had mixed feelings as she returned from the excitement of the London protest to the relative quiet of the English countryside. It would be easy to be moved by the colour and spectacle of the march through the city's streets, buoyed by its demonstration of power and unity, but were those feelings an accurate reflection of the occasion and its impact on the suffrage campaign?

The newspaper coverage may have been sympathetic, full of gracious and encouraging words, but the Asquith government had simply ignored the event, the sounds of defiance quickly vanishing as the marchers strode out of Whitehall, beneath the solemn lions of Nelson's monument toward Hyde Park, flanked by silent police officers and followed by supportive but bemused crowds. There were no politicians inside the Albert Hall to hear the rousing speeches of Millicent Fawcett and Charlotte Despard or the thunderous applause of those who needed no convincing.

And where exactly did the Women's Freedom League fit into the suffrage jigsaw? It was clear that Despard had strategically placed the League closer to the ranks of the suffragists rather than the suffragettes, although no one really knew what the difference between the campaigns might be, at least at street level. The WFL had been created because of a division of internal politics in the WSPU rather than because of opposing manifestos, and the two organisations had been engaged in similar, pestering activities that would pale by comparison with the violence that would follow.

Was it a mistake? Was the WFL in danger of being suffocated, its message of activism on behalf of all classes of women squeezed between the broad flanks of Millicent Fawcett's NUWSS and the moneyed authority of Emmeline and Christabel Pankhurst?

The importance of the caravan tour had become clear. It was the one activity that set the WFL apart from the other societies, a grassroots campaign that won attention by its simplicity: an engaging message delivered from a wooden van in a grassy field or from the plinth of a town hall statue to be seen and heard by a gathering crowd.

The NUWSS had established branches or affiliates in some of the towns Muriel and Lilian visited, but the WFL was fresh, and fronted by a golden-tongued spruiker who could connect with women – and men, for that matter. Although she had battled angry opposition, taunts and even the threat of violence, Muriel had found an increasing interest in the message that women needed a voice beyond the opinion of their husbands, fathers and brothers.

The first stop after resuming the tour was the strangely named village of Angmering, where the battle against ingrained attitudes about women and their place in society had Muriel reaching for the words of Henrik Ibsen: 'There, as in other parts, the women seemed so much more intelligent than the men, and it was surprising to hear the words of wisdom coming from a simple old mother, whereas the son of the same betrayed his ignorance in every word he uttered. More than ever are we convinced that, as Ibsen says, "We must look to the women for reform." It is a great joy to speak with these simple women, to hear their life experiences and to be able to point out to them the connection between their conditions and the parliamentary vote. These women are indeed ready for the gospel of freedom for their sex.'[1]

In the village of Findon, once a stronghold of smugglers, Muriel was reminded of another complexity – fighting the hostile, media-created perception of suffragists as ugly witches and dour spinsters:

> It is wonderful to watch the effect this campaign is having
> upon these country people, who hitherto have known nothing
> of the movement, save what they have read in the newspaper
> columns. When we tell them that we really are the same
> women of whom they read such strange accounts in the
> London press it makes them pause and reflect. And so our
> campaign, if doing no other good, is surely causing these
> country folk to take a kindlier view not only of our movement,
> but of the women who are in its ranks.[2]

She and Lilian Hicks climbed from the coastal plains, up through the chalk hills of the South Downs to the wooded tops of the Sussex Weald, stopping in towns and villages with names like fairy tales – West Grinstead and Cowfold, Pease Pottage, Partridge Green and Faygate – and countryside to match. The van's appearance sparked 'no little excitement', as the *Sussex Agricultural Express* reported at their arrival in the town of Rye, after the van had headed back toward the coast. Muriel – 'the Australian' as she had now been identified, prompting the occasional Antipodean to call out 'Cooee' from the crowd in gentle support – was now firmly the star attraction, as Lilian Hicks returned to London, her place taken by a rotation of women who would act as Muriel's assistants.

The crowd gathered at Landgate, a fourteenth-century entrance to the fortified town, was large, Muriel's arrival anticipated as

word spread of the van and its war cry. There were still pockets
of opposition, but here, at least, the critics were vocal rather than
violent, as the paper's reporter noted: 'That the lady was eloquent
no one will deny, and the way she handled the crowd was excellent,
her repartee was of a pungent description, and more than one "mere
man" must have been sorry he spoke.'

The mood changed two nights later when she spoke again, this
time on the Town Salts recreation ground where another large
crowd had assembled: 'Miss Matters spoke at great length. The
crowd seemed to treat the matter as a huge joke, and when 'Noah' –
a local celebrity – commenced to question the lady, laughter was
general. At the conclusion of the meeting Miss Matters thanked
her hearers for the courteous hearings she had been accorded and
stated she and her friend had thoroughly enjoyed their stay in
Rye. A large crowd followed the ladies to their abode, which they
experienced little difficulty in reaching, but anything in the nature
of unpleasantness was luckily averted.'[3]

Behind closed doors there was more encouraging support, as
Muriel would recall several years later: 'One of the most valuable
memories I shall always retain is my meeting with Henry James,
the great novelist. It was at Rye. After my speech at a drawing room
meeting he spoke warmly in favour of women's suffrage.'[4]

Opponents inevitably targeted the marital status of 'Miss'
Muriel Matters: 'The best thing you can do is find yourself a
husband', 'Marry a working man and have a family and then see if
you can talk like it', 'You'll alter your tale when you've been married
a bit and have three kids'.[5] The refrain was constant, her only
defence to ignore and remain above the insulting chorus.

While Muriel struggled from day to day on the road, donations
barely covering daily expenses, back in London applications had
begun to arrive to launch WFL branches in half a dozen towns. 'The

cause has made great strides since the arrival of the van,' reported East Grinstead, while Southborough called it 'a splendid and lasting lesson'. Petworth had 'many converts', Chichester was 'more enlightened' and Midhurst women were 'a family, all for the WFL'.[6]

Buoyed by the response, Charlotte Despard formalised the tactic as 'our next step'. The only way to force Herbert Asquith to acknowledge women's voting rights was to cover the country with branches.

'Britain is our map,' she wrote in the *Women's Franchise*:

The recognition of our citizen rights is the point we have to reach. The enemy, as we have proved lately, is not only strong but subtle. He can make use of every sort of cover: he can hide behind many an evasion. What we have to do is study him at home – to convince him of our numbers, our strength, our determination, and to bring over to our side those upon whom he relies for his own success. I really think even Mr Asquith, assailed on all sides by members of his own government and party, would presently find his position untenable. I am perfectly well aware that such a series of campaigns, as I propose, not only in the great centres but in small towns and villages, will mean money and sustained enthusiasm and much individual sacrifice. This is our next step. It will take much doing, but it has to be done.

* * *

It was late afternoon on Monday, June 30 when 'Asquith' hauled the heavy wooden caravan and its passengers up the last slope and into Tunbridge Wells, a hilltop town on the edge of the High Weald famed for the chalybeate waters bubbling in natural pools from beneath its surface for which it would soon receive a rare, royal prefix.

Muriel steered the horse into a field at the edge of the first row of houses, a now practised procedure after more than six weeks on the road. The weather had been kind, warm rather than hot and largely free of the rain clouds that frequently scudded across English summer skies, but the travel remained exhausting, bouncing for hours over rutted country roads on wooden, steel-rimmed wheels.

As usual there was a crowd to meet them, word racing ahead of their imminent arrival. As Muriel carefully dropped to the ground to unharness Asquith, a knot of women approached. One of them stood out: Violet Tillard was taller than the others, slender, almost birdlike, with sad eyes and an easy smile. She was the daughter of a retired English army colonel, George Tillard, who was serving in India when his first daughter was born in 1874.

Violet's was a childhood marked by tragedy as much as the privilege associated with the life of the family of a senior army officer. The death of her mother at the age of nine clearly impacted on her later choices in life as she trained as a nurse at the Poplar and Great Ormond Street hospitals and then spent three years in the United States nursing a paralysed boy with special needs.

Violet, or Tillie, as she preferred, had been back in Britain for two years when the WFL van rolled into Tunbridge Wells where George Tillard had retired in relative modesty. Violet was not there to listen, needing no convincing about the suffrage cause and having already made up her mind that she wanted to join Muriel Matters on the road.

The meeting would remain vivid in Muriel's memory, as she recalled more than two decades later: 'As the caravan made its way slowly up the hill to Tunbridge Wells, Violet Tillard came forward with her sister Irene and greeted us. We became friends from that moment, although we did not foresee all that the future would hold for us.'[7]

A reporter from the *Kent and Sussex Courier* had also watched the van's arrival and was among the huge crowd which assembled that evening on the Common, astonished to witness how Muriel was able to control a potentially unruly crowd with the power of her delivery:

> By the time Miss Matters mounted a chair to address the crowd it had swelled to a thousand and was growing larger every moment. A considerable portion of the crowd was composed of lads and youths who scented the opportunity for creating a disturbance, but when Miss Matters commenced to speak even the hooligan element was silenced. Two or three policemen remained in the vicinity of the speaker, and comparative quiet reigned for nearly half an hour. Probably the hobbledehoys were disappointed to find that Miss Matters was not the suffragette of the comic papers. As she herself put it, she was 'neither freak nor a frump', but she certainly was a lady of amiable demeanour and a speaker able to put her points with a great deal of force and forensic skill.[8]

But sections of the crowd were growing restless as still more people arrived. The crowd now numbered over two thousand. Trouble-makers began to move forward toward Muriel: 'The dense mass of heated and perspiring people became denser still. An ominous swaying to and fro of the crowd was noticeable, as the lady vainly endeavoured to continue her speech. "Do you want to hear me speak," she asked of the hooligans. "No," they yelled. "Then you can go away elsewhere," she replied.'

The reporter could sense there was trouble looming: 'Despite efforts and appeals from the respectable part of the gathering, the roughs, many of them distinguished by cigarettes, high collars, straw hats and unintelligent faces, made a rush for the chair. Miss Matters was swept from her feet but, fortunately, was caught as she fell by a gentleman.' Police reinforcements arrived and despite Muriel's protestations that she wanted to continue her speech, they escorted her to the police station, followed by a jeering throng, until the crowd dispersed.

The intrepid reporter went to the caravan the next morning seeking Muriel and her companions. He wouldn't have been surprised to find the field empty, the women gone, after their fortunate escape. Instead he found that, far from being cowed by the experience, Muriel was busy writing notices about the next night's meeting.

'Was that your first encounter with hooligans?' the reporter asked.

'No. I've been through it before and I'm getting hardened to it now,' she replied. 'I do not mind a bit of heckling, but their brutality gets on my nerves. One man had his head fractured at one of our meetings.'

'So you won't tempt providence by going to the Common again, I suppose?'

'Well, I don't know. We may have a farewell meeting on Wednesday evening. All this sort of thing brings the women on our side and all the decent men. We shall have a meeting tonight for women and for "guaranteed" men; that is to say, men who accompany their wives and so on.'

The reporter paused, intrigued by this woman who seemed happy to risk so much for a cause that stirred so much passion.

'What did you think of the rougher section of the crowd?' he asked finally.

Muriel stopped writing and thought for a moment. 'My feeling was that they resembled a herd of buffalo. Once emotion crosses them, it is like a wind at which the animals take fright, and these people are really no higher than the animals. But I saw many intelligent and sympathetic faces in the crowd, and here and there, as one walked to the station, little knots of women cheered us. I think the women were on our side.'

There was one last question: 'Have you suffered imprisonment for the cause?'

'No,' she smiled. 'I think I can do more by educating the women, as I am trying to do; but if I thought I could serve any useful purpose by being imprisoned I would be willing to undergo it.'

* * *

Violet Tillard had joined the crusade by the time the van rolled into Hastings a week later. The journey had been relatively quiet compared to the 'exciting campaign', as she described it, in Tunbridge Wells. But the pleasant respite from the violent exchanges they'd endured worried Muriel. Combating apathy, she feared, was far more difficult than confronting and overturning impassioned opposition, as she would write in a report that revealed a sense of wry humour and patience at her task:

We found Goudhurst very peaceful and comforting. But lack
of opposition generally goes with apathy, and to a great extent
this is what we had to confront. We quite understand these
country folks' point of view. It is difficult to feel strenuous-
minded or militant in the midst of cornfields scarlet with
poppies, and hedges of dewy honeysuckle and sweetbriar
surrounding the caravan, and wide horizons showing purple
shadows, save where the sunlight makes gold the distant hills.
But notwithstanding the lotus-eating tendency, we girded on
our armour and went off to the fray.

We met it next day in Cranbrook. The rest of our officers had returned home, leaving Miss Bennett and myself to fight the foe alone. We took up our stand in the market place beneath the shadow of St Dunstan's. Our strongest opponents were a sore-headed Liberal and a fat old lady who clung to the market cross and made an impassioned declaration against us and our disreputable behaviour. However, we rallied ourselves against the opposing force and soon victory was ours. We decorated between fifty and sixty soldiers with the Legion of Honour – 'Votes for Women' badges.

On to Tenterden where we had a victorious meeting. All the men were prepared to lay down their arms and make peace with their women comrades. We made our way to Wittersham where we laid siege to the town in the midst of slow-falling rain. With enthusiasm we make a further attack tonight.[9]

Hastings was a new challenge, a town already softened by the appearance the previous month by Emmeline Pankhurst as the WSPU began its own foray into the south of England. Hundreds gathered in Wellington Square near the beachfront where the French–Norman army of William the Conqueror came ashore nine centuries before in a battle that would create the structure for modern English society.

'Miss Matters made a very long speech full of pungent witticisms at an unfortunate man's expense,' a local paper reported. 'Her smart sayings met with good-humoured appreciation. She wanted them all to free their minds of prejudice in this matter. At present they were not half represented, and yet the tax collector did not pass women by. They wanted to have a hand in deciding about those taxes.'[10]

It would be the first of several meetings in a town that in years to come would embrace Muriel as one of their own. As the weather deteriorated the meetings were forced inside, first to the market hall 'which held a cosmopolitan crowd and outside raged the storm and rain' and then inside the fish market 'amongst the weather-beaten old sailors and fisher folk'.

The hastily convened venues may have opened up a new audience, but they also provided a new type of ammunition for hecklers as Muriel and Violet found themselves donning mackintoshes when fish heads and entrails from the slop buckets were hurled from the crowd. The colourful disruptions continued as an 'inebriated monk' tried to interrupt proceedings, only to be hauled away by his wife who promptly burned her husband's costume.

Confrontation would continue as the van followed the coast south. At Herne Bay, a bodyguard of fishermen escorted the van along the beach road against an angry mob calling out 'Chuck 'em in the sea', then stayed 'as sentinels by the gate whilst outside the mob howled like wild beasts till a late hour'.

For the most part, Muriel was able to contain, even harness, angry elements within a crowd, often using humour to settle and turn opponents, or use their philistine arguments to convince others, always holding on to a calm defiance. In front of several hundred spectators at Bexhill she made an impassioned plea to accept that the world had changed, mechanisation had forever altered industry and women did not just belong in the home to be treated like 'half idiots and half angels', grateful to have kind husbands. 'We are neither,' she insisted, continuing:

Men might say they don't want a petticoat government but
women have had enough of the coat and trouser government.
People talk about woman's beautiful influence but it is only

a pussy cat's influence, a back stairs influence, a pulling-the-string-behind-the-throne influence. We ask to be allowed to exert influence openly and not to rank with lunatics, criminals, paupers and children. I had the privilege of being allowed to vote in my own country and want English women to have it also. I urge those women who do not want to vote not to stand in the way of those who would almost give their lives for it.[11]

Then came the questions. A Mr Harry Cockett stepped up, demanding to know why 'an alien' was involving herself in the English suffrage question. Muriel didn't hesitate: 'I was born under an administration of the British flag. How on earth then can I be an alien. It is the best we can do, now we have got the vote, to come and help our unfortunate sisters in England.' The crowd cheered.

'My old woman is boss over me,' another called out to general merriment. 'Well,' countered Muriel, 'If she's a good old woman I'm very glad she keeps you in order. Many of you men wouldn't do your duty if it wasn't for your wives, but if you won't help us, we are going to leave you to stew in your own gravy.'

And so they continued: Why were they attacking the Liberals who were pro-suffrage? Why should a man and a woman in the same house both have the vote?

'How about window smashing?' one antagonist challenged Muriel. 'You men burned down the whole town of Bristol when you sought the franchise,' she shot back. 'Give me a sensible argument against female suffrage.' None was given.

There was a change of rhetoric in Eastbourne a few days later as Muriel – 'who has a very sharp tongue and speaks with considerable force and fluency' – and her co-speaker Maud Arncliffe Sennett, a former actress, went on the attack against the leaders of the

newly formed Women's National Anti-Suffrage League and, in
particular, its president, Lady Jersey. The colourful exchange would
be reported by the *Eastbourne Gazette*: 'How could Lady Jersey
know anything of the enormous suffering which goes on in the
slums?' Mrs Arncliffe Sennett asked, comparing a woman battered
by her violent, drunken husband, who kept her three children fed
and clothed on twenty shillings a week, with guests at Lady Jersey's
garden party where ladies wore hats that cost ten guinea and dresses
ten times as expensive.

Unbeknown to her there was a supporter of Lady Jersey in the
crowd, a Mr Warren, who bristled with indignation as he stared
down Maud and Muriel: 'Are you of the opinion that if women had
the vote the country would be benefited?'

Onstage, Muriel smiled and took the question: 'If I did not
believe from the bottom of my heart that it was going to do good
I should not be working at by-elections and making myself a
laughing stock for men, women and children to jeer at.'

Mr Warren wasn't finished: 'Do you happen to know that Lady
Jersey is the daughter of the late Lord Leigh, Lord Lieutenant of
Warwickshire? His Lordship was one of the finest Liberals and one
of the best philanthropists that ever lived in this country. How is it
that Lady Jersey belongs to the Anti-Suffrage League?'

'Oh, my friend,' Muriel laughed, 'I cannot answer that!
Goodness knows! There is no telling. God only knows! If that
woman is the daughter of a Liberal man I am surprised that a
Liberal man should bequeath to women such illiberal ideas.'[12]

Mr Warren retired, furious. The next day, Muriel ended her
stint on the caravan and headed back to London while Charlotte
Despard took Asquith's reins. The battle had just begun.

13.

A POETIC LICENCE

The establishment of the Women's National Anti-Suffrage League (WNASL) created an extra complication for the WFL in light of Herbert Asquith's demand for proof of an overwhelming desire among British women for the vote. A group of credible women speaking against their cause would only add to their task, even if the Anti-Suffrage League was made up entirely of society women and blue-blooded aristocrats.

Lady Jersey was soon made aware of the derision of Muriel and Maud Arncliffe Sennett and launched an extraordinary attack of her own: 'The speech is an amusing instance of one of the dangers foreseen by the opponents of women's suffrage. Women are always apt to be swayed by their personal likes and dislikes rather than by the broad views of what would be beneficial to the community at large.'[1]

She continued in this vein a few days later, writing for the *Daily Express* in which she declared: 'We have already enough voters who are swayed by sentiment rather than actuated by careful consideration. Moreover, since there are more women than men in the United Kingdom, the result would be that the casting vote in government would rest with women, a climax that many of us would consider most undesirable.'

The wife of the 7th Earl of Jersey was well known in Australia, having lived in Sydney for three years in the early 1890s when her husband served as the Governor of New South Wales. Despite her first-hand knowledge of the colony, the fact that Australia and New Zealand had granted women suffrage held little sway with her because they were only, in her words, 'small nations'. She added insult to injury by continuing: 'More than one Australian lady has told me that she strongly objects to women's suffrage because the uneducated, common woman will use her ballot without thought.'

Neither did Lady Jersey believe that women should pursue careers in literature, art or science, as she told a function in 1891 soon after her arrival in Sydney: 'Could she do so without forfeiting her dignity as a woman? Could she do so without neglecting those duties which were bound up with her truer life? If there is a section of people who wished to study the professions and qualify themselves in the sciences it is to be deplored.'[2]

Although Lady Jersey was the movement's figurehead, the real driving force was Mary Augusta Ward, an Australian-born British novelist whose choice of pen name – Mrs Humphry Ward, after her husband – was indicative of her attitude to women's rights. As author of the league's manifesto, she concluded: 'The admission to full political power of a number of voters debarred by nature and circumstances from the average political knowledge and experience open to men would weaken the central governing forces of the State, and be fraught with peril to the country.'[3]

The WNASL's formation seemed to confirm Asquith's argument, that the vast majority of women were either apathetic or did not want the responsibility of voting forced upon them. Within a year there were one hundred and four branches and sub-branches across the country, with nine thousand members, rivalling the

WSPU in size. It seemed from the numbers alone that for every society woman in favour of the vote there was another against it.

Privately, though, the WFL sensed that its establishment would eventually drive more women toward the cause of suffrage, and behind closed doors, in their 'kindergarten moments', chose to refer to their nemesis as the Anti-Suffrage Society, if only to be able to refer to it by the acronym of ASS.

* * *

Muriel Matters, too, had become a person of influence. In the six months since she was noticed and then embraced by the WFL leadership, Muriel had transformed herself from promising stage actress and literary darling to prominent suffrage crusader, meeting the challenge of Peter Kropotkin and William Stead who had tapped into her social conscience.

She would never take to the professional stage again, other than for charity functions, swapping the footlights of West End theatres for the rustic halls of outer London boroughs, where she had become a regular speaker, and the plinths and benches of Hyde Park on which she would perch herself to draw a weekend crowd.

The Permain's flat in Bloomsbury was long gone as she now shared rooms with other suffragists in the less salubrious inner city neighbourhoods, keeping body and soul together by private tutoring. It would be a recurring theme over the next five or six years of her life, often advertising her expertise in the pages of newspapers, as she had in Adelaide.

Back home in Australia, Muriel's change of lifestyle had been noticed, and drew mixed reviews. The *Sunday Times* in Perth noted simply that she had joined the suffragists 'and has made several stirring speeches', while a columnist for the *Truth* labelled

her a leader of the shrieking suffragettes and penned a rough ditty
lambasting her audacity in referring to male opponents as a herd of
buffaloes:

> *When Muriel 'mags', she ruffle-ohs,*
> *And hurts the herd of buffaloes;*
> *No doubt to them it matters much,*
> *When Muriel Matters scatters much*
> *Of this loud yell.*
>
> *Around the place of many miles,*
> *O, do not call them animals*
> *Don't lead them to slaughter, Miss*
> *For each may have a daughter, Miss,*
> *Named Muri-el.*[4]

The Women's Freedom League was also on the move, forced from
its Buckingham Street premises by a lease problem, but using it as an
opportunity to find larger rooms around the corner to accommodate
its expanding operations: 'Members, friends, reporters and anti-
suffragists will henceforth find us at Adelphi Terrace House, no.1
Robert Street,' the executive announced in the *Women's Franchise*,
somewhat cheekily, in September. 'Our rooms are four in number,
are on the first floor, and are in every way more convenient than
our old ones. The rent is about double, so we shall expect all friends
to help us by doubling their annual subscription, and by getting us
new subscribers.'

The shoestring nature of the WFL budget was evident, the
organisation surviving largely on donations: 'We have not had to
spend any money on new furniture, thanks to the kindness of Mrs
Herringham who has given us the linoleum, and of Dr and Mrs

Drysdale who presented us with electric light fittings. However, we are much in need of shelves and cupboards, and those friends who intend to take this occasion of showing their interest in the league are asked to note this, and send us any cupboards, old or new, or money with which to buy them. We are almost glad that circumstances compelled us to move, as our work has so much increased, and in our present offices it will be easy to expand. Those friends who would like more details should come and see for themselves; but let no one forget that as we intend to do much more work, so we shall require a great deal more money.'

The determination of the WFL leadership to 'do much more' was immediately evident, as it launched a campaign to free Daisy Lord, a teenage laundry worker from Croydon who had admitted murdering her newborn illegitimate daughter and been sentenced to hang for her crime. It seemed likely that the young woman, herself illegitimate, had been raped, then hidden her pregnancy and delivered the child alone. In her shame, despair and fear she had strangled the baby with a piece of cloth and hid the tiny body in the sleeve of her only coat. At her trial she simply said, 'No one is to blame but me. I did it all. I thought I would put an end to it, so that it should not have the trouble I have had.'[5]

Tearful jury members recommended mercy, but the judge insisted he was obliged to pass a sentence of death despite the fact that no woman had been executed for infanticide in almost sixty years. Daisy languished in solitary confinement for a month before her death sentence was commuted to life imprisonment, despite the fact that a similar case in Glasgow – where an orphan girl had strangled her newborn baby – had resulted in a prison sentence of just a few months.

The Daisy Lord case had raised the ire of the *Daily News* which editorialised: 'Where is the justice, human or divine, in such a loathsome process of barbarity? We may be told that the whole thing is just a solemn farce – that the judge and jury knew that the poor creature would not really be hanged. If it is only a solemn farce, in the name of human decency let us do away with it. And yet Mrs Humphry Ward and her friends in aristocratic and literary circles go about wondering why women want the vote.'

The WFL, with Muriel, recently returned from the caravan tour at its head, took up the cause with relish and campaigned furiously, insisting that Daisy Lord had been treated abominably, and would have been treated differently if she had been a man. Noted art patron and feminist Christiana Herringham was one who noted the importance of the case for the wider issue of suffrage: 'At present in such cases the fathers usually escape both in reputation and pocket – the girl-mothers, with a blasted name, have almost no means of honest livelihood. This is one of the great questions that make women demand political power. Only when women are valued equally with men will it be possible to find a solution to the problems of modern life, without any unequal law.'[6]

The WFL held a demonstration in Trafalgar Square and started a petition that swelled to 60,000 signatures within a month. Miss Lord's sentence was eventually commuted to three years and she would walk free in 1911. The Women's Freedom League was establishing itself as an organisation which was a champion of women's rights and not merely enfranchisement.

14.

CHAIN GANG

It had appeared relatively innocuous, humorous in fact for the attending police and reporters who watched the motley cluster of suffragettes, trying to be anonymous among the crowd as they waited, stamping their feet in the cold outside the prime minister's residence at 10 Downing Street, for the arrival of Cabinet ministers. It was January 1908 and Muriel's trek with the equine Asquith was still some months away as the women braved the wintry weather.

A Press Association reporter approached the group, more out of boredom than anything else. It was clear they were there to clamour for the vote. The police had already identified some of the women and were ready for more than loud voices. 'Where are you from?' the reporter asked. The reply was terse, the women surprised and disappointed they had been recognised as agitators: 'The Women's Social and Political Union.' The reporter smiled: 'Planning any demonstration?' One of the women turned to face the inquisitor and smiled back: 'Wait a bit and you'll see.'[1]

A few minutes later two taxi-cabs pulled up and a familiar figure stepped out among the new group of arrivals. Flora Drummond was a flamboyant character, even among the Pankhurst warriors, an organiser who often dressed in a general's outfit, complete with cap and epaulettes, and was known to ride a horse up and down the flanks of WSPU protest marches. She had earned the nickname 'the General' and would proudly serve nine stints in Holloway Prison, including a period during which she was pregnant.

Her appearance changed the situation. There were now a dozen protesters milling outside the prime minister's front door. Something was afoot. The police line stretched like an accordion as a carriage pulled up. Herbert Asquith, then the deputy Prime Minister, alighted and made for the black door, clearly aware of the women on the other side of the road. He disappeared inside as half a dozen suffragettes sprang forward, police cutting them off before they could reach the door.

But it was not over, the protest more sophisticated than a single rush. Several women had hung back and watched as police resources were drawn to the main protest. As officers tussled with their comrades, two suffragettes moved forward and chained themselves to the iron railings outside the house. As the first group, still shouting, was bustled away, burly officers turned their attention to the snap-lock chains, later described as 'similar to those used by bank messengers'. Their initial efforts failed to break the chains as the women screamed about being roughly handled, but as more men joined in the links finally gave way.

Flora Drummond, meanwhile, had stood aside from the crowd and now rushed to the door of no.10, managing to wrench it open and leap into the hallway, where a startled hall porter stood in her way. 'We want votes for women. We have a perfect right to be here. Let me see them,' she yelled as officers caught her and dragged her back outside, pleading with her to co-operate: 'Come Madam, you have got inside. Let that satisfy you for today.' The General continued to struggle, tripping over another suffragette as she was finally evicted.[2]

The demonstration had finally been quelled, although the women refused to disperse, continuing their vocal protests until five of them, including Flora Drummond, were arrested, and marched off to Cannon Row Police Station to face a magistrate on charges of disorderly conduct. In court, Edith New and Olivia Smith admitted chaining themselves to the railing and defiantly challenged the idea that they had done anything illegal. The magistrate disagreed, offered them good behaviour bonds, which they refused, and sentenced them to three weeks each.

Outside the court their colleagues expressed frustration that the plan, although impressive in its strategy, had fallen short of their hopes, because another group of protesters had arrived too late. 'We are not done yet,' one remarked.

And whose idea was it to use chains? asked a reporter. 'That we are not at liberty to state. The intention was that those who chained themselves to the railings should be able to make a speech before being removed, but the chains seem to have given way – probably they weren't so strong as we thought they were. Next time we will make sure of their strength.'[3]

The media pounced on the novel chain tactic, the satirical *Punch* magazine joking about bargain-priced, specially made suffragette equipment: 'Chains chains chains. Very strong, with automatic police-proof padlock and railings attachment complete.'

But others were watching with more serious intent. There *would* be a next time, but it would not involve the WSPU and would not take place in Downing Street. The Women's Freedom League had noticed the intriguing new tactic and began to work on its own strategy. The target would be much bigger and the chains would be much stronger.

* * *

If there was a single object that was symbolic of the fight for female suffrage, it was the brass latticework known as 'the Grille' that shielded women visitors from Members of Parliament as they sat in the Ladies' Gallery in the House of Commons. Designed by the architect Charles Barry as part of his plans to rebuild Westminster Palace after fire gutted most of the building in 1834, the eighteen panels of metalwork decorated with ivy and hearts formed a gilded, claustrophobic cage for those inside.

The gallery itself was set high above the Speaker's Chair, reached via two flights of stairs or a lift, with seating for only thirty or so. Only the occupants of the front row could see anything of the activity in the chamber below, their vision confined, according to one wag, 'to the Radicals below the Gangway, the Irish Members, and such remnants of the Fourth Party as still hovered around their old position. They never by any chance caught a glimpse of the Whig Members except on the occasions of critical divisions.'

Stuffy and remote as it was, the gallery, with a tea room at one side, was regarded as an 'improvement', given that women had previously been able to follow proceedings only by listening at the top of a ventilator shaft, dubbed the Lantern in apparent reference to a light shining over the heads of the MPs.

But it was a disingenuous offering. Despite being welcomed along the Strangers' benches of the neighbouring House of Lords, the mere presence of females in the Commons would be the subject of furious and at times ludicrous debate in the latter half of the nineteenth century, opponents arguing that women would interfere with the running of the House and cow the MPs from free, unfettered discussion about the affairs of state. If they were to be tolerated, then the Grille was required to at least prevent the women being seen.

Over the next sixty years similar arguments continued to be raised, frequently in mirth but always with a tinge of embarrassment and recorded in the Hansard. The first complaints emerged in 1858, then again in 1864. In 1866 the member for Dundalk, Sir George Bowyer, took up the cudgel: 'The place is too limited for comfort and health, and besides being cramped up in a place which really might be compared with the Black Hole of Calcutta, the ladies have the benefit of the foul air which ascends from the body of the House ... there is no reason for such concealment.' But Henry Cowper, member for Hertfordshire, who headed the House Committee, would not budge: 'If there is an open and visible gallery for the reception of the ladies, the influence exercised by that gallery over the proceedings of the House would be such as not to be altogether desirable.'

Three years later, Henry Herbert, member for Kerry, tried again, arguing that the Ladies' Gallery was a disgrace. The temperature was always four degrees warmer than in the chamber, and 'they have to breathe the air that passes through all the lungs of the House'. But the First Commissioner for Works, the dour Austen Layard refused to renovate, although he conceded: 'I must confess it is extremely bad. If it were not for those who occupied it, I would be inclined to call it a Chamber of Horrors.'

In 1876 there would be another extended debate, led this time by Mr William Forsyth, the member for Marylebone, who condemned the Grille as 'a piece of prudery' that should be pulled down: 'If those who were in favour of the grating desired it for the protection of the ladies they paid but a poor compliment to the House; while if, on the contrary, they thought it necessary for the protection of the House, that was but a poor compliment to the ladies. The House of Commons is the only assembly in the world in which it is found necessary to shut up the ladies the way we do.'

In 1885 the issue erupted again, the conditions in the gallery allegedly so bad that the women in the back rows could barely breathe, let alone see or even hear proceedings. But Mr Herbert Gladstone, MP and Deputy Commissioner of the Office of Works, dismissed the complaints, insisting that the viewing problems were caused not by the lattice but by the supporting stone mullions, and musing that the Grille might even improve the spectators' hearing 'by breaking the waves of sound'. And the ladies did not want light, he added: 'Ladies come to the gallery to hear and see what is going on in the House. I do not think the question of light applies in the matter.'

And on it went, as the Grille itself became the barrier – metaphorical and physical – which separated the conservative belief that women did not belong anywhere near political debate and the growing sense among more liberal members that the opposite was true, that it was important that women were kept well informed, if only to encourage their sons and to support their husbands.

Throughout the rest of the century and into the first decade of the twentieth century, the Grille stayed firmly in place, heartily despised by the growing number of suffragists who made the climb into the ceiling to catch a glimpse of proceedings they were desperate to join. As Millicent Fawcett noted, 'One great discomfort of the Grille was that the interstices of the heavy brass work were not large enough to allow victims who sat behind to focus … it was like using a gigantic pair of spectacles which did not fit, and made the Ladies' Gallery a grand place for getting headaches.'[4]

It was little wonder then that the Grille would become a target for the suffrage movement. In mid July 1908 the Women's Freedom League executive committee sat down to discuss a bold plan to make the Grille a centrepiece of its campaign.

* * *

Teresa Billington-Greig's fervour for gender equality had its foundations in a stormy relationship with her religious-minded parents including a violent father, and an education that insisted her only role in life was that of good Catholic girl. Lessons involved silent rote-learning with little discussion, less analysis and no questions. She turned to writers like Byron, Shelley and Milton for hope and was inspired by the writing of the Italian activist and journalist Giuseppe Mazzini, 'with his worship of humanity and his vision of universal and continuous "natural" progress'.[5] She left home as a teenager, disavowing religion and social expectations, and became a teacher despite her own experiences, or perhaps because of them.

Her involvement in the suffrage movement began in 1903 when she was recruited by Emmeline Pankhurst as a speaker. In 1906 she worked with Annie Kenney as an early demonstration organiser when the WSPU moved to London, earning the nickname 'Parnell in petticoats' after the Irish nationalist Charles Parnell. Her commitment to the ideals of feminism was evident the joyful day in February, 1907, when she married the businessman Frederick Greig, who agreed to lengthen his own surname to Billington-Greig in order to recognise the union as a marriage of equals: 'Bride retains her name', said a headline in the London *Daily News*.[6]

In an essay published in 1911 she would write: 'I seek [women's] … emancipation from all shackles of law and custom, from all chains of sentiment and superstition, from all outer imposed disabilities and cherished inner bondages which unite to shut off liberty from the human soul borne in her body.'[7]

To Teresa as much as anyone the Grille represented the 'sex-subjection' at the core of disenfranchisement; it was a symbol either to be torn down or used to tether a great protest in the heart of enemy territory. Inspired by the events outside Downing Street in

January when Flora Drummond rushed the front door, TBG, as she signed herself, hatched a plot using a series of diversionary tactics to allow two WFL members to get into the Ladies' Gallery and then chain themselves to the hated Grille, creating a protest that would not easily be forgotten.

The biggest diversion would be a mass protest beneath the statue of Richard Coeur de Lion, the twelfth-century monarch, astride his steed, arm raised in triumph, which dominated the Old Palace Yard facing the House of Lords. There would also be a disturbance organised at the other end of the building, outside the entrance to St Stephen's Hall, which led to the House of Commons, and another inside the hall itself, provided that enough members could gain entrance. Finally, there would be two male supporters who would raise a disturbance in the Strangers' Gallery, which sat at the other end of the House to the Ladies' Gallery.

'The plan of attack could not really fail,' she later wrote. 'Whatever attitude was taken by the House, whichever alternative it chose, the women would triumph. To talk the House out would have been a triumph indeed. To remove the Grille had even greater symbolic value.'[8]

Diversions aside, the most important question was who should lead the protest, chain herself to the Grille and make a historic speech to the parliament. None of the national executive, including TBG, who had spent time inside Holloway Prison, could be chosen, because they would be instantly recognised by the police. For the same reason, they could not select a member who'd already been arrested and charged. And it had to be someone who could make a speech, otherwise the opportunity would be lost.

The answer was clear – Muriel Matters, the mercurial Australian who had so successfully managed the caravan tour. She was largely unknown, given that her most prominent public involvement until now had been in Manchester, Peckham and the counties south of London. It was unlikely that London police would know her face and she had a voice like few others, one that could soar above the male anger that would inevitably accompany her discovery once she was chained to the Grille.

Muriel, who had just returned from her stint on the suffrage caravan tour, was hurriedly sent off to join the campaign in East Anglia, the counties immediately north-east of London where she could be useful but safely out of the way, a star performer kept under wraps – although her work would not go unnoticed: 'Miss Matters is an attractive, polished and popular speaker and has made many converts,' one paper reported after a series of meetings in Colchester and Sudbury, adding that one society woman, Lady Pearson, had made a substantial £100 donation to the cause.[9] But there was always the threat of violence. At another event, this time in a packed town hall in Woking south of London, angry men rushed the closed doors. Failing to get inside, they set off sulphuretted hydrogen canisters, releasing a highly flammable and poisonous gas, which forced the hall to be evacuated and the meeting abandoned.

Back in London, the executive set the Grille protest for the evening of October 13, keeping the planning and details from all but a few and excluding mention of them from the minutes normally kept meticulously by TBG. But it was hastily abandoned a few days before the event when news came of a separate parliamentary protest being planned by Emmeline and Christabel Pankhurst. Unlike the WFL's covert operation, the Pankhursts made no secret of their intention, widely advertising the 'rush' in handbills distributed across the city, even stating that it would begin at 7.30 pm.

On the morning of the protests, Emmeline appealed through the media for people to help the WSPU break down barriers and force their way into the House of Commons. The police responded by revealing there would be five thousand officers deployed, including two hundred on horseback. Anyone loitering or making a speech near Westminster Palace faced arrest.

In the end, forty people were arrested, including Emmeline and Christabel Pankhurst and the General, Flora Drummond, who had been taken in the day before for inciting the protest. The police lines largely held, although one woman managed to get into the Commons. Margaret Travers Symons, a secretary to the leading Labour politician, Keir Hardie, had been on her way to the Ladies' Gallery at the invitation of a member when she looked through a peephole which gave a view of the parliamentary floor. Acting on the spur of the moment, Mrs Travers Symons walked through the swinging door and onto the floor of the House. She was quickly grabbed and taken back outside, yelling as she left, 'Attend to the women's question.'[10]

The WFL held back its own plans, instead launching a provocative campaign on October 12 in which an estimated thousand members pasted thousands of posters – 'proclamations' – calling for the vote on public buildings across London and other major cities. Posters were glued to the walls of Parliament House and 10 Downing Street, the doors of Cabinet ministers, on pillar boxes the length of Whitehall, on Nelson's Column in Trafalgar Square, and the walls of Guildhall, Mansion House, the Bank of England and even Holloway Prison.

Muriel and Violet Tillard were told to 'decorate' the House of Commons, but fled into the back streets when a side door opened and a phalanx of police rushed out. In the chaos they weren't seen, and they crept back after dark to finish their work, even clambering up statues to glue their posters.

They would wait another fortnight – until October 28 – before launching their most provocative action. On the morning of the protest, on the other side of the world, a columnist in the South Australian magazine the *Gadfly*, published by the poet C.J. Dennis, made note of the activities of the former Adelaide elocutionist:

Most South Australians who read daily of the eccentric and athletic behaviour of the suffragettes in London will be surprised to learn that an Adelaide maiden is among the most strenuous clamourers for the cause. Muriel Matters, whose talent for elocution took her fame-hunting a few years ago, is the culprit, and Australians in London report that she addresses meetings, both in and out of doors, chalks pavements and draws crowds like the most hardened veterans. To the ordinary and everyday Australian feminine mortal, who got her vote without having to smash Parliament House into atoms or resort to such trifling amusements as that, the conduct of the British woman seems nothing more than a bid for notoriety. Still, one can't help admitting she knew a thing or two more than her alphabet when she lassoed the interest of the gifted Muriel, who has a quantity of charm besides what is known in high and culchawed circles as the gift of the gab.[11]

Muriel Matters' gift was about to be put to the test.

15.

HEROINE OF THE GRILLE

Muriel Matters sighed and sat back on the bare wooden seat. There was no point leaning forward to peer through the brass lacework Grille in front of her and see what was happening ten metres below. At best, she could spy the despatch boxes and the shoes of the speaker in his chair.

Anyway, they were just a group of trussed-up, pompous men, and the sight of them was almost as tedious as their self-righteous speeches emanating from the floor of the House of Commons. She would later sum up the experience thus: 'Sitting behind the hideous obstacle, listening to the lifeless and monotonous twaddle that was being loosed below.'[1]

Muriel and WFL compatriot Helen Fox had been sitting quietly in the Ladies' Gallery for almost three hours, increasingly uncomfortable in the stuffy room set in the rafters of the Palace of Westminster for the moment her carefully planned protest would begin and make this night – October 28, 1908 – one of the most important in the history of the women's suffrage movement.

London's autumn chill had been an important accomplice when they presented themselves at the St Stephen's entrance of parliament at 5.30 pm. Their chains wrapped in calico knitting cotton and hidden beneath dark, heavy overcoats, the women asked to see the member for Kennington, Mr Stephen Collins. Neither had ever met the 61-year-old, God-fearing man of temperance but they had no qualms about taking advantage of his naivety in the suffrage game of cat and mouse.

A few days before, Mr Collins had taken a call from a 'Miss Adler', who asked if the two women could be allowed to see the workings of parliament, given that they were employed by the civil service. Mr Collins blindly accepted the story and agreed to sponsor their visit, meeting them in the building's Central Lobby between the House of Commons and the House of Lords.

From there the MP escorted Muriel and Helen in an internal lift to the door of the Ladies' Gallery, and handed them their tickets: 'I expressly warned them as to their conduct, stating that it had been found necessary to be cautious as to the admission of ladies,' he gravely told the press the next day in his defence. 'I wanted their assurance that they would behave themselves, and that they contemplated no mischief. I wish I had been there when the disturbance occurred as I should have had something to say to them for having broken their promise.'[2]

Muriel, clutching a book of Robert Browning's poetry and a box of chocolates, had smiled sweetly. Of course she and her friend would behave themselves, she laughed, sweeping past the MP and hoping he would not ask for their coats.

Stephen Collins wasn't the only MP to be duped by WFL women to get into the parliament that night. Mr James Gibb, the Liberal member for Harrow, was one who received – and believed – a letter from the Kensington Fabian Society stating that two cousins of a member were visiting from Lisbon and wanted to see parliament. There were others too, like Mr James O'Grady, the Labour member for Leeds South East, who allowed two other sympathisers into the lions' den.

By the time Muriel and Helen reached the gallery it was more than half full. Some of the faces in the crowd were familiar, and friends would become important when the action began. Violet Tillard was one who had managed to get inside, a WFL poster carefully rolled up beneath her cloak. The friends passed each other without acknowledgment in order to maintain the ruse.

Muriel had hoped to get seats in the front row but all had been taken so she settled on the second row. Given the tedious debate below it seemed remarkable that no one moved when the sound of Big Ben chiming 8.00 pm outside reverberated through the chamber.

At least she was on the aisle, and if no one vacated a closer seat in the next thirty minutes she would simply have to force her way to the front. Timing was crucial, given the diversionary protests about to erupt outside and the effort required to unwrap the heavy chains hidden beneath her coat, the ends of which were attached to a wide leather belt around her waist. It was the sort of contraption normally used to quieten troublesome patients in a sanatorium, but tonight the chains would be used not as a restraint but to give her the freedom to launch an unforgettable protest, latched to the Grille using 'burglar-proof' padlocks so she could not be easily arrested and hauled away by security.

It was a nervous wait, made worse by the appearance of a police inspector named Charles Scantlebury whose job it was to keep order inside the House of Commons. The sheer number of women making their way into the House on a cold Wednesday evening had raised his suspicions. The Ladies' Gallery was normally all but empty at that time. Tonight it was almost full, even though the debate on a Licensing Bill was hardly riveting. He looked at the faces, trying to sense if there was trouble ahead, even though he thought it unlikely that women's suffrage protestors could have managed to get so far into the building. All the protests were outside, beyond his scope of responsibility.

The women, he decided, seemed to be genuine onlookers: middle-class women, nicely dressed, even if some were still in their overcoats. Still, he couldn't be sure. Talk was kept to a minimum, beneath signs that demanded silence even though the women's voices were unlikely to interrupt the proceedings below. High above the gas lamps suspended from the ceiling, the gallery was so far from the MPs that many women had brought opera glasses for a better view. Satisfied, Scantlebury withdrew and went to report to the Serjeant-at-Arms that he intended to keep a watch on the gallery.

Muriel breathed a sigh of relief. She glanced around the room again, trying not to dwell on familiar faces and arouse the suspicions of the attendant at the door. Violet was nearer the front, ready to unfurl her poster once the protest began. Helen, who sat nearby eating chocolates, would reveal later that she was worried that a woman seated behind her might have been a police officer in plain clothes, placed there to quickly stifle any trouble. The woman had been 'looking at me hard',[3] so Helen had pulled the chocolates out of her bag to put her off – after all, a determined protester wouldn't be munching chocolate, would she? The woman eventually moved away.

In her worry about getting to the front, Muriel had begun to suspect that police had stacked the gallery. As she contemplated the problem the attendant appeared next to her. She would have to move, he said, to make way for several well-attired women – probably MPs' wives, Muriel silently fumed as she was wedged into a seat at the back of the room. The Grille was now further away and as Big Ben chimed 8.15 the game seemed gone.

'The minutes dragged, then flew, alternately, according to the beats of my heart,' she later wrote to a friend. 'Yet but two minutes to the half hour and I was quite unprepared for the task.'[4]

Then a miracle, or so it seemed. As the parliament clock on the opposite wall ticked past 8.30 a tired-looking woman seated at the front stood and left the gallery, weary of the politicians' voices below. Muriel had her chance. Dashing forward, she stripped off her coat, slipped beneath a railing, pushed aside the legs of two women and threaded the thick chains through the Grille before snapping the padlock shut on one of the centre panels.

'It was over, done in a second,' she later told the *Daily Express*. 'I had a leather belt around my waist and around that was padlocked a chain. Just one snap of another, self-locking, padlock and another chain had fixed my belt to the Grille.'

In fact she used two padlocks: a keyed lock to attach the chain to the belt (hiding the key down the back of her dress) and a spring lock to shackle the chains to the Grille. It merely added to the immediate confusion in the chamber below where Mr James Remnant, the Honorable Member for Holborn, had just begun to speak on an amendment to an amendment: 'The Solicitor-General has said it would be impossible to borrow beyond the compensation fund, but loans could be made on the future instalments of the levy under the bill ...' he droned.[5]

Suddenly a voice was heard above – a woman's voice. Shocked eyes shot skywards to the row of arched windows below the roofline, hard to see in the shadows cast from the gas lamps that would light the seat of democracy for another four years, despite the growing use of electricity across the city.

Muriel's commanding tones rang out across the great hall in what history would mark as the first speech ever by a woman in the House of Commons, her words instinctive rather than rehearsed, but the message loud, clear and effective:

Mr Speaker, members of the Il-Liberal government. We have
sat behind this insulting Grille for too long. It is time that
you ceased to legislate merely on effects, it behoves you to deal
with primary causes. You are discussing a domestic question,
and it is time that the women of England were given a voice
in legislation which affects them as much as it affects men.
We demand the vote.

Mr Remnant stopped. So did the Hansard reporter, sitting
immediately beneath the Ladies' Gallery, his transcript ceasing
mid-sentence with the explanation: 'The remainder of the speech
was inaudible in the Press Gallery on account of a disturbance in
the Ladies' Gallery, where two ladies had chained themselves to the
Grille and endeavoured to address the House in favour of woman
suffrage.'[6]

On the contrary, Muriel's speech was more than an endeavour
to speak; it was a triumph and it was audible above the uproar that
followed. Various versions would emerge over the next few days
as the British Press got itself in a lather over the audacity of the
protest. The House of Commons, the bastion of democracy had
been brought to a halt by a woman with a unique perspective and
credibility, a colonial rebel who had done what no English woman
had been allowed to do – she had voted in a federal election.

Now exultant, Muriel continued:

We have listened too long to the illogical utterances of the
men who know nothing about it. Attend to the women. We
demand of this government calling itself Liberal but which
is really illiberal to show its liberalism. For forty years we
have listened behind this Grille, and we are going to do no
longer...[7]

Helen Fox, who had followed Muriel's lead and shackled herself to panel no.11, had never made a speech before but, spurred by the adrenalin of the moment, suddenly found her voice: 'The women of the country demand the vote,' she shouted, her mouth pressed to the Grille as Violet Tillard also sprang into action, revealing the hidden poster from beneath her heavy coat. It was one of five thousand that had been printed to paste on pillar boxes and buildings around the city. This one had been glued onto cloth and fixed, top and bottom, to pieces of bamboo to allow it to be rolled up. Violet squeezed the scroll through the Grille and let it unfurl above the heads of the media who had all stood and turned in their seats to see what was happening. The bold capitalised text was clear, even from a distance:

PROCLAMATION

WOMEN'S FREEDOM LEAGUE

DEMANDS

VOTES FOR WOMEN

THIS SESSION

The whole chamber was now in commotion, a rustle of millinery and jumble of voices from behind the Grille and shocked, flummoxed anger from the floor below. Then there was another disturbance. A man stood in the Strangers' Gallery at the other end of the chamber. Heads swivelled. 'I am a man and I protest against the injustice to women,' yelled Thomas Bayard Simmons as he threw a handful of pamphlets over the railing onto the MPs below. It was a diversion in a clearly co-ordinated attack.

Members didn't know where to look next as Simmons, who was already known to police as a suffragette sympathiser, was quickly bundled out of the gallery and evicted. He had been recognised when he'd arrived a few hours earlier and the two men who subdued him were plain-clothed police.

Attention swung back to the Ladies' Gallery where attendants and the police had arrived to quell the women's protest. There was a babble of voices, but Muriel's was commanding above the fray.

The attendants and police grabbed Muriel, hoping to pull her off the Grille, only to discover the chains. Her head was jerked back, hitting a chair, and a male hand reached around to cover her mouth and silence the historic speech. 'Oh, don't hurt her,' called out Helen Fox who had been in mid cry with another appeal for the vote.

Helen Bourchier, a WFL member, who had been sitting at the back, leaped onto the man's back, her weight dragging him to the ground and loosening his grip. 'I should have been badly hurt if it wasn't for her,' Muriel said later. Another WFL member, identified only as the 'grande dame' also put herself between Muriel and the men.

In the chamber below, Mr Remnant had given up, replaced by the member for Cambridge University, Mr John Rawlinson, a former amateur footballer who had won an FA Cup with the Old Etonians. Rawlinson tried to continue the speech but no one was listening, their necks craned upwards, watching the struggle, the flash of faces and hands behind the lace-work Grille as two beefy men tried to pry loose a woman from the brass railings.

Muriel revelled in their attempts: 'You can't do it, you can't. You cannot get me away,' she cried gleefully before turning her attention back to the dumbfounded men below. 'We demand in the name of justice that the women of England shall be heard ...' she began, ready with another verbal volley before the mood suddenly changed.[8]

Two more men had joined the skirmish, now intent on forcing the Grille from its stone anchors and silencing the woman in chains. In the struggle, one of the men grabbed hold of Muriel around the throat while a second man tried to gag her with a handkerchief over her mouth. Muriel was furious. 'You dare touch me,' she cried angrily. 'You bully. I'll have you up for assault.' Some newspapers reported that they heard the sound of a man being slapped.

A reporter from the *Dundee Courier* would observe: 'Nothing more comical has been seen in the history of the parliament than the dismay on the faces of the authorities after they recognised that no key would undo the spring lock which the dauntless two attached to the Grille.'

The gallery had been cleared of the other women, including Violet Tillard, whose poster, wedged in the Grille, would be collected and kept rather than discarded by staff – a fragile but powerful reminder of a unique day in the history of democracy.

The space was instead filled with frantic men in tailcoats, armed with wrenches, trying to unscrew the Grille panels. With the fastenings finally removed, the Grille suddenly gave way and the men collapsed backward in a heap, eliciting more mirth from Muriel who couldn't help but cry out 'Hurrah, hurrah' – not to cheer for the rattled men but in triumph at their incongruous position. 'Votes for women!' added Helen Fox as the men turned their attention to her section of the Grille.

Muriel was led from the gallery, still attached by her chain to the Grille panel being carried by one of the attendants. It was a farcical scene, described in *The Times* as 'an absurd procession' and later captured in artwork for the front page of the *London Illustrated* magazine. Helen Fox followed soon after. The sounds of the women's cheers and laughter were heard and recorded by reporters as they were herded down a staircase and along a corridor to one of the committee rooms.

Another WFL member, Gwendolen Lally, watched the struggle and later wrote in the *Women's Franchise*: 'Muriel Matters is a young

Australian girl, with masses of golden hair, the face of a dreamer and an enthusiast. Dishevelled, overcome and panting after the exertions of her struggles, she was conquered but not subdued. She is a modern day Joan of Arc.'

Muriel would later recall an elderly MP standing at the entrance to Room no.15. Seething with outrage, he glowered as the two women were escorted inside. Muriel, relishing the moment, returned his stare and retorted, 'Yes, it is perfectly scandalous that we women should have to behave in this way but we must do something vulgar to attract your vulgar attention.'[9]

Inside the ornate room with its wood-panelled walls and tessellated-tile floor, an agitated Inspector Scantlebury waited with a cluster of officers. It seemed ludicrous that so many men were needed to curtail the activities of two women. When Muriel and Helen refused to produce keys and unlock the padlocks, a smithy was called from the maintenance department and strong hands sawed through the chains with a file, eventually removing the pair from their manacles.

Muriel waited, expecting to be charged and escorted to the police cells. It would be her only disappointment of the evening: Scantlebury refused to take action, keen to ensure he didn't make martyrs or heroines out of the women who had already made him look like a fool. Of the fifty or so breaches of parliamentary security achieved by women protesters over the next decade, this would be the one to make the greatest impression, highlighting Prime Minister Herbert Asquith's steadfast refusal to legislate for the enfranchisement of women.

Instead, Muriel and Helen were peaceably escorted to the Westminster Bridge exit, well away from the crowds that had gathered near the St Stephen's entrance. They were evicted with just a polite 'Good evening'.

Back inside the chamber, however, there was another disturbance. MPs had flocked back in the wake of the melee, partly out of curiosity but also because a division had been called and a vote was necessary to determine the outcome. As the 'Ayes' and 'Nays' gathered, ready for the count, a second man, later identified as an actor named Victor Storr, leaped to his feet. 'Why don't you give votes to the women and attend to the unemployed?' he called, throwing out yet more pamphlets smuggled into the parliament inside his coat. Reporters, this time with a clear view of the protest, described it as a 'snowstorm' of paper.

Other men who tried to quieten him by placing their hands over his mouth grabbed Storr, but he resisted and the struggle turned violent. 'Do justice to the women and the unemployed,' Storr yelled as eight police intervened and threw him out.

* * *

While Muriel, Helen and Violet were causing their uproar, there had been another two protests, one inside the lobby and the other outside in the street, one timed to erupt at 8.33 to provide some distraction and protect the planned main event inside the chamber.

Between 6.00 and 7.00 pm, a group of women had quietly gained entrance to St Stephen's Hall. They filed past watchful police on the pretext of waiting to interview Stephen Collins, the MP who admitted Muriel and Helen, and, it turned out, had vouched for another four women. There were hopes that some of the women might even get further, perhaps into the Central Lobby or even as far as the Members' Lobby, but security was too tight for all but two, a Miss Taplin and a Miss Newlands, to progress.

Once inside St Stephen's Hall, the women stationed themselves on the benches along the walls, half-hidden between the great statues of important men that guarded the portal to democracy, and sat patiently, careful to avoid any acknowledgment of each other. They were dressed smartly, in their best tailored costumes, in order to appear as if their business was genuine. The ruse was relatively simple in construction, but brilliant in its execution.

At the appointed time, and assuming that the Grille protest inside had gone to plan, the women stood on the benches and began a loud protest, interpreted later as an attempt to 'rush' the Central Lobby beyond the next doorway. Police played down the incident, saying they had quickly snuffed out the protest, but an account in *The Woman Worker* saw the episode very differently:

> Miss Henderson, Miss Sidley, Miss Bremner and Miss Neilans jumped on the side benches in St Stephen's Hall and began to speak there. It took some minutes to put them all out. Others made a rush for the doors leading to the Central Lobby, but these were slammed and held against them. Doubling back along the corridor, one or two were chased by policemen, whom they out-paced; and then, outside the House, there was another game of tig which left the men in blue much blown. It was all they could do to keep some of the demonstrators from slipping in [to the Hall] again.

Outside there was a third protest, this one timed for 8.45 in case the St Stephen's Hall protest had been quelled. It began with Dorothy Maloney climbing onto the plinth of Richard the Lionheart's statue in the Old Palace Yard, followed quickly by three other WFL members who shouted 'Votes for women' and 'We want freedom for women'. As the crowd grew around the statue, it made access difficult for the police officers who had finally begun to arrive.

Maloney was a fiery Irishwoman who lived in Dundee and had gained notoriety earlier in the year when she forced Winston Churchill to abandon a meeting in her hometown by repeatedly ringing a bell as he spoke. On this night, she wasn't going to go easily, clinging tightly to the bronze horse as two officers tried to wrench her free, one working on prising her grip apart while the other reached from below to grab her ankles.

The Times observed that police attempts to dislodge Miss Maloney 'provided the crowd with considerable amusement', although the *Daily Mail* had a more considered take: 'The women clung tenaciously to the legs of Richard's horse. Were not the cause so serious the scene would have been slightly ridiculous. Those brave women hung on, gripped the iron hard, and shouted out their speeches, demanding justice for women.'

By now, Muriel and Helen had been released, a throng of reporters waiting for them as they walked out into Bridge Street, angry that they hadn't been arrested. Muriel, in particular, was determined to be taken into custody, as she told a journalist, Charles T. King, who watched the eviction. Reflecting on the night two years later, he wrote:

Inspector Scantlebury and his men gently escorted the girls out to Bridge Street, bade them a cheery 'Good-night', and disgusted them by declining to take them into custody. 'Never mind,' said one of the girls to me, brightening up, 'I am going to have another go. They will have to arrest me.' So she crept round to the St Stephen's entrance where the police were keeping back a little crowd, and flung herself against a row of big constables. They told her to go away. She ran back and flung herself at one of the biggest. He pushed her back. She had another attempt, and they swung her round and round

to calm her down. She leaned against the stone wall for a
moment, got her breath, and threw her light form against
a long heavy row of constables for the last time. Then they
simply had to take her away.

Muriel's version differed slightly from the reporter's, but with the
same end result: 'Reporters anticipated my exit and besieged me,
but I had more business to attend to and rushed around to St
Stephen's where I raised my voice again and demanded admission
to the House of the people: "It is as much a House of women as it
is of men," I cried. Then I was arrested. The Grille has, at last, been
used for some good purpose.'[10]

16.

HOLLOWAY

They arrived like a battered army, hats askew, sleeves torn, and bloodied from physical clashes, but somehow victorious in their disarray, and cheered by a crowd that grew so dense that the gates of the Cannon Row police station had to be closed.

By 10.00 pm on a cold but clear Wednesday night, fifteen protesters – fourteen women and one man – had been arrested outside parliament and marched around the corner to the station where they were bailed and ordered to appear in court the next day on charges of disorderly conduct and obstructing police.

The biggest cheers were reserved for Muriel Matters who was among the last to arrive, nursing bruises on her arms and around her throat but smiling broadly as she was closely escorted by two burly officers who didn't seem to understand that they were aiding the suffragist propaganda by manhandling her in front of the throng of newspaper reporters.

Teresa Billington-Greig, the architect of the protests, had danced with joy when Helen Fox, who had not been arrested, dashed back to the WFL headquarters in Robert Street to give an excited account of the chaos inside the House of Commons. It was hard to see how the protest could have had a more satisfying result, particularly when word filtered through that Prime Minister

Asquith had decided to shut down both the Strangers' Gallery and the Ladies' Gallery in response to 'the disorderly and discreditable proceedings'. And the hated Grille – the despised symbol of their campaign – had been pulled down, at least in part.

The next morning the suffragists woke to a mix of responses, the more conservative voices like *The Times* condemning their actions variously as disgraceful, a violation of democracy, childish and a setback for the movement. Other more liberal papers like the *Daily Mirror* applauded the 'lion-hearted bravery' of the women and the clever strategy of their leaders. All crowned the newest star of the women's movement – Muriel Matters – as the 'Heroine of the Grille'.

By 9.00 am, the street outside the Westminster Police Court was a crush of women, their hats aflutter with ribbons of gold, green and white. As had become a habit, the members facing prosecution were escorted by dozens of their suffragist sisters, who waved placards and sang as buses trundled past filled with city workers. Others bore mugs of tea and posed for photos. *Deeds Not Words*, the main banner demanded as the crowd marched into the courtroom to fill the public gallery.

In the corridor outside the hearing Helen Fox stood talking to a reporter from the *London Evening News*, disappointed now that she had avoided arrest and frustrated that she could not go to prison with her friends: 'What have I done that I should not be arrested?' she complained. 'I chained myself to the silly old Grille and I wrestled some policemen in trying to get back into the House. I thoroughly deserve to be locked up. Other people have got it for doing nothing. It's too bad to be standing here while all the others are inside getting ready for prison.'

The reporter pressed further, the young woman happy to oblige with details about the plot and the careful, and at times lucky, execution. Planning had begun in July, she said, when a group of members chained themselves to the Downing Street gates as a test run. They had set October 13 to get inside the Ladies' Gallery but had aborted the protest because it clashed with the WSPU rally: 'That spoiled it.'

Contrary to the claims by Mr Collins, she and Muriel had not promised to behave themselves in the Ladies' Gallery. In fact, he had barely looked at them, let alone asked their names or their business, his condescending attitude evident when he pointed out the prime minister: 'He did point out Mr Asquith. "That's the prime minister," he said. I thanked him and tried to look as if I didn't know.'

In fact, she had been in the gallery before and had listened to debates – 'really interesting debates, not like this ridiculous licensing nonsense'. The gallery attendant had recognised her and asked if she was 'going to be good', to which she had replied: 'If you let me sit in the front row.' He guided her to the middle row.

'Some men are very stupid,' she mused. 'The attendant might have known very well that I wouldn't sit two hours and a half listening to futile talk about "clause 13 and clause 14" and "this amendment and that", and watching a lot of petty divisions without some plot being on.'

Helen had been nervous, but Muriel's calm demeanour had made her determined: 'She was marvellously cool. I saw them struggling with her. I thought they would break her back.'

Attendants had tried to muzzle her as well, but she struggled free, now so comfortable in the fray that 'I could admire the acoustic perfection of the House. My voice carried splendidly. I didn't shriek. Never mind what the newspapers say. Whenever a woman makes an unexpected speech the reporters say, "She shrieked."'

She laughed at the men's attempts to use dummy keys to break open the padlocks, and both she and Muriel were gleeful when, instead of getting a file to free them, the attendants decided to remove the Grille panels: 'We had thought they would adjourn the House while they filed our chains. We never dreamed they would really break the absurd old Grille. I was delighted when they wrenched away two pieces of the Grille, each as big as a door.'

Once outside she had tried to get arrested until a Labour MP appeared and escorted her away: 'I'm just going to write to him and tell him I'll thank him to mind his own business in future,' she declared cheekily. 'Only for him I should have gone to gaol and been quite happy.'

* * *

Inside the courtroom, the prosecutor, Mr Muskett, painted the situation as grave, in fact 'the most disgraceful yet enacted in connection with the suffrage movement'. He asked an equally grave Magistrate Hopkins, peering down from the bench, that the punishment meted out be stiff fines or prison sentences.

The only man arrested, Arnold Cutler, was dealt with first. 'A respectable looking youth in a dark coat and cap,' according to the *Sheffield Evening Telegraph*, Cutler had been in the crowd surrounding the Richard Coeur de Lion statue and shouted 'Shame! Let the women alone' when the police arrived and tried to remove them from the plinth. When officers chased him away, Cutler stood in the middle of the road, removed the belt from his trousers and 'assumed a threatening attitude'.

'Why did you mix yourself up in a rowdy scene of this sort?' the magistrate asked. 'I have a weak heart and am very excitable,' Cutler replied, to the amusement of the public gallery. Magistrate

Hopkins fined him twenty shillings which was promptly paid by Charlotte Despard.

Marguerite Henderson maintained the defiant attitude of the suffragists, insisting that she had gone to parliament not to create disorder but to make a speech inside St Stephen's Hall.

'But surely addressing people in the vicinity of the House of Commons is a very serious offence,' Magistrate Hopkins offered.

'I supposed you'd think so,' retorted Miss Henderson.

'You go down there making disorder—'

Miss Henderson interrupted: 'We were not responsible for disorder. I went down there to make a speech inside St Stephen's Hall.'[1]

The magistrate had had enough: 'Pay a penalty of five pounds.'

'I'm not paying it,' came the resolute reply, Henderson knowing full well that she would be spending the next month inside the notorious Holloway Prison.

Marion Leighfield was next in the dock, questioning the behaviour of the police who had pushed her and sprained her ankle: 'If an offence is committed it is surely the duty of the police to arrest the wrongdoer, not to assault her.'

Magistrate Hopkins stopped her: 'Does it not strike you that this farce is about played out?'

'Not as far as I am concerned', Leighfield assured him before being escorted to the cells below, where Marguerite Henderson waited for her friends.

The 'Bellringer' Dorothy Maloney, who had spent a month inside Holloway Prison earlier in the year, was another who raised cheers and laughter from the public gallery when she explained her reasons for climbing onto the Richard Coeur de Lion statue: 'To tell you the truth I thought it was safer to trust myself to Coeur de Lion than to the police.'

Mr Hopkins was not amused and stated the obvious: 'This is all for effect, you know.'

'It may be, but it is for a good cause. We intend to keep up our agitation until we are satisfied,' Maloney confirmed, drawing more laughs.

'You are very unrepentant,' Mr Hopkins observed, again stating the obvious.

Maloney had the last word: 'I don't recognise the authority of this court.'[2]

And so it continued through the morning. Almost half the WFL offenders to appear in court that day were married with husbands who supported their activism, contrary to the public perception of the suffragette movement as a club of ugly, bitter women who were unattractive to men. And among those arrested were mother and daughter Emily and Barbara Duval who appeared in the dock together.

'Are you bringing your daughter up to be an agitator too?' the magistrate asked.

Mrs Duval was resolute: 'I have four daughters, sir, and it is the most sensible view of life to take. We all want freedom for women.'

Mr Hopkins sighed. 'I am sorry you take such a pessimistic view,' he said, banging the gavel to confirm a £5 fine for Mrs Duval and a caution for her daughter who was under age.

On and on it went, defiant women facing down unyielding male opposition. 'You may sentence me today but tomorrow when we are making the laws you will be ashamed,' thundered Dinah Bowman-Welles before she was led away. The details differed only marginally for the others who followed. Edith Bremner, Jane McCallum, Marion Holmes, Dorothy Spencer and Mary Manning were fined, refused to pay, and were sent off to wait for the police van – the 'Black Maria' – which would take them to prison. Violet Tillard was almost overwhelmed in the dock, unused to being the focus of attention and barely able to be heard over the hubbub of the court until she was fined when she suddenly found her voice. 'I will not pay,' she shouted as she was led back down to the cells.

Muriel, the knobs of bruises on her arms from the previous night's tussle at the Grille now an angry purple, had waited in a holding cell below for her turn in the dock, accused of obstructing two policemen – 'one 6 foot 2 and the other 6 foot, and little me was the obstruction,' she would recall years later.[3] She listened patiently while the taller of the two arresting constables recounted their conversation on the way to the station during which Muriel had told him 'that being an Australienne with a vote in my own country I am trying to do my best to get votes for my English sisters'. The constable paused to check the scrawl in his notebook: 'She also said, "I am sorry, Constable, to give you this trouble. I would much sooner fight Mr Asquith."'

When the constable finished and stepped down, Muriel turned to the magistrate: 'Your honour, I'd like to have the case remanded please.'

Mr Hopkins was wary of her motives: 'I will do so with great pleasure if you can alter the evidence against you. I am not, however, going to do so for the purpose of giving you time to prepare a speech. I would be glad to have an expression of regret and the assurance that you would go back to Australia where you can vote.'

Muriel stood her ground: 'No sir, while I am here I must do my absolute best to improve the conditions of the women in this country. I am not going back to Australia until we have the vote in England.'

The magistrate had heard enough, aware his protestations were merely aiding her grandstanding: 'Pay a fine of five pounds.'

'What, no option?' she replied, to snickers from the public gallery and inviting the obvious response.

But Mr Hopkins didn't answer, now weary of the parade. Rather than fearing the consequences of their actions, these women willingly embraced imprisonment. It was a badge of honour rather than a social burden.

Instead, his clerk answered the chief protagonist who stood proudly in the dock: 'One month imprisonment.'[4]

* * *

It was called Suffragettes In and Out of Prison, a cheaply made game of chance mounted on a cardboard sleeve in which four players rolled a dice in a race to move their suffragettes as they tried to escape Holloway Prison by evading walls, warders and police. The game sold for one penny from street traders, and was sponsored, according to an advertisement on the back of the game board, by the *Morning Leader* newspaper, whose slogan, 'The paper for the busy man and the home', reeked of the misogyny the suffragettes sought to end.

The game and others like it that would emerge, among them a challenge to get suffragettes into the House of Commons and another to negotiate the passage of their cherished women's suffrage bill, were indicative of the comic attitude that met the protesters' desperate efforts. Rather than be outraged that a woman would be jailed simply for ringing the doorbell at the home of a politician, the papers tut-tutted or, worse, laughed and welcomed the punishment.

Holloway Prison had been built half a century before, designed as an imposing ragstone imitation of the great medieval fortress Warwick Castle, although the grand turreted exterior, complete with battlements, suggested a palatial residence rather than a grim penitentiary. It was originally a mixed-sex prison, the playwright Oscar Wilde among its most famous inmates, until it was converted to a women-only prison in 1903.

The first suffrage protesters to be incarcerated at Holloway in 1906, Teresa Billington-Greig among them, had been granted the status of political prisoners and treated as first-division inmates, which meant they could wear their own clothes, congregate away from other prisoners, and even receive visitors and food parcels. But by late 1908 there was a marked change in the attitude of the judiciary which, as a group, wanted to quash the increasing militancy of female protesters.

Suffrage prisoners, including Emmeline and Christabel Pankhurst who were still behind bars for their roles in the October 13 uprising, were no longer regarded as political prisoners and were stripped of their first-division classifications. They and their WSPU colleagues were in the second division, still segregated from the general prison population but with fewer privileges and poorer food, clothing and accommodation.

But Magistrate Hopkins had gone one step further and ordered that the WFL miscreants serve their time as third-division prisoners. According to some reports, he had even considered sending them to hard labour.

The hard edge of prison life soon became evident once Muriel Matters, Violet Tillard and the others arrived in the Black Maria on the morning of October 30, having spent the night in the cells below the court. Once inside the grand gateway, they were stripped, medically inspected and then interrogated, semi-naked in an open hallway. They were then washed and ordered to pick out a dress and undergarments from piles lying on the floor. Second-class prisoners wore green serge and third-class wore brown. All wore white caps and blue-and-white checked aprons. The underclothing was coarse, ill-fitting and ill-made, the stockings thick and shapeless and the shoes heavy and clumsy – and rarely in matching pairs.

A yellow cloth badge bearing the number of the cell and its block number was then stitched roughly to the inmate's dress. It not only signified where a prisoner belonged but became her only identity while behind bars. Muriel Matters, assigned to Block 2, would be known by warders simply as '36'.

The cells in which they would spend twenty-two hours each day were barely wide enough to contain their simple wooden beds, each raised slightly off the concrete floor and covered with a mattress and pillow stuffed with something akin to and as uncomfortable as dried grass. Although the tiny window was sealed, there was no heating and winter was approaching.

The only other furniture was a shelf on which the inmate placed a tin pot for gruel, a wooden spoon, salt cellar, piece of soap, a Bible, prayer card and a booklet of prison rules called *The Narrow Way*. There was also a book called *Health of the Home*, a guide to cleanliness that offered advice on the dangers of open windows and a dark warning that the night's blackness in the dank cells was a reminder 'of the narrow bed in which they might soon be laid'.

'Every day seemed a month and every night an eternity,' Muriel would later tell audiences. 'Ill-ventilated, ill-lit, foul-smelling and small almost as a doll's house. There are no thoughts in life as long as one's thoughts in those prison cells at Holloway. It was here that I learned to read new meaning into the prayer "Lord make haste to help us", and to understand that the cries of those unfortunate prisoners for all their lives had been for help.'[5]

Curiously, Muriel, Emmeline and Christabel Pankhurst were all photographed in prison by a London studio. Clearly it was something sanctioned by prison officials, perhaps to demonstrate that the suffrage protesters were being treated humanely in the face of claims of poor conditions inside the prison.

The portrait of Muriel – a suffragist in prison dress – is posed, Muriel seated with a piece of fabric in her hands as if she is mending a kerchief, her thick hair trying to escape the white prison headscarf and a look of calm bemusement on her face. Emmeline Pankhurst later described the experience of incarceration as feeling 'like a human being in the process of being turned into a wild beast'.

Prison life began each morning at 5.30, the inmates woken by a bell and given an hour to scrub and clean their cells for inspection. Breakfast, served in the cell and eaten alone, comprised tea and six ounces of brown bread with a small portion of butter. The day's silence was broken, only briefly, during prayers in the prison chapel. It was the only time that the third-division prisoners saw one another and they were at all times forbidden to speak. Baths were weekly. There were no visitors and no correspondence.

Chores were also divided by class, second-class prisoners usually sewing or knitting and third-class women picking and shredding the mattress stuffing or cleaning the prison. Likewise, second-class prisoners could exercise daily, walking silently in the gravel courtyard, while third-class women walked only three times a week, exercise that Muriel complained loudly was 'ambling around in an asinine way', for which she was immediately sent to solitary confinement: 'I was the lowest prisoner because I gave sauce to the matron,' she later said with some pride.

According to family stories, she took her protest one step further when the guards refused to provide her with toilet paper, instead tearing pages from the cell Bible until the authorities relented. Her sentence was lengthened by a couple of days.[6]

The food was poor, but eating all meals alone in the cells was worse. Lunch was at noon: boiled potatoes, carrots, egg and a pint of milk. Dinner at 5.00 pm was a mutton broth, brown bread and a cup of cocoa. By contrast, second-class prisoners were given combinations of bacon and tinned meat with potatoes, beans or soup. Lights were turned out promptly at 8.00 pm.

'The worst punishment of the confinement was its dreadful mental stultification. It was a system of hopelessness that made no attempt to raise the moral and spiritual standard of the inmates, but rather to depress and deprave them,' Muriel said on her release.[7]

The Labour politician Keir Hardie tried to have a newspaper delivered to her but it was refused. Allowed only one book from the prison library, Muriel chose a volume of poetry which contained the verse, by an author unknown, found inscribed on the pillar of a Roman cemetery in Canterbury:

> *Where is the man who has the power or skill*
> *To stem the torrent of a woman's will?*
> *For if she will, she will, depend on't –*
> *And if she won't, she won't, so there's an end on't.*

* * *

Beyond Holloway's walls, the Australian media's response to Muriel's protest and imprisonment was, typically, mixed. It created a feast of sensational headlines in Adelaide, where the correspondent for the *Observer* described the protest as an outrageous fiasco and accused the suffragists of being a disorderly rabble. Muriel was shrill and aggressive, he said, dismissing the protest as futile: 'While effective in calling public attention to their pet ideas, it has not gained for them more sympathy or support from level-headed electors.'

There was the inevitable ditty, like 'The Song of the Suffragette' which appeared in the Queensland magazine *Figaro*:

They regard us at home as a lunatic crowd
In Australia they know us as 'hatters'
But let women-enfranchised Australians please note
We've got with us Miss Muriel Matters.

Though the obdurate males with self-satisfied 'side'
Only smile when a petticoat flatters
We shall weary their patience and humble their pride
By the methods of Muriel Matters.

Some regard us unequal to man
Such folly a suffragette scatters
While importunate widows continue to fan
The flame lit by Miss Muriel Matters.[8]

In Perth, there was ardent support from the social editress of the *Western Mail* who wrote that Muriel's friends were not surprised when she joined the suffrage movement:

She has thrown herself with the same heart and soul into what seems to be becoming a burning question in England that she has shown in her profession. She has been reported in the press as having extraordinary power over hostile audiences and of possessing marvellous courage. In reading the local accounts of the journey through the provinces lecturing in the cause of women's suffrage – of the rage of the gatherings of people, the struggles, the stones thrown, the absolute danger to life and limb experienced at the hands of unsympathetic mobs of people – it is difficult to realise that one is living in the prosaic and commercially inclined twentieth century. The facts that the cables have

sent forth this week, however unpalatable this may seem
to conservative minds, go to show that the martyr spirit is
as much alive as ever it was, and there are still to be found
spirits who have the courage to be fanatical in their cause
they have espoused and devotion to suffer for the opinions
that they hold.[9]

The *Register* in Adelaide took a different tack. Although disagreeing
with the protest as a 'diverting, if reprehensible comedy', the
correspondent believed it had probably achieved more for the suffrage
cause than any action before: 'With hundreds of other episodes,
it emphasises the irrepressible courage and perseverance of the
suffragettes,' he wrote, adding: 'The idea of sending women to gaol
because they are endeavouring to obtain a share of democratic powers
is as repugnant to British ideas as the unfeminine demonstrations
which are thus punished.'[10]

There had been an outcry in London too, not over the jailing
of the women as much as the decision by Magistrate Hopkins that
they should serve their time in the third division, 'with drunkards
and vagrants', rather than in the second division. There was a protest
outside Holloway the night after the jailing and an unsuccessful
appeal to the Home Office to have the women transferred to the
first division as political prisoners.

Indicative of the official attitude was an exchange between
Elsie Cummin, a young woman who'd been among the crowd in
the town of Midhurst when Muriel was on the caravan tour. Miss
Cummin had since helped establish a branch of the WFL and now
wrote to her local MP and youngest member of the House, Lord
Winterton, in the hope he might use his influence to have Muriel
transferred from the third to the first division.

Lord Winterton's reply was emphatic:

Madam, I have to say that I shall most certainly not use
any influence that I may possess to have Miss Matters
transferred from the third to the first division. I consider that
Miss Matters richly deserves the punishment which she is
undergoing. I may further add for your information that the
attitude and behaviour of the leaders of the women's suffrage
movement have entirely alienated the strong sympathy which
I personally have hitherto felt for the cause of women's
suffrage. I shall support the present government in any step
that they may take to put an end to the intolerable nuisance
caused by the so-called demonstrations by leaders of the
movement.[11]

17.

A PAIR OF DIVAS

At 8.00 am on November 28, after a month and two days of virtual solitary confinement, Muriel was released from Holloway along with four others, including Violet Tillard. They were greeted by a cheering throng waiting on the manicured lawns outside their cheerless cage, and escorted back to central London where they joined the other women who had already been set free.

The group gathered in an upstairs room at the Cottage Tea Rooms on the Strand, a modest establishment with an incongruous Dutch windmill on its signboard, nestled among the tobacconists, barbers and restaurants that dominated the streetscape. Outside, a mix of motor cars, omnibuses and horse-drawn carts clattered along the busy road as the women toasted success with a demure round of tea and cakes, and planned for the future.

In a single night of co-ordinated mayhem, the Women's Freedom League had found its place and voice in the suffrage jumble, without the arrogance of the WSPU and its public call to arms, which was designed to antagonise police as much as deliver a political message. The WFL leadership couldn't help feeling that the tactics of their suffrage sisters were as much about feeding the ego and promoting the image of Emmeline Pankhurst as they were a campaign strategy.

As Teresa Billington-Greig mentioned rather pointedly: 'Militancy as designed and carried out by Miss Pankhurst and her mother has tended not to work a revolution by the enslaved woman, much less to work a revolution in her.'[1] At any rate, the WFL's experience had shown that covert operations – using the element of surprise – were going to work best, and protests had to be more imaginative than merely standing up in political meetings and drowning out the speaker.

The Grille protest had become the most potent weapon in their public relations arsenal, a meticulously planned and executed operation that had caused confusion and conservative outrage and for which fourteen of their members had served a month in third-division prison. It had also created a new champion in Muriel Matters, the exotic Australian performer who had become the first woman to make a speech in the House of Commons. People would want to see and meet the woman who defied the entire parliament and caused its closure, to hear her story, what was said and how she forced attendants to remove the object they hated most. The Heroine of the Grille was a suffrage drawcard.

Teresa Billington-Greig could not hold back her delight. As she boldly declared in the November 5 edition of the *Women's Franchise*:

> October 28, 1908 will be marked as a red-letter day in
> the history of the women's suffrage agitation … for it will
> be remembered that on that day the Women's Freedom
> League made it necessary for the House of Commons
> to choose between the adjournment of business and the
> removal of the insulting Grille. If women cannot enter the
> House of Commons by force, they have demonstrated the
> fact that they can and will enter its precincts by strategy
> and secrecy.

The names of Miss Muriel Matters and Miss Helen Fox may not go down to the future ages. They may be forgotten, but their deed will never be forgotten. They were instrumental in removing the Grille – that sign of sex subjection, of women's exclusion from citizenship. The thing they did will stand as a sign of the breaking of barriers, of the shattering of sex-slavery.

For our own women words can scarcely suffice. Their protests were extraordinarily successful; the work to be done was carried out with dignity, courage, initiative and unswerving loyalty. I was never prouder of my fellow members than on the evening of the protest unless it were on the following morning when I listened to their speeches on the dock. The meaning and purpose of our agitation was never more clearly placed before the public through the agency of the press and the magistrate on that day. Our women, committed to prison in the third division, classed as the worst of common criminals, are still the victors. They have achieved something; they have brought the day of our liberty appreciably nearer. They have assisted at a symbolic ceremony; they have prepared the way for other women passing in freedom where they passed in chains.

The Ladies' Gallery had been ordered closed and the Strangers' Gallery cleared after Muriel's protest. Both would eventually be reopened with tighter security, but akin to closing the gate behind a bolting horse, the damage was already done. The night before Muriel's release from Holloway, debate in the House of Commons had been dominated by discussion on the proposed introduction of proportional representation.

The chief proponent was the prime minister, Herbert Asquith, the greatest stumbling block in the female suffrage cause, who pointed out that in the election of 1895 the Conservatives had won 411 of the 670 seats in parliament – and a clear majority – on just 49 per cent of the national vote.

Asquith told the assembled MPs: 'There can be no question in the mind of anyone that is familiar with the working of our Constitution that it permits a minority of votes, whether in the country at large or in particular constituencies, to determine the actual representation of the nation and in defiance of the opinions and wishes of the majority.'[2]

The sheer hypocrisy of the speech, given his anti-suffrage stance, was not lost on the huddle of women at the Cottage Tea Rooms. Their agitation had only just begun.

* * *

Some weeks earlier, in the late afternoon of November 12 as Muriel nursed a bowl of mutton broth and an oily cocoa she couldn't stomach to celebrate a lonely thirty-first birthday in her cell, the soprano Dame Nellie Melba was posting a letter from her London hotel to a hard-working newsboy who had thrown his pile of papers onto the ground as she stepped from a taxicab, rather than allow her to get her shoes wet. She enclosed a £5 note in gratitude for the chivalrous act.[3]

The story created a sensation in the press, as had her farewell concert a few days earlier in the splendour of the Royal Albert Hall, the great amphitheatre filled to its regal gunwales. Dressed in a shimmering cinnamon gown, Australia's greatest cultural export was drowned in floral adulation as she gave a dozen encores after singing Tosti's 'Goodbye'.

The diva was off to America and then to her homeland after having toured mainland Europe and Britain during the latter half of 1908. She would not be back for two years and London's opera lovers were sad. But it was not the great cities and concert halls that had left an impact on Melba, rather the north of England and its grim industrial landscape where she had witnessed the struggle and poverty of ordinary people, normally hidden from her eyes.

As she was preparing her departure, Melba granted a final newspaper interview in which she revealed that she had signed a petition, addressed to King Edward VII, opposing the jailing of suffragettes and suffragists as second- and third-class prisoners. Asked what had influenced her to take this step, Melba replied that it was a question of humanity: 'I believe that the lot of the woman worker would be bettered if the influence of women could be used in the selection of our parliamentary representatives,' she said simply.[4] The benediction of such a celebrity was an unexpected and welcome boon for the WFL and other agitators.

Punch magazine could not help but publish a ditty contrasting the fortunes of the two Australians dominating the suffrage headlines in London:

Where sounds through all the tiresome day
The suffragettes' determined bray,
Comes forth a fine, pellucid note
It's high and clear, and loud and long –
'Tis Nellie Melba, Queen of Song,
Who in a voice sublimely strong,
Demands a vote.

To Muriel who matters much,
The cute Miss Austral Fox and such,
Old England turns a dummy ear
The sentiment that Muriel quotes

None heeds. The yells of fifty throats
Don't count: but all prize Nellie's notes –
They are so dear.

That voice that now cries woman's woes
Is worth, as every John Bull knows,
A quid a second. So Punch bets
When it is raised for any cause
To back up or oppose the laws,
It is received with loud applause,
For 'money talks' when Nellie pets
The suffragettes.[5]

In her days on the stage, the tone of newspaper coverage had been all-important for Muriel, the slight of a reviewer akin to a potential death knell for her career but, as Muriel would write in a letter to her family back in Perth in the days after her release, for a political agitator infamy was a blessing. Newspaper headlines kept the issue in the spotlight, reached thousands and helped to change minds. Perceptions could be rebuffed and ignorance corrected – but to be ignored was death.

Plans were hastily made for Muriel and others to go on a speaking tour across England, Scotland and Ireland as the WFL sought to make the most of their time in the spotlight. 'I have come to understand the power of the press,' Muriel wrote. 'I believe I can achieve great things by reaching the people with my voice.'

One of the tour's first calls was the town of Tunbridge Wells where Violet Tillard had become something of a cause célèbre. Although never having made a speech in her life, she quickly warmed to the task, as the local paper reported: 'After being forbidden to speak while in prison it seems quite strange to be permitted to talk again freely,' she said to laughs from the curious crowd. 'The conditions had a curious mental effect on us all. It was an experience I would not have missed for anything. Now I am released I feel that we need the vote to fight this terrible prison system. Our prisons seem to be constructed and governed so as to develop an evil tendency in a person's nature.'[6]

Muriel spoke last and had the crowd in stitches:

The last big indoor meeting I attended was that meeting in the British House of Commons [laughter]. Of course, that action of mine, and also the action of that other creature of the Grille was just the action that you might expect from an unsexed, ferocious woman, the sort of action that a woman like myself would do [laughter]. That, I know, is what a great number of the people are thinking today. 'Goodness knows what they will do,' they say. I admit that on the surface it was the act of a lunatic [laughter]. I chained myself to the Grille. Let me tell you that it had been very well thought out by one much wiser than myself. It was Mrs Billington-Greig, the 'Parnell in Petticoats', who considered the idea of putting that unsightly Grille to some use. The idea could not be carried out for some time and when it was suggested that I should do the work, I was very pleased to accept [laughter]. I had never been in the British House of Commons before, but I hope to go again; and don't be surprised to hear that I have done something very much worse than I have done before [applause].

Muriel's sudden stardom would also help to fill WFL coffers. In early December she packed out St James's Hall in Regent Street and raised £2000 for the cause, as she regaled the audience with the story of the protest, how she had sat behind the Grille 'listening to the lifeless and monotonous twaddle that was being loosed below', until she saw her opportunity when the attendant's back was turned. 'In a moment I was through,' she exclaimed to the cheers of the crowd. 'The experience was simply delightful. The Grille was broken away, symbolical of all conventionalities being broken away. Women must continue in their great spiritual movement, for they were animated by a great spiritual idea. I don't have any liking for the methods we employ, but although distasteful they are necessary if women wish not to remain doormats.'

Her speech drew a standing ovation but, more poignantly, a series of 'Cooees' echoed from various corners of the hall as Australians in the crowd saluted their compatriot; to their delight Muriel returned the call.[7]

The *Women's Franchise* also reported the evening, gushing in its praise: 'Miss Muriel Matters was accorded a special reception, and by her earnestness and simple eloquence she lifted the subject to a high plane of thought and aspiration, carrying the audience along with her: "When you see the light, follow it," were her concluding words, and the storm of applause which broke out as she resumed her seat seemed not only a tribute to her powers and heroism, but also sounded a note of gratitude to one who could thus touch the heart while satisfying the intellect.'

The unnamed author had made an important point. Muriel was more than an actress and polished elocutionist, professions that required skilful delivery of someone else's prose. Rather, she was a woman of powerful intellect and rare intuition. Attuned to her audience, she could read their mood and take them with her. Muriel could excite and inspire, appease unruly mobs with unscripted composure, dismiss clumsy objectors with finely honed put-downs and razor-sharp wit. Miss Muriel Matters was a born leader.

As the evening drew to a close, Charlotte Despard made a presentation to Muriel of a silver badge to commemorate her imprisonment. Shaped like a shield with an embossed relief of the Holloway portcullis and a loop of chains hanging from the bottom in reference to her Grille protest, it would be the first of dozens handed out to WFL protesters who would go to prison over the next decade. Four months later, the WSPU would come out with its own version of the 'Holloway brooch'. (Muriel's brooch, along with the chains with which she shackled herself to the Grille are now in the Museum of London.)

More than one thousand women would eventually spend time behind bars for the cause between 1905 and 1914, the movement emboldened rather than defeated by the political and judicial crackdown, as Muriel had presciently pointed out one night at a rowdy public meeting in St Leonards-on-Sea during the caravan tour: 'The spirit of the suffragists could not be crushed by sending them to prison because then they were made martyrs, and it was the blood of martyrs that made a movement flourish and grow.'

* * *

When the House of Commons rose on December 21, prorogued until mid February, it effectively killed off the Women's Enfranchisement Bill approved so overwhelmingly by members ten months before. Although expected, the formal declaration not to carry the bill through to the new session of parliament only served to further enrage suffrage groups as, yet again, the government had stonewalled on legislation that most MPs supported but seemed to have little chance of bringing into law.

A fortnight beforehand, the Chancellor David Lloyd George had attempted to appease women suffrage campaigners when he fronted a meeting of the docile Women's Liberal Federation at the Albert Hall to explain the government's position. Instead, the meeting was overrun by suffragettes and suffragists who proceeded to howl down the MP for almost two hours, and some chained themselves, Muriel Matters-like, to furniture as three hundred and fifty stewards attempted to gain some sort of control.

Dozens of women and men were evicted and at one point organisers even tried piping an organ rendition of 'Oh Dear, What Can the Matter Be' through the hall to calm the masses, all to no avail. For once there was unity among rival suffrage groups as members of both the WSPU and the WFL chanted 'Deeds Not Words' and accused Lloyd George of empty promises – 'You run with the hare and hunt with the hounds.'

When he was finally able to speak Lloyd George tried to assure the crowd that the government intended to address the suffrage question, but was hamstrung because of a powerful minority in the cabinet and within senior ranks of both the Liberal and Conservative parties, which was opposed. Neither party wanted to risk internal splits by sponsoring the legislation. Instead, an Electoral Reform Bill would be introduced, 'which will not comprise woman suffrage but will be so drafted that a woman's suffrage amendment will be in order'.

'I do not believe we will ever carry women's suffrage in parliament unless and until it is treated as an open question by either one or other of the great political parties,' he finished to a now almost-silent audience as they digested the ramifications of what the chancellor was promising.[8]

He appeared to be saying that the prime minister, Herbert Asquith, despite personal reservations, was quietly supporting the proposal but could not introduce government legislation directly because of internal division inside the Cabinet. Likewise, the Tories were torn at the senior levels, despite general support for women's enfranchisement in their MP ranks. Instead, Lloyd George was proposing that a legislative framework would be put in place under a reform bill in the hope that someone would independently sponsor a woman's suffrage amendment that could be voted on in open parliament, where 420 of the 670 members were in favour. Mr Asquith 'could not resist' such a vote and would be prepared to take responsibility for the bill.

But, he warned, the protesters' militant behaviour threatened to derail the proposal. This was the greatest chance they ever had and if they threw it away it would be entirely through the folly, the lunacy, of some of those who thought that they were helping the cause through militancy.

The response from the suffrage movement would be disbelief, the sense that they'd heard the promises before and that Lloyd George had offered nothing concrete to assuage their fears. And for Lloyd George to admonish them like obedient dogs and threaten to withdraw the promise if they didn't lie down and behave was pouring petrol on a bonfire.

Three weeks later, just after the New Year as the streets of London turned to ice and the Pankhursts headed to the Swiss Alps resort of Villars-sur-Ollon on a skiing holiday with a clutch of wealthy supporters, a strange procession made its way to Trafalgar Square. Muriel Matters and Charlotte Despard led the solemn line of women, shrouded in black and leading a light wagon drawn by what was described as a decrepit-looking horse.

It was a mock funeral for the Women's Enfranchisement Bill, 'killed by the government', and represented by a roll of linoleum draped in a white cloth. It was pure theatre, free of the growing anger of many of the protests, but still designed to generate media coverage as a resolution was passed calling for the government to include the vote for women in the King's Speech and carry a new bill in the next session.

The crowd gathered around the Nelson lions in the cold – a mere handful at first – had grown considerably by the time Muriel was introduced, her voice carrying down Whitehall toward an empty Westminster Palace. Herbert Asquith had demanded that they prove women wanted the vote, she said, and yet William Gladstone, who served four terms as Liberal prime minister, believed the best governments acted on instinct: 'The great Gladstone once said, "We must not wait until the majority ask. It is for us, as politicians and statesmen, to anticipate the needs and requirements of the people." That is what the Women's Freedom League is doing on behalf of the women in this country.'

The hecklers couldn't help themselves: 'Why don't you get married and stay home,' one called loudly. Muriel was quick to cut him down: 'Let me give you a tip, my friend; we cannot all do that because if we were to try to get married tomorrow there are not enough men to go around.'[9]

Until now Muriel had held no formal administrative position within the WFL, but that was about to change as she was appointed 'Organiser for Branch Development and Formation'. It gave her a measure of seniority in the league's structure and even a modest wage, the money earned from her stage career now long gone, which helped pay for her modest shared room in Bayswater on the northern fringe of Hyde Park. Single women in the suffrage movement often lived together and shared their minimal resources, particularly as organisers like Muriel were frequently on the move, travelling and making speeches across the country.

Muriel's enthusiasm seemed boundless as she also helped form a new group, the Actresses' Franchise League, which staged propaganda plays as a fundraising vehicle for the suffrage movement and whose members included stage stars like Lily Langtry, Sybil Thorndike and Decima Moore.[10]

But Muriel's first responsibility was with the WFL and in her first month as an organiser she was rarely in London, sent south to reform a branch at Eastbourne and then north to Liverpool, where she received a standing ovation after addressing the stock exchange from the rostrum, gavel in hand, and into Scotland where she opened branches in Edinburgh and Helensburgh.

By the beginning of February, she had returned to the periphery of the capital, giving town hall speeches almost every night at places like Chelmsford, where she made a rousing call for the government to include women's enfranchisement in the King's Speech, set for the opening of parliament on February 16.

'The present agitation is only the beginning of great things in this country. We, ourselves, do not like the methods but we love the cause. A vote is nothing in itself but it is a means to an end,' she told the crowd.

'It is not a war of the sexes. That could never be because we are not anti-men. God bless them, the dear souls, they do the best they can but they do not understand women, and women do not understand them. We do not want a petticoat government. If they could but scatter the petticoats behind the present government then all would be well.'[11]

Back at the Robert Street headquarters, Teresa Billington-Greig and the others were planning their next covert operation. If the ruse to get into parliament and remove the Grille was regarded as scandalous, then the next idea was truly madness. The minutes of their meeting of December 12, 1908 would mention a 'flying machine'.

18.

MURIEL TAKES FLIGHT

The Conquest of the Air

On the last day of the old year, Mr Wilbur Wright
made a final effort to surpass all his previous performances
in the direction of serial flight. Remaining in the air for
a continuous period of 2 hours 22¾ minutes, he covered a
distance of over 77 miles and thereby succeeded in carrying
off the Michelin Cup by a record far in advance of any
achieved by his competitors. This aeroplane flight taken in
company with Count Zeppelin's memorable 12 hours' voyage
in his dirigible balloon accomplished last July render the
year 1908 memorable in the annals of human attempts to
achieve conquest of the air.

Gloucestershire Echo, January 4, 1909

Powered air travel was in its infancy in the first years of the
twentieth century. The experimental airship LZ-2, forerunner
to the famous Zeppelin, was trialled in 1906 and the following
year the British army flew its first dirigible over London before
abandoning it, deflated, at Crystal Palace. The prospect of aerial
warfare was still confined to fiction, described in the H.G. Wells
novel *The War in the Air*.

Fixed–wing travel was even further distant. The American brothers Wilbur and Orville Wright had made the world's first powered flight in December 1903, one of their mechanics became the first passenger five years later, and the first scheduled air service – a bi-plane flying boat – would only take off in 1914.

It seemed incredible then that in the winter of 1908–09, the executive of the Women's Freedom League was plotting a spectacular campaign in which one of its members would be asked to risk her life by climbing into a basket beneath a rickety bamboo-framed airship and fly, Mary Poppins-like, over the capital's rooftops.

Only a handful of women had ever ascended the skies in a powered flying machine, much less been taken onboard for a purpose other than sitting quietly and praying that they would get down in one piece. The first British woman to fly in an airship was nine-year-old Marie Spencer who, in 1906, rode with her Uncle Stanley, one of five brothers who ran an aeronautical business in Highbury. The family had been building gliders, balloons and airships for three generations and was credited with a series of firsts, including the first airship flight over London in 1902.

It was the Spencer brothers to whom the WFL now turned, hoping to be able to charter their latest airship to launch an outrageous and dangerous protest as the King opened the new session of parliament on February 16.

After some negotiation, the Spencers agreed to a £75 fee for what they hoped would be a two-hour flight from the Hendon airfield in the north of the city, buzzing over Charing Cross, Trafalgar Square and down Whitehall to catch the King's procession as it neared the parliament. All going well, the chosen suffragist in the gondola would then use a megaphone to speak to the crowd, diverting all attention from the pomp and ceremony of the occasion.

The airship was 27 metres long and held together by an open framework of ashwood and bamboo. Its gondola was barely big enough for two people. It was powered by a 35-horsepower petrol motor which drove a pinewood propeller mounted at the front to pull rather than push the machine through the air. It flew well enough in a straight line, but manoeuvring was a challenge as it was shunted around at the whim of the weather. Stanley Spencer had once tried to circumnavigate St Paul's Cathedral in the airship, only to be foiled by strong winds, and now these crazy suffragists wanted him to try again, only this time around Big Ben and with one of them aboard.

And who would that be? There was only one choice as far as the executive was concerned, and in late January, as she toured Scotland opening new branches, Muriel Matters was given 'first right of refusal' to ride in the airship. She accepted without hesitation and returned to London.

No one would ever lay claim to the idea, but it had all the hallmarks of Teresa Billington-Greig's imaginative thinking. The plan was ingenious in its madness, the intention to fly over the head of the King as he made his way in the golden state coach, guarded by Beefeaters from the Tower and horse guards mounted on jet black steeds, and then drop hundreds of 'Votes for Women' leaflets over their heads like confetti from heaven.

It had been foisted on the WFL in a sense because the police had banned the league from distributing its literature at street level along the parade route, presumably in retaliation for the success of the Grille protest, as Muriel would later reveal: 'Others could use it, but we were denied the privilege. As we could not get a footing on earth, we thought we had better secure one in the heavens. Accordingly, I went up in an airship and, needless to say, I was quite unmolested by police as their regulations do not extend up there. You see, there are still some limitations to man's authority.'[1]

As with the Grille protest, secrecy was paramount, not because the airspace above Westminster was controlled but so that the police could not stop Muriel from flying by putting pressure on the Spencer family to pull out of the deal. As minutes from the league's meetings would show, their security fears would be discussed numerous times over the next few weeks as preparations were made, including printing twenty-five kilograms of the leaflets to be scattered to the winds.

On the eve of the protest, satisfied that the police could do nothing to stop them, the WFL issued a public notice: The Women's Freedom League will signalise the opening of parliament by an airship trip. The airship has been chartered and will ascend from Hendon at 1.30. The aeronaut and his assistant will be accompanied by Miss Matters, who distinguished herself in connection with the Grille incident in the House of Commons. There will be attached to the airship banners and streamers forty feet in length and they will bear such inscriptions as *Votes for Women*, as well as the title of the particular organisation under whose auspices the trip is being arranged. Miss Matters will carry a megaphone and as the voyagers pass over London an attempt will be made to address the crowds. It is not intended to attempt a descent in London, but it is proposed that the journey shall cease in the neighbourhood of Epsom on some convenient space in the downs. As the airship passes over the House of Commons handbills will be thrown down.

* * *

Muriel waved to the crowd below, one hand gripping the basket edge, as the airship rose over the trees. 'Goodbye,' she called through the megaphone before her voice was lost as the airship was carried southwards.

Any fears she may have harboured vanished, the cold forgotten as she gaped across the wooded landscape toward the rooftops of the city, a view many had imagined but few had seen: 'It was like nothing on earth, quite wonderful',[2] she would exclaim to an eager gathering of journalists. Henry Spencer, by contrast, had no time for views, already hard at work trying to swing the airship eastward, across the wind, so he could later turn directly south and allow the ship to drift lower over the city.

The hope was that the winds would stay light, although they were forecast to slowly shift north-west, which would push the airship away from the target. Still, they could not wait for better conditions, as the protest was timed to coincide with the King who would shortly leave the gates of Buckingham Palace.

The delay caused by the engine problems meant they might miss the King, but even so, the crowds would still be lining the streets and showering them with the handbills would be spectacular.

They had quickly reached Wormwood Scrubs, another belt of green, as Henry Spencer continued to wrestle with the steerage sail at the back of the structure, keenly aware of his brother's earlier, ill-fated attempt to fly the machine into the wind around St Paul's Cathedral.

He was like a spider in a web of rigging, clambering across the bamboo as he adjusted the ballast to keep the ship aloft and on course. Muriel was transfixed, as she later told reporters: 'What worried me was to see Mr Spencer get out onto the rigging. I was afraid that he would say at any moment, "Just climb out there and see to the ballast." Of course, I should have gone had I been asked.'[3]

Spencer's efforts seemed to work as they tacked like a yacht sailing windward toward the suburb of Cricklewood and closer to the line they needed to fly over Westminster, but the breeze was gusting more sharply and he was forced to turn the airship back south.

Muriel's first sense that they would struggle to get to their target came ten minutes later as the airship flew over Hyde Park and the Albert Hall, the scene of so many boisterous suffrage rallies. Muriel could see Buckingham Palace and Big Ben as well as the mass of people who typically lined a royal procession route. But they were still too far to the west, the wind holding them on a course that would miss the parliament.

They were also too high, the megaphone useless. 'We were about 3500 feet high and although we could see the House and the people quite plainly, I don't expect they could see us,' she would later say.[4]

But on the ground the airship had indeed been noticed. It looked like a 'generous German sausage', according to one reporter standing outside the parliament, its brazen message readable, although it was only a background distraction as the procession passed through the royal gates and into the Palace of Westminster.

It was now or never as they flew over Chelsea. Muriel began hurling handfuls of leaflets over the side – 'yellow, green and white floating down to the people like beautiful birds'[5] – as Henry Spencer scrambled around the rigging, cajoling his craft to defy the wind and fly back to the city.

But it was all to no avail as they were shoved by the wind across the Thames and on toward Tooting. Their target gone, the aviators relaxed and Spencer brought the airship closer to the ground. People came out to see the strange contraption and the lady with the megaphone: 'Now and again, when we got down to 500 feet, I leaned over the side of the basket and asked through my megaphone where we were. I was greatly amused because the only answer people ever gave me was "Votes for Women".'

They had been in the air for almost two hours when Henry Spencer looked for a place to land, rather than swing further west to Epsom where they had originally planned to set down. They had cleared the most southern suburbs of London and farmland stretched below. Croydon slipped past in the west at 4.00 pm as the airship dipped to a few hundred feet above the ground.

The journey would come to an inglorious end, the airship landing in a hedge at Coulsdon, not far from where Muriel's caravan tour had begun nine months before. When it threatened to lift off again, a farmer grabbed a guy rope and grimly hung on, preventing it from sailing away and into a copse of trees while Muriel 'was clawing onto the side of the ship like a monkey'.

Muriel was safe, although stranded for an hour as she waited for her compatriots to catch up. The airship had travelled about thirty kilometres, but the WFL members who followed by road, led by Edith How-Martyn, had to zig-zag their way through London, stopping occasionally to make short speeches and distribute more leaflets. They would travel almost ninety kilometres.

The press was waiting in the evening gloom when they got back to Robert Street, anxious for a colourful quote from the new queen of the suffrage movement. Muriel didn't disappoint. The elements had been against them, but the protest had been a success, she insisted, if only because it gained attention, notoriety and headlines.

'You may take it from me that after today's experience we shall not do much on earth again. Think of us landing on the House one of these nights and giving the members advice through the window by megaphone,' she laughed, before turning serious. 'If we want to go up in the air, neither the police nor anyone else can keep us down, and if we can throw handbills we could easily throw anything else.'[6]

The reporters had their story.

19.

ACCLAIM ACROSS THE ATLANTIC

Propaganda by airship

The latest and most ambitious exploit of the militant woman suffragists

New York Times, February 17, 1909

The daring stunt fronted by Muriel Matters had reached across the Atlantic and made headlines in the biggest city in the United States. Far from considering it a failure, the *New York Times* splashed on its front page the story of not only the flight but of the Grille protest of a few months before. Within a week, the story had been repeated across America, from large cities like Los Angeles and Washington to the plains of Ohio and small southern towns. The fact that Muriel hadn't managed to pepper King Edward with suffrage flyers was largely irrelevant compared to the event itself – the world's first aerial protest.

American suffrage groups, hitherto unwilling to tread the same militant path, looked on in amazement and with some admiration for their British sisters. Writing to Millicent Fawcett, the NUWSS head who was dubious about the growing level of militancy, the prominent US suffragist Alice Stone Blackwell observed: 'You are far better qualified to judge of the suffrage situation in England than any of us here in America can be; still, perspective sometimes enables one to get a different view of the thing, and to me it does seem as if the militant tactics are doing good. At all event, when so many thousand women are boiling hot on the subject (as is evidently now the case in all the English societies) it is only a question of time when they will carry their point, no matter what mistakes individuals may make. I only wish our American women were half as enthusiastic.'[1]

Australia, too, was softening its often harsh attitude to Muriel's activism. The previous derision and lamenting by some journalists that she had traded the stage for the agitator's pulpit was subsiding, replaced, at least in part, with a grudging pride that a small-town girl from Adelaide and Perth (depending on which paper was reporting) was now rivalling, if not overshadowing, Emmeline Pankhurst as the most prominent figure of the suffrage movement.

The *Western Mail* columnist 'Zadig' was effusive: 'She has pluck and dash and her recent exploit in an airship has naturally concentrated upon her considerable public attention. But Miss Matters by no means depends for her popularity on dramatic incidents. She is an effective and impressive speaker and her flights in the air are nothing compared to her flights of oratory. She is argumentative, eloquent and humorous, besides being remarkably piquant in manner and attractive in appearance.'

The *Critic* in Adelaide was perplexed by a propaganda postcard being circulated by the WFL of Muriel calmly reading a book. On the back it read 'Premier Aeronaut. Advance Australia!'. 'The portrait shows how deceptive are appearances,' declared the newspaper. 'This lady looks quite incapable of the Boadicea sort of action she has recently indulged in. Adelaide friends remember her as a quiet and unassuming maiden.'

It contrasted sharply with the coverage in London papers where the protest, like the Grille incident, was largely dismissed, some editors interpreting Muriel's warning that the WFL would try again as a threat to drop a bomb on the parliament. Rubbish, she told a packed house at Caxton Hall the next day: 'We women do not intend to make martyrs of the members of the Cabinet. We simply are going to make them look like a set of drivelling idiots.'

But not all the British coverage was negative. The *Daily Express* declared her a 'determined warrior' and the *Belfast News* applauded an 'enterprising plan', while the *Observer* published 'The Airship Poem', a four-verse ditty that gently mocked the suffrage movement while acknowledging the 'masterful Miss Matters'.

> *High above our heads suspended*
> *pamphlets, megaphone and all*
> *In a big balloon distended*
> *with the gas of Caxton Hall*
> *Soars the masterful Miss Matters*
> *chained securely to her seat*
> *While her circulars she scatters*
> *at our feet.*
>
> *Far below policemen, trembling*
> *gather closely round each gate*
> *Of that palace where assembling*
> *Lords and Commons legislate.*
> *These do well to stand in fear of*
> *an incursion from the heights*
> *Where she floats, the pioneer of*
> *women's rights.*

Far below her feet the teeming
thoroughfare rounds 'Wyndham's' shows
Patriotic Britons streaming
to 'what every German knows'.
Scouting this dramatic sermon,
she'd invade the land we love,
Dropping like the dew of Hermon
from above.

Woe is me! What man proposes
providence at times resists.
And the way an airship goes is
crooked as a suffragist!
Adverse breezes that today from
Westminster to Croydon blow
Waft Miss Matters miles away from
Cannon Row.

What a lesson for each maid is
to be learned from such a case
Of the foolishness of ladies
who fly in nature's face
Who to such mad lengths are going
by the winds of folly fanned
That there's certainly no knowing
where they'll land.

But it was the regional coverage that was especially important for an organisation trying to raise its profile, membership and finances beyond the fringes of London, and it was there that Muriel's exploit was greeted with hefty praise. The *Western Gazette* in

Somerset hailed it as 'the most remarkable event in the whole of their propaganda', while the *Lincolnshire Echo*'s front-page headline declared: 'The Lady who Cannot be Kept Down'.

The *Norfolk and Suffolk Journal* described Muriel, albeit tongue-in-cheek, as a young warrior in a campaign of ingenuity: 'The suffragists, not content with their infantry assaults, cavalry parades, motor car and char-a-banc demonstrations and steamboat trips took to the air on Tuesday. Miss Muriel Matters, one of their youngest warriors, sailed aloft from Hendon in a diminutive basket of a cigar-shaped dirigible balloon for the very latest thing in suffragist dashes to Westminster. Miss Matters meant to teach the government that there is still another way by which suffragists might one day find their way into the House – a descent on the top of the Victoria Tower.'

The meeting at Caxton Hall on the morning after the airship stunt did not dwell on Muriel's flight but its aftermath, her derisive description of MPs as drivelling idiots the call to arms for a march on the parliament in the hope – as forlorn as it was – of forcing a meeting with Herbert Asquith.

But the hastily convened protest wouldn't get far, the marchers confronted by police as they left the hall. Two dozen were arrested for displaying banners and declaring their intention of marching on Downing Street as the constabulary, using a wide interpretation of their powers, attempted to crack down on the disturbances before they occurred. The remaining marchers regrouped behind closed doors and emerged soon afterwards. Instead of heading to Downing Street, Charlotte Despard led one hundred women to Westminster Police Court, flanked by dozens of mounted police.

It was soon evident from the addresses of those arrested – women from Birmingham, Manchester, Glasgow, Cardiff and Sussex among them – that the call to the suffrage movement was gaining momentum. As one report noted, 'The women who were charged with obstruction came from various parts of the kingdom in answer to the call recently issued by the London women to come forward if they did not mind prison.'[2]

The morning's fun and games were far from over as the delegation, now numbering one hundred and fifty, left the police court and marched on Downing Street, this time getting as far as the gates to the street before police lines held them back. When the prime minister sent a message via police commanders that he would not see a delegation, there were several rushes on the gates and another six protesters were arrested.

A third attempt to speak with Asquith would be made later that night, this time outside the parliament, but with the same result. Far from crushing the spirit of suffrage militancy, tougher prison sentences and a point-blank refusal to include the women's franchise in the new session of parliament had merely toughened resolve within the WFL.

* * *

It is a two-hour journey by train from the heart of London to the rural tranquillity of Sevenoaks, a market town built at the intersection of two ancient roads and famous for having arguably the oldest cricket ground in England. The landscape had begun its vivid winter-to-spring transformation on the morning of March 11 as Muriel Matters sat alone in a carriage, pondering her own remarkable life transformation since turning from fledgling actress to prominent agitator. If the caravan tour had announced her arrival and the Grille protest revealed her capability, then the airship jaunt had showed her audacity and bravery. What on earth was next in this increasingly complex campaign for democratic recognition?

She was due to speak at a WFL branch rally later that night, but had decided to travel early for a different purpose, to attend a meeting of a volunteer organisation set up to help the thousands of men and women discharged from asylums each year.[3]

The Mental After Care Association had been established in 1879 to deal with the consequences of an ill-fated attempt to treat mental illness by building and filling asylums across the country in the belief that institutionalisation would address and even ameliorate the problem. Instead, the policy had done the opposite: therapy had stagnated, staff were over-worked and under-trained and new guidelines filled the asylums not only with the chronically insane but with society's misfits – from the homeless and hopeless to abandoned pregnant women and the intellectually handicapped.

The After Care Association offered hope and care to the hundreds of men and women tipped back into the streets each year as the institutions overflowed, by providing short-term accommodation either in halfway houses dotted around the country or in private homes where they were given advice, money and clothing and assisted to find suitable work. The group also introduced a system of visiting ex-patients in their homes, an early form of psychiatric social work.

The association's work resonated with Muriel's Wesleyan roots, reviving childhood memories of performing at fund-raising events for the poor organised by her uncles and of the practical social care that was such a cornerstone of parish activity in Adelaide. It also spoke to her experiences inside Holloway Prison where most of the women serving time were suffering some form of mental instability, and were harmed further by a system intent on degradation and humiliation. For Muriel, incarceration had confirmed once more that the achievement of democratic rights was not the end of the suffragist struggle, but the necessary means by which to fight the myriad of social problems facing not only women, but society in general.

The Daisy Lord case had been a glaring example of the system being incapable of understanding the individual: 'She was a mere girl who under the stress of the dreadful situation in which she found herself had done away with her child,' Muriel would tell her audience that night. 'And yet every bishop in the House of Lords turned down our request that her sentence should not be of death but detention.'

One of her fellow prisoners had been a mother of four, working as a seamstress in a grimy sweatshop where she was paid just ninepence for sewing together a dozen shirts, and was required to pay for her own cotton thread. In utter desperation she had stolen what was described in court as a trifling sum and yet had been sentenced to several months imprisonment, away from her children, an experience that had shattered her psychologically.

'There shouldn't be one law for men and another for women,' Muriel said: Every child born, whether in or out of wedlock, should, in the eyes of the law, have two parents so that the father shares equal responsibility with the mother. Divorce laws are a disgrace in a civilised community, the awful curse of sweats [sweatshops] is another evil which could be remedied if only women had a hand in framing industrial laws. As a matter of fact, nine out of ten laws passed in the House of Commons are of a domestic nature and affect the wife, the mother or the working woman in an industrial world. We are asking for the vote not merely that we might once every few years register a cross on the ballot paper but that we might improve the conditions not only of the women but the men and the children of the Empire.[4]

Back in London, Muriel's position within the WFL had been cemented. At the Suffragettes Fair in April the executive presented a theatrical sculpture of famous women, known as a tableau, in which Charlotte Despard took the role of Queen Elizabeth with Teresa Billington-Greig as Boadicea. Muriel was cast as Joan of Arc.[5]

She was also prominent in the WFL's continued campaign of political disruption, first at a series of by-elections, including in Croydon where Muriel and Marion Holmes attempted to exploit what appeared to be a loophole in nomination proceedings. Women might not be able to stand as candidates, but could they nominate a candidate to stand?

The Mayor of Croydon, Major John Fox, seemed stumped: 'I must ask my legal adviser that question. What occurs to me for the moment is that if ladies cannot vote and are not on the parliamentary register I do not see how they are entitled to nominate.'[6]

The town clerk, Mr Lloyd, was also unsure: 'I do not think you can determine the question. It is merely an abstract question of law at the moment. If the ladies give in a nomination paper, then we will deal with it.'

He then handed Muriel a form, almost certainly the first time a woman had been invited to nominate a candidate to sit in the House of Commons. Her response was typically brazen. Given that she was not about to nominate a male candidate, she asked instead, 'Are you prepared to hold back the election until the thousands of women citizens of Croydon have a voice in it?'

'No,' replied Major Fox. 'I recognise your position and I say honestly that you have my sincere sympathy. Personally, I have always been strongly of the opinion that the ladies are entitled to their votes. This is a historic occasion.' With that, he posed for photographs with the two women much to the astonishment of journalists, whose coverage the next day would focus on the suffrage byplay.

* * *

If Muriel was discovering a level of sympathy among some election officials, then there would soon be a harsh reminder of the political bulwark against female suffrage. Another Bill in favour of women suffrage had passed the House but would soon be shelved as MPs debated the conclusions of a working committee set up in the wake of the Grille protest. The 'Brawling Bill' would seek to punish 'disorderly strangers who disrupt proceedings' with prisons sentences of six months and fines of £100.

Sir William Robson, the Attorney-General, pulled no punches: 'In order to keep those unsexed hyenas in petticoats from disturbing the deliberations of the most majestic assembly in the world (loud cheers) we propose to pack them off to the police court, the very first word they utter, there to be sentenced to at least six months'.

He then targeted Muriel personally: 'For this House to be interrupted in the discussions of high matters of State by persons who are not persons, who have no country, no rights and yet are harboured and permitted to exist in the Land of the Free ... only confirms my former opinion that females are something less than human and herein lies our difficulty.'[7]

The extraordinary attack would be continued by others but the Bill would eventually fail, essentially because MPs feared being dragged into court to give evidence, allowing protesters the opportunity to make more grandstanding speeches.

There were other examples of interference by officialdom. In the early summer of 1909, the playwright George Bernard Shaw, who had helped during Muriel's first years in London, prepared to open a new play in the West End, a satire on the suffrage debate called *Press Cuttings*, only to be halted by official censors claiming he was making fun of 'real individuals'.

The objection was mainly to his use of fictional names: Prime Minister Balsquith was clearly a combination of the actual prime ministers Arthur Balfour and Herbert Asquith, and an army general named Mitchener was assumed to be a caricature of the famed General Kitchener. Shaw managed to get around the ban by staging the play in private clubs but eventually relented and changed the names to Prime Minister Johnson and General Bones.

The play touched on Muriel's Grille campaign, opening with desperate officials ordering all railings be removed to prevent protesters from anchoring themselves to government buildings. In a departure from numerous suffrage plays produced at the time that attempted to justify the arguments for women's votes, the play instead used farce to poke fun at the arguments of politicians and anti-suffrage groups.

Shaw, a member of the Men's League for Women's Suffrage but a critic of 'grotesque' violent protest, also predicted the eventual rise in spontaneous instances of individual hostility that had begun the previous summer when WSPU members began throwing stones through windows. Encouraged and even endorsed by Emmeline Pankhurst, they would eventually turn to bombings and an attempt to burn down a theatre being attended by Herbert Asquith.

The Shaw production coincided with the catalytic case of Miss Marion Wallace Dunlop, a WSPU member jailed for wilful damage for using a rubber stamp on the stonework of St Stephen's Hall, began a hunger strike in protest at not being classed as a political prisoner.

Her 91-hour fast ended when panicked prison officials released her rather than risking the young woman dying as a martyr, but it would be the beginning of a sustained campaign of hunger strikes embraced by suffragettes that would lead to torturous force-feeding of prisoners and the controversial Cat and Mouse Act under which hunger strikers were released and then re-arrested and jailed once they had recovered.

The stakes were getting higher.

20.

RICE, POTATOES AND SODS

While the Pankhurst group was escalating its campaign, the Women's Freedom League had lowered its profile, at least in terms of spectacular stunts. Teresa Billington-Greig, the architect of the Grille campaign, had taken ill, then been injured in a train accident and would spend a year recovering from both. In the absence of her ingenuity, WFL activities adopted a quieter, more traditional pace – traditional town hall meetings, fund-raisers, membership drives and the like, one of the few exceptions being the picketing of parliament, night and day for almost four months, in the hope of confronting Herbert Asquith as he arrived or left the building.

Muriel would take her turn on the picket line when she wasn't travelling the country; among her destinations were Glasgow, Birmingham, Chelmsford, and Chichester. She would travel into Wales for the last four months of the year, without the caravan and Asquith the horse but with Violet Tillard as her lieutenant, on a quest to harness the support of the women of the western flank of Britain.

The missiles in Wales were not eggs and stink bombs, but rice, potatoes and sods of turf. Instead of bell-ringing to drown out the speeches, men set off fireworks outside the halls. On the docks in Cardiff, five hundred men sang music hall ditties to stop

Muriel's speech, while police guarding the stage were pelted with bags of flour.[1]

More than three thousand turned out in Neath: 'A frantic rush was made by women and men to get at the speakers,' the *Evening Express* reported, adding that police had to stand guard at the railway station until their midnight train to Swansea arrived.

At Carmarthen, the oldest town in Wales and supposed birthplace of the mythical wizard Merlin, a crowd of men outside the local guildhall threatened to pull down the gates and rush the stage. Police, fearful for the safety of Muriel and Violet, surrounded the speaker's box and shuffled the two women out a side gate before the howling mob broke through. Reporters followed Muriel back to her lodgings to find her 'pale but not noticeably agitated'. She said 'she had had a rough time but was not daunted, and hoped for greater things in future from Wales'.[2]

There was a different atmosphere the following night at Mumbles, outside Swansea, where the crowd of one thousand or more cheered when Muriel called for the political demise of Herbert Asquith. The *Cambrian*, which described the speech as 'haranguing the crowd', lauded her: 'She is an Australian, clear-minded mistress of happy phrase, has physical attractions, enthusiasm, courage and a sense of humour. The Women's Freedom League made no mistake in importing her.'[3]

Muriel spoke from lorries and horse carts, lectured on chairs in halls and took questions clinging to statue plinths in parks, gamely using anything that would raise her 160-centimetre frame above the heads of her audience, frequently numbering two thousand or more, so they could see and hear her. At one meeting in Cardiff's Victoria Park there was a crowd of over five thousand, mostly well-wishers.[4] She was disarming, her appearance and manner deceiving; the woman dressed in 'pretty light blue and dainty lace' was capable of standing up to unruly men and delivering powerful, unscripted put-downs.

When men started singing a music hall number 'Oh! Oh! Antonio' about a woman pining for her lover, she turned it onto the crowd. The reporter from the *Cardiff Times* was impressed by her ability to cajole a mob: 'This Miss Matters neatly turned to advantage by saying she always understood that music had the effect of soothing the savage beast, and she hope this occasion would prove no exception ... Miss Matters then spoke for nearly an hour.'[5]

On another occasion, when challenged by a man about her experiences in Holloway she retorted, 'It might have been nice when you were there but it was far from nice when I was there.' As the man left the meeting, humiliated, another was overheard asking his son, 'Say laddie, how would you like to have a mother who could talk like that?'[6]

She railed against the House of Lords as a 'House of Masters', labelled anti-suffragists as 'dear old aunties', and met the argument that women were too weak with the question: 'Then why is Lord Roberts, a physically weak man, in command of the army?' And as for the local favourite, the member for Carnarvon Boroughs and Chancellor of the Exchequer, David Lloyd George: 'We are going to send a body of women to Carnarvon and I'm going to lead them; we are going to beard your pet lamb in his own den.'[7]

In return, she endured jibes about marriage and insinuations that she was a prostitute; she debated taxation policy with ignorant loudmouths; embraced the label of rebel and outlaw as part of 'the Welsh blood in my veins'; and queried why women should be paid less than men for the same task.

At times Muriel focused on the demands made of women: 'We are being asked to develop all the best qualities of our natures but are not granted the necessary power to do so. We are regarded by some men as half idiots and half angels, and not allowed to be 'persons' within the meaning of the Act of Parliament. Then what are we?'[8]

At others she described suffrage opponents with a hint of asperity. 'They are divided into several camps,' she told a crowd while she stood in a horse cart during her third speech of the day in late August: 'There is the dear old gentleman who wants to put women in glass cases and protect us and there are the unchivalrous men who allow women to pay silly calls, play afternoon bridge and go about gossiping, but tell them their place is in the home if they put their nose outside the door to discuss politics. Of the women there are those who have all they want in life and are overdressed and overfed, and the other the women, including wives and mothers, who want peace at any price, not peace with honour. We want to inspire women with self-respect.'[9]

In Cardiff, the *Evening Express* reported a sharp change in her message: 'While attacking men for their materialism and the absorbing passion for money, her most violent criticisms were reserved for those members of her sex who belonged to the anti-suffrage league. She characterised them as "un-sexed echoes of men". Women, she said, were political slaves and she and those who thought with her pleaded for greater freedom. Miss Matters concluded with the sinister prognostication that blood would be shed before the vote was won.'[10]

In another speech she criticised the hypocrisy of anti-suffrage Jewish MPs who had only won their place in the Commons half a century before, and also took a shot at 'foreign' MPs who were 'the first to declaim against the rights of women'. In particular, she named 'Monsieur' Hilaire Belloc, the French-born writer and historian, and member for Salford South, who, despite having a mother and sister who were strong advocates for women's rights, regarded women getting the vote as immoral, because 'it disturbs the relations between the sexes'.[11]

Belloc wasn't the only writer with whom Muriel would joust. Marie Corelli was a British novelist (real name Mary Mackay) who, at the time, sold more books than Arthur Conan Doyle, H.G. Wells and Rudyard Kipling combined and yet could not accept that women needed a stronger voice, claiming she influenced 'forty males' without having a vote herself. Her opinion boiled down to this passage, printed in a pamphlet titled *Woman, or Suffragette?*: 'The clever woman sits at home, and, like a meadow's spider, spreads a pretty web of roses and gold, spangled with diamond dew. Flies or men tumble in by score, and she holds them all prisoners at her pleasure with a golden strand as fine as hair. Nature gave her at her birth the right to do this, and if she does it well she will always have her web full.'

'I do not believe that fly-catching is a satisfactory occupation,' Muriel retorted to a meeting of businessmen and their wives at the Hotel Metropole in Swansea. 'We are asking for the vote in order that we might get out into the sunlight and have a direct and pure influence on the political and social life of the nation.'[12]

She pursued the fight further in a 'vigorous reply' through the letters pages of the *Daily News*:

What a relief it is to read in the papers that the eminent novelist, Miss Marie Corelli, is not one of these unsexed creatures, a suffragist! The suffragists have made the declaration that women's influence should be accompanied with full responsibility, and they deprecate the use of 'back stair' influence. It would be difficult to reconcile such a declaration with the views expressed by Miss Marie Corelli in her pamphlet. Also, in reference to a certain countess who once enjoyed the smile of her monarch, Miss Marie Corelli suggests a really clever woman would have caught another King, and made the first King jealous. A suffragist could

never live up, 'or down', to such a moral standard as that
which the novelist cleverly advocates. The whole rend and aim
of the suffragist movement is to inculcate a morality founded
on the fundamental greatness of humanity, which strikes the
death blow at power obtained through petty intrigue and
jealousy by working on the baser passions of mankind.

In a rare interview, Violet Tillard was asked about the campaign in
South Wales which, despite a hostile response in some areas, she
said had opened at least half a dozen branches, and why they were
opposing David Lloyd George in his re-election bid. 'You know
Mr Lloyd George is in favour of women's suffrage. Why do you
oppose him?' the reporter asked. 'Because the Cabinet – and Mr
Lloyd George is a great power in the Cabinet – could have done
something for us and they did not. We hold the whole Cabinet
responsible,' she replied firmly.

As Christmas approached Muriel and Violet headed back
to London, to prepare for a much bigger journey together – they
would travel halfway around the world to Australia.

* * *

Muriel was going back to the stage, not as an elocutionist reciting
the intricate words of Robert and Elizabeth Browning or the
marathon odes to fictional fishermen set to music by Strauss, but as
a celebrity speaker on a cause célèbre circuit. Women's rights would
be the subject of talks by the most famous suffragist in London.

The idea was the brainchild of a former Adelaide journalist
named Beaumont Smith, who was in London in the summer
of 1909 with his new boss, the wealthy theatre owner William
Anderson, to find acts to bring to Australia the following year. They

had signed up the British humourist Jerome K. Jerome, famous for his comic novel *Three Men in a Boat*, and Lavinia Warren, wife of the celebrated circus dwarf General Tom Thumb. There would also be pantomimes and several dramatic plays with themes of class division, although George Bernard Shaw, the man about to write *Pygmalion*, the classic of such tales, turned them down.

Muriel was chosen as a serious curiosity, her journey from aspiring small town actress to soap box queen hopefully enough to entice an audience, let alone her part in the struggle for women's rights in Mother England. The crowds she drew across Britain, often in their thousands, were heartening, but the challenge was to translate that into packed theatres in Australia.

There were plenty of cynics, of course, typified by the author of this syndicated column, who showed extraordinary ignorance in the space of a single paragraph: 'She was prominent in the chaining incident in the House of Commons; she has smitten a policeman; and travelled in a caravan organising and preaching suffragette principles, but there is one great drawback that limits her chances of success. She has never been to gaol [and] a prominent suffragette who has not been gaoled is regarded in London as lacking in spirit. Besides, what can Muriel Matters have to say to enfranchised Australian women that really matters? Bringing a suffragette to suffragists is worse than carting coal to Newcastle.'[13]

But Smith painted a very different picture. The suffrage story was not one to be sneered at but admired, he insisted; it was the tale of a group of women who, far from the often snide media coverage, were struggling to survive, some of them even starving while fighting loyally for something they believed in. Muriel and her colleagues were often treated badly by police. He had watched one police officer on horseback slap a woman across the face and another ignore a protester when she was assaulted by a man in the crowd. And the most famous of these women, after her recent exploits, was the Adelaide-born Muriel Matters: 'All London knows her name and South Australia should be proud of the enviable position she has gained by sheer hard work and dauntless courage,' he trumpeted.[14]

With some months until their Antipodean adventure would begin, Muriel had just been voted onto the national executive in recognition of her deeds, and Violet returned to Wales for the first two months of 1910 to run the WFL campaign against Lloyd George. He would retain his seat in the general election, although the Asquith government was barely returned. The campaign had been robust and angry at times, finally erupting into violence on the eve of the poll when the suffragist protesters were attacked in the street and then had their headquarters threatened, as Muriel wrote to a friend in Perth:

> Our days in Carnarvon are nearly ended. In the early hours of Friday morning, a mob of some hundreds stormed our rooms and commenced smashing in the front door. The howls were terrific. The police arrived quickly and repulsed them with a heavy baton charge so that many went maimed in Carnarvon the next day. They had the most serious riots on polling day, however. The crowds took the police and locked them up in twos and threes. One hundred stalwart police from Manchester had been specially drafted in, but they seemed hopeless to cope with those rough quarrymen.[15]

Muriel then headed west to Dublin where she addressed the newly formed Irish Women's Franchise League, highlighting the improvement to men's wages since the franchise was extended to 'respectable working men', while women's wages stagnated.

But her visit was more telling because of her host, the Lord Chief Justice of Ireland, Lord O'Brien, whose daughter Georgina had invited Muriel to stay. Lord O'Brien would later recount a conversation with the 'charming militant' over the dinner table. Muriel was clearly not intimidated by her wealthy and important host, sparring over the effectiveness of militant action without which, she insisted, the suffrage question would have been left 'in some obscure corner'.

The discussion then turned to the former British prime minister William Gladstone, whom both admired. Lord O'Brien had known him personally, describing him as 'a pre-eminently great Liberal statesman, a man of surpassing intellectuality, of stainless moral character'.

In doing so, Lord O'Brien had painted himself into a corner. Muriel pointed out that it was Gladstone who had understood that although abhorrent, the notorious bombing of Clerkenwell Prison in 1867 by the Irish Republican Brotherhood had later forced his government to look at the issue of Home Rule and try to forge peace in Ireland.

Lord O'Brien could not help but be impressed: 'Then, with a lofty wave of the hand, the young lady added, "You were not born to be a statesman; you are a mere judge." "Well," I replied, "statesman or no statesman, mere judge or no mere judge, if you were brought before me for a criminal offence I will sentence you to imprisonment." "Sentence me if you will," she cried. "Gladly will I go to gaol to attest by my sufferings the sincerity of my convictions."'[16]

Back in London, Muriel took on another senior legal figure, this time lambasting the President of the Probate, Divorce and Admiralty Division of the High Court, Sir John Bigham, who had pompously declared that adultery by a husband wasn't grounds for divorce, and 'a wise wife should shut her eyes to many things'. Muriel took him to task at a Trafalgar Square rally: 'Women don't want to be told what ladies of refinement should do if their husbands are unfaithful to them,' she told the crowd. 'If women get the vote they will ensure the laws are amended to recognise marriage equality.'

She would continue the theme of social equality in private, during a send-off hosted in a city flat, in which she implored colleagues to 'dwell more on the necessity for the removal of the social evil and an improvement in the economic position of women, rather than on the political side of the question'.[17]

Four days later she and Violet boarded a steamer for the six-week voyage to Australia via Cape Town. They left behind a truce of sorts, the WSPU and the WFL having agreed to end militant protest to give a cross-party group of MPs time to draft a women's suffrage Conciliation Bill. It would last eight months.

21.

A VOYAGE HOME

Muriel stood on the deck of the steamship, transfixed by the scene unfolding before her. After three weeks at sea they had finally reached land, at first a strip of purple on the horizon, then strands of white as the shoreline widened. Hills and trees appeared, black and grey rocks and the sounds of surf above the noise of the engines. But it was when the vessel entered the heads and Muriel could see the West Australian settlement of Albany that her heart responded. She was home: 'I realised with a tremendous rush of feeling what my own land meant to me, as never before,' she would write: Environment works mightily on the spirit of a people, and here in full view were to be seen factors which make Australians what they are. Colour everywhere – in the depth of the sea, the delphinium blue of the sky, the ruddy hillside tracks descending from rocks a combination of purple and brown. On every side the eucalyptus showed its individual form; beneath its shade tangled masses of wild violet, scarlet runner and yellow wattle gorse ran wild whilst, sentinel-like, the flaming waratah kept guard. One felt inclined to shout, 'Had sunny Greece a clime more fair? Surely no!'[1]

Her wonderment continued the next day, as she boarded an early morning train for the city of Perth, where her family and supporters waited. In England, travelling between London and the

next speaking venue, she might sit for a few hours contemplating
the changing landscape, but this would be a journey through night
and day:

> One sees the country in varying moods. The spirit of the
> bush takes possession as of old; for once apprehended it is
> never really lost. Sunrise comes after the journey starts,
> tremulous at first, as the dawn in other lands, but quicker
> and fuller it bursts, flooding the world in flame. No cloud
> appears in the vivid turquoise sky. Through miles of gum
> and scrub we pass; no English green is seen, but tones of
> blue and grey. Towards noon not a breeze is stirring; though
> winter 'the gum leaves hang lifelessly down', and in the
> distance a purple haze blends pulsing with the mystic blue
> and grey. When evening comes the stillness is intense, and
> despite the noise of our slow travelling train, one hears
> distinctly the sounds heard only in the Australian bush –
> the mocking laugh of the kookaburra, the liquid lament of
> the native magpie, the myriad whirrs and croaks of insects
> and frogs which come from the rapidly drying waterholes
> and creeks; birds fly silently from tree to tree; a wallaby,
> like the sun downer, is fleeing to its rest. This is the magic
> hour of the Australian bush; and, like all things magical,
> 'tis swiftly gone. No twilight here. Land of the sun it truly
> is, for as he sinks the land obeys and darkness covers all.
> Then come the stars, cut out of the heavens, so near, so
> brilliant and emerging from the purple night the Cross of
> the Southern Land stretches athwart the sky. It is useless to
> expect English friends aboard the train to see or feel as we
> do. They are in the position of the old lady who stood by the
> Whistler and watched the scene on the canvas grow beneath

his touch, and then exclaimed: 'I don't see it like that!', bringing the artist to reply, 'No madam, don't you wish you could!'

Muriel's thoughts would be published four months later in the WFL's newspaper, *The Vote*, as she pondered a return to London after crossing the continent twice, visiting four states and speaking to thousands in packed theatres, at quiet social afternoon teas and even rowdy industrial meetings. It was reflective, an ode to her home and family rather than a report to her suffrage colleagues on the obvious success of her tour, the 'delphinium blue' of a northern hemisphere flower a sign of the impact Europe had made on her life, but also a yearning for what she had left behind. A century later, the observations for an Australian who has left to explore the world hold true:

Nature has been lavish, and her children have responded. Independent, enterprising ones she has reared, vigorous to a fault, intolerant and self-assertive. See that young sapling rearing its frame insolently to the sky? – a prodigious growth for years – and you see the young Australian, man or woman, as much a product of the country as the gum tree itself. One must remember this in dealing with our people. Springing from pioneers who faced and risked all, aided by environment and spurred on by necessity, Australians are what they have been made. The defects in their qualities – because of their individualistic force – are apparent everywhere; and the first feeling on return to them is one of intense disappointment. But as one learns to view the whole, the great possibilities for the country and the people present themselves, and the drawbacks sink to their native insignificance.

* * *

Leonard Matters was waiting when his older sister stepped off the train sixteen hours later to start her national tour. The 29-year-old reporter at the *Daily News* would begin his own international adventure the next year when he struck out for the United States and the wilds of Canada, but for now he basked in the success of Muriel's fame. Some of the details of her adventures had found their way into the columns of his newspaper via her letters home, but on this occasion he stood aside from the media excitement about her tour as journalists fell over themselves in adulation and greeted her as a loving brother.

Where once there was quizzical mockery, the media had now mostly decided that Muriel Matters was a warrior woman to be admired and celebrated, albeit in the shadow of the sudden death of King Edward VII, who, like his mother, was a vehement opponent of women's suffrage and had once referred to the suffragists as 'those dreadful women'.

Three sold-out events were scheduled for the Perth Literary Institute in the heart of the city. With flamboyant titles like 'The Torch of Feminism' and 'Within the Walls of Holloway', they would be illustrated with lantern slides provided by the *Daily Mirror* newspaper in London that showed, close up, the battle on the streets.

'Rarely is the opportunity given to an Australian woman to become famous as has been given to Miss Muriel Matters,' crowed the *West Australian*. 'The best woman speaker in England,' boasted the *Truth*. 'Miss Matters addressed over two million people and enrolled thousands to the cause', applauded the *Western Mail*. The *Sunday Times* cheered the daring young West Australian: 'the first time in history that the voice of a woman had been heard above a society whisper in the House of ancient usage and musty tradition'.

But while the admiration flowed it was an interview with a critic, the aptly by-lined 'Cynicus' in the *Daily News* that proved most revealing: 'I did a terrible thing today, I interviewed Miss Muriel Matters', he began, describing it as a meeting between the heavyweight boxer John L. Sullivan and Grace Darling, the British heroine who braved huge seas in a rowing boat to help her father save nine survivors of a shipwreck.

> The Heroine of the Grille is not the slightest degree like the typical suffragette. She is not big, she does not talk in a loud voice, she does not brandish an umbrella and she does not look as if she were ready to form part of an infuriated crowd to level tyrant man and all his works in the dust. On the contrary, she is petite, has a fascinating soft voice and she chats away with all the easy grace of a well-educated woman. No doubt she is the typical suffragette to the best of her ability. She says she hopes the day will come when man and woman will be very much the same. And you simply look at her and hope that day is a delusion. She declares that she has no sympathy with the excessive femininity of the modern woman and you simply stare in amazement, for she is all woman to the very tips of her fingers. She declares herself in favour of the militant movement, but the statement does not upset you. You feel perfectly certain that if an army of Muriel Matters were to make an assault on man he would not run away. On the contrary, he would stand his ground and the only arms would be open arms.[2]

For all his misogyny, Cynicus then embarked on a free-wheeling conversation which captured Muriel's fears and hopes for the future. Holloway had been tougher than she'd admitted publicly and she had no real taste for militancy, but felt the league's activities were a reasonable compromise on doing nothing and being violent: 'The government really decides our tactics. What we do depends on what it does – or rather what it doesn't do. We dislike those tactics far more than our opponents do for we have to pay the penalty. But they are forced upon us. If you want John Bull to listen to you then you must take him by the nose and pull – hard.'

The militant suffrage movement was growing, with 150,000 or more active supporters and branches across Britain. She was weary, but buoyant and determined; the workload was at times overwhelming, as she often gave four speeches a day: 'I don't think that's my record. I once addressed fourteen meetings in one day. That was when we fought Winston Churchill in Manchester.'

'Then you are very hopeful of the future,' the journalist observed.

'Very. There is, I am sure, a general awakening of women right through the rest of the world. The movement is bound, in my opinion, to end in the establishment of equality for women and that, in turn, will lead to the elevation of her status, intellectually, morally and socially, and the final consequences of all must be the permanent betterment of the race, for the position of women is the supreme test of civilisation.'

Muriel would speak for more than two hours on the first night, taking as her theme her journey to London and her involvement in the militant suffrage movement, which at first, she said, she regarded as vulgar, but then became convinced was the only course of action to affect change given that Millicent Fawcett's passive tactics had achieved nothing in half a century. But she drew the line at violence, as she made clear in later interviews while recounting the only time she had lost her temper: 'My temper at one time was a little peppery. A young man struck me in the chest during one disturbance. I retaliated by taking his hat and throwing it into the crowd. They said: "How dare you touch that young fellow!"'[3]

The *Daily News* described her as having 'the zeal of a reformer and the humour of a satirist', holding the packed hall spellbound. According to the *West Australian*, 'She was at times impressive, at times satirical, at times scornful, but whatever she said, she said earnestly and in a manner which to many doubtless showed the suffragettes in a light somewhat different to that in which they had previously stood. Applause and laughter were frequently aroused during the course of the lecture, and at its conclusion Miss Matters received an ovation which cannot have failed to have been pleasing to her.'

The *Truth* was more poetic: 'Listening to Muriel Matters, the charming, young, piquant mistress of satire, one realises how far we have got away from the old ideas of suffrage cranks and cartoons, the vinegar-visage dames with baggy, ill-fitting clothes and large knobs of hair, and their dogmatic "Down with the men, down with 'em, the wretches." One can only wonder at the hard-hearted magistrate who could imprison such a rebel.'

If Muriel's first performance was a mixture of personal story and history lesson, then the second lecture five nights later was pure storytelling as she recounted her experience behind bars. With Violet at her side in drab prison garb, she poked fun and mimicked the 'senile growl' of the police prosecutor, the 'shrill, angry scream' of the prison wardress questioning their womanhood, the 'surreptitious whispers' of the prisoners and the 'benevolent futility' of the prison chaplain. 'Although Miss Matters takes the suffrage movement very seriously, she has the valuable faculty of being able to see the humorous side of things, even of her own troubles,' the *Daily News* critic concluded.

Between appearances she was fêted at social events and sparred with opponents through the letters pages of local newspapers, ridiculing those hiding behind names such as 'English Woman' and 'Radix' and agreeing to another, matinee appearance to debunk her critics.

She also spent time with family members who had settled comfortably into the rhythm of West Australian life and had no intention of returning to Adelaide. Muriel was particularly close to her older sister Elsie, who would accompany her and Violet as they travelled around Australia, but her relationship to the younger ones like Isabel, who was 12 when Muriel left in 1905, was more distant; an adult who tended to lecture her about pronunciation.[4]

Muriel's delivery changed dramatically for the third lecture. Her personal reflections now exhausted, she instead traced the 'torch of feminism' through civilisation, from the Egyptians of 5000 BC, when inheritance passed from the maternal rather than the male line, through the empires of Greece, when women were economically independent, to Assyria which demanded fidelity from both sexes in marriage, and Rome, where women could own property, to medieval Europe, and on to modern America and Britain. 'We have not the space to follow the lecture,' the *Daily News* reported. 'To give a condensed report of what was necessary would be to imitate the man who carried around a brick as a sample of his house.'

* * *

The lasting image for Muriel as she left Perth two weeks later was not the welcome or adulation of her visit but the spread of ages of the women who flocked to her speeches: 'those who had fought in the Old Country, the fighters of today and in the faces of the young girls one could see our hopes for tomorrow'.[5]

It was a five-day voyage to South Australia aboard the 'mail boat', the only transport link between the two states. She arrived at Port Adelaide, just as her grandparents, Thomas and Mary Matters, had done almost six decades earlier. Muriel could relax a little now, relieved that her first two weeks had been a sell-out and that the press response was overwhelmingly positive. Although her immediate family was in Perth, it was in the streets and cafés of North Adelaide that she felt most comfortable, and little had changed, at least physically, save the appearance in the city centre of electric trams.

She was billed to speak in the Town Hall where Samuel Clemens' wit and charm had captivated the city. Her publicity machine had already cranked up by the time she arrived with Violet and her older sister, Elsie. Advertisements lauding *The Lady of the Grille, England's Foremost Woman Orator* and *That Daring Australian Girl* greeted them.

As in Perth, Muriel sat through a series of newspaper interviews, relating her story with practised ease and answering questions that rarely strayed from a formula, although there was the occasional probe that gave pause for thought, such as the obvious question asked by one reporter: Why would British MPs refuse to grant women the vote?

'It is regarded as an innovation, and English politicians are so conservative that they look upon any change with horror,' Muriel replied. 'They consider the women of the United Kingdom are happy without the franchise, therefore it is inadvisable to give it to them.'[6]

Was it too much to expect equality? 'We don't expect to bring about the millennium but we do expect to bring the millennium one step nearer. We can do without men's chivalry but we cannot do without fair competition in the outside world.'

There were some detractors, mostly hiding behind nom de plumes, like 'Dria', a female columnist who insisted: 'Miss Muriel Matters and her gaol companion, Miss Tillard, propose dilating upon their weirdly wonderful proceedings in the "glorious" cause of "Women's Rights". Hundreds will doubtless flock to hear them, but we do not expect our sympathies to be roused. The mad and hysterical behaviour of the suffragettes in England has in no sense appealed to the women of South Australia, who, although they possess the much coveted vote, still feel convinced that the government of the country is safer in the hands of men (poor job that they make of it sometimes) than it would be with us.'[7]

Others felt conflicted, like letter pages contributor Agnes Goldsworthy: 'I am willing to believe that the women of England have been shamefully treated politically, but they are extreme in their methods of retaliation. I think I voice the opinion of all Australian women when I say that we sympathise with the suffragettes but strongly disapprove of their tactics. It is hard to believe such clever, sincere women could be guilty of doing such silly, hysterical things. But since I have read some of Miss Matters' views, I begin to doubt many of the tales that have been cabled out. I think in our hearts we Australian women do not want to believe any ill of the suffragettes in England.'[8]

Muriel could not resist replying in the same pages two days later, observing: 'May I return the compliment with this addition, on behalf of English women – We do not want to believe anything ill of the Agnes Goldsworthys of Australia, but we shall feel constrained to if they form their opinion of a movement and its leaders from meagre newspaper accounts on an untruthful and prejudicial nature.'

The most vocal media opponents insisted that the women of South Australia had won the vote peacefully and, therefore, so should British women refrain from protest and wait patiently. It was an argument that ignored the fact that political expediency, and not the quest for social change, had persuaded the South Australian parliament to grant women the vote. That same desire to retain or win power was also the reason that Herbert Asquith continued to deny women the vote in Britain. He feared that granting moneyed women the vote, the most likely first step, would hand power back to the Conservatives.

Muriel's lectures in Adelaide followed much the same format as they had in Perth, although she could not help but hark back to her Wesleyan roots and weigh in to local issues like prison reform, alcoholism and prostitution, challenging audiences to tackle government policy on those subjects. 'How much do you know about local prisons?' she called from the stage, almost admonishing the well-heeled crowd that remained silent. 'I have only been in Adelaide a week but I have been finding out things.'[9]

True to her word, she had asked city elders for a tour of their gaols, as she had in Perth and would again in Melbourne, rebuking the political leaders she met for not addressing the disparities in conditions between men's and women's institutions. In Adelaide she would also be introduced to the early education system developed by Friedrich Froebel, a nineteenth-century German pedagogue who coined the term 'kindergarten', recognising the importance of play and activity in childhood learning that would influence educationalists such as Maria Montessori and Rudolf Steiner. 'Magnificent work which opens up a new era in the life and training of the child,' Muriel would report.

Adelaide audiences had been expecting speeches about the battle for democracy. Instead, they were taken to the heart of a humanitarian movement which wanted to rehabilitate as much as punish:

Some people are keen on temperance. So are the suffragettes. Some work hard in the cause of social purity. So do the suffragettes. But we say drunkenness and prostitution are very often the effects of a cause, and if the evils are to be remedied we must get to the root of the matter. The question of prostitution is more a question of economics than morals. If women had equal chances – that is, if they received equal pay for equal work – and if they were taught at their mother's knee to regard a woman's life as equal to a man's life it would not be as likely that they would sell their bodies.[10]

Then there was the humour, in the form of biting quips and anecdotes delivered with the timing of a stand-up comedian. It somehow fitted snugly, and even enhanced, an otherwise serious message:

'I admit that some women are foolish, but that's only because God made us to match the men.'[11]

'Men are not able to mother a nation as well as father it.'[12]

'Lord Cromer told us that women should remain disenfranchised because we are not capable of bearing arms. This coming from a man lame in one leg and with a squint in one eye.'[13]

'We women are classed with criminals, lunatics, paupers, aliens and children as regards the franchise. Yet when it comes to paying rates and taxes, our money is as good as any man's.'[14]

'Mr Chamberlain has told us that nature has made men and women different and parliament can never make them the same. That is a great joy to us.'[15]

* * *

If Perth and Adelaide were homecomings, then Melbourne was a political opportunity for Muriel, who had made it known when she first arrived in Australia that she wanted to take a message back to the British parliament from its colonial offspring that female enfranchisement should be embraced, like 'the child turning round and scolding the parent',[16] she said in an early interview, clearly relishing the idea of a stinging rebuke for Herbert Asquith.

The opportunity arose two days after arriving in Melbourne when she was the guest of the Women's Political Association, led by Vida Goldstein, who had not only become the face of feminism in Australia in the years since Muriel's absence but was prominent on the international stage, and had met the American president Teddy Roosevelt in the White House.

Among the guests at Muriel's reception was Josiah Thomas, postmaster-general and senior member of the federal Cabinet, who told the room that he not only supported the cause of female suffrage but also the methods of the suffragettes, and hoped he would see women elected to parliament. Privately, Thomas would tell Muriel that if a resolution of support from the Australian parliament would help, 'then I would be glad to act on the matter', paving the way for a remarkable vote in the Senate five months later.[17]

Charles McDonald, Speaker of the House, also spoke at the event, insisting that when great principles were at stake it was necessary to make the fight 'bitter'. In reply, Muriel disagreed with the notion of bitterness, and put forward her own thoughts on behaviour: 'We have been told by our opponents that the first thing for a woman to be is ladylike. We reply that "no", the first thing is for her to be a woman in every sense of the word.'

Vida Goldstein moved a resolution that cemented their bond which read, in part: 'That the Women's Political Association ... asks Miss Matters to assure her militant colleagues that this association has always supported, and always will support, the brave women who are ready to risk their own lives in the attempt to win for all women the means of self-protection, and recognition of the mother as the chief factor in moulding national character.'[18]

She had been accepted as a significant influence in mainstream politics, and her position was confirmed at a lunch a few days later when she would meet the Australian prime minister, Andrew Fisher, recently victorious in the 1910 election that made him the first Labor Party leader in the world to form a majority national government. When asked later about women's suffrage, Fisher responded that he was 'delighted' with the results.

If there were any doubts about Muriel's appeal outside Adelaide and Perth they were swiftly answered in late June when she filled the 1500-seat Princess Theatre in Spring Street over three nights. The lectures would repeat her earlier themes, but the anecdotes and side discussions would change with the audience. Where prison reform and prostitution dominated in Adelaide, here she talked about the revolution of art and literature that had risen from the oppression of politics.

She hated the hypocrisy of the British, who were afraid to confront issues and 'wrap them up and pretend they are not there',[19] deplored the survival of petticoats as 'an odious convention of medieval times and the symbol of women's thraldom' and defended socialism: 'There can never be equality but we can all have equal chances.'[20]

The plaudits came: some flowery and declaring her to be the 'new woman'; other reviews, although favourable, were laced ignorantly with old views: 'Behind that femininity, that musical voice, that pretty smile and gentleness there is a brain of masculine strength.'[21]

There were those who maintained pious antagonism, most notably *Punch* magazine whose correspondent took umbrage at one of Muriel's most popular lines that women were not entrusted to vote for MPs but allowed to choose a husband. The writer retorted: 'If women were really intelligent in taking husbands there would be no divorces and wife-beating would be a rare entertainment.' The remark not only implied that it was a woman's fault if she was beaten, but that the practice was rampant and, in the writer's mind, could be described as 'entertainment'.

The Age newspaper took the middle road: 'Miss Matters has evidently broken through the conventions and narrow interests of the mid-Victorian days. She is occupying herself strenuously in politics and the improvement of women's position and economic usefulness. May her efforts in that direction be successful.'

The interviews would raise another issue, the categorisation of suffrage protesters. Although the Women's Freedom League tried to distinguish itself from Emmeline Pankhurst's group, the WSPU, by calling themselves militant suffragists, Muriel did not shy away from the term suffragette or its impact on the campaign.

'What is the difference between suffragists and suffragettes?' inquired a reporter from the weekly magazine *Table Talk*. 'The suffragists just want the vote and the suffragettes get them,' Muriel replied, using an adage about the boy in the street. 'The difference is they have worked for it quietly for sixty years with little effect; we are the militant body, and the name suffragette was first applied to us in derision, but we have taken it for our own and wear it with pride.'

Muriel's warmth toward suffragette tactics and their impact would soon change.

If audiences in Sydney were any smaller, it was by a marginal amount, although Muriel only spoke twice, both times to positive reviews, and attended a series of private meetings and a conference of New South Wales trade unions before heading back to the southern capital where demand was so high that she repeated her lecture series at the Independent Hall and the Gaiety Theatre and was invited to speak from the pulpit of the independent Australian Church where her subject was 'Prison Reform and Individual Responsibility for Corporate Sin'.

While in Melbourne, Muriel stayed at the aptly named Whitehall, the stately home of Vida Goldstein. The pair had become close, with one newspaper lamenting: 'An interesting pair. Both have charm and brains and it is really hard to understand why either of them insists on fighting the entire male sex when they look so eminently fitted to make at least ONE happy.'[22]

After a second meeting with Prime Minister Andrew Fisher,[23] who confirmed he would support a parliamentary motion to call on the British parliament to support female suffrage, Muriel and Violet took a train back to Adelaide for another round of speeches and then took the mail boat to Western Australia for further appearances, touring the rough and ready goldfields and addressing a meeting of hundreds of women at His Majesty's Theatre in Perth in support of striking tramway workers.

On September 12 the pair boarded a steamer back to Britain. 'In this country the progressive forces have it, and the reactionaries are going to the wall,' Muriel wrote ahead of her arrival back in London, a few days before her thirty-third birthday. 'The democratic ideal is the one toward which the Australians are moving. Here democracy is more than a theory; it is fast becoming reality.'[24]

* * *

On November 17, Andrew Fisher's promise of political support came to pass with a resolution prepared by Vida Goldstein and introduced to the Senate by Arthur Rae, a former shearer, journalist and trade union leader from New South Wales who would later write to Muriel: 'I sincerely trust that it will be of some slight service and I am pleased to see, at any rate, the suffrage has become a live political issue in British politics.'

The resolution, which passed unanimously, read:

> That this Senate is of the opinion that the extension of the suffrage to women of Australia for state and Commonwealth parliaments, on the same terms as men, has had the most beneficial results. It has led to the more orderly conduct of elections, and at the last federal elections, the women's vote in the majority of states showed a greater proportionate increase than that cast by men. It has given a greater prominence to legislation particularly affecting women and children, although the women have not taken up such questions to the exclusion of others of wider significance. In matters of defence and imperial concern they have proved themselves as far-seeing and discriminating as men. Because the reform has brought nothing but good, though disaster was freely prophesised, we respectfully urge that all nations enjoying representative government would be well advised in granting votes to women.[25]

A second proposal, to cable the resolution to Herbert Asquith, was passed 15–4 despite objections by some senators that it was 'impertinent'. Asquith acknowledged it immediately and succinctly: 'I have to thank you for your telegram conveying an expression of the opinion of the Senate on the result of the enfranchisement of the women of Australia.'

He would not yield.

The next day Westminster exploded in crisis as the eight-month truce with the suffragettes was abandoned. Angry that Asquith had dissolved parliament and with it the Conciliation Bill, Emmeline Pankhurst led a rally of three hundred members to parliament to confront the prime minister who refused to see a delegation. Over the next six hours in bleak, cold conditions and while debates continued inside parliament, protesters clashed repeatedly with police. There had been bigger rallies before but they had usually been quelled by swiftly arresting the ringleaders. This time, police made no arrests but resorted to physically battering the women, at times throwing them between officers like rag dolls, in the hope they would retreat. They did not.

The brutality was brazen and happened in front of hundreds of onlookers and reporters who defied the Home Secretary, Winston Churchill, and covered the bloody riot. A front-page photograph in the *Daily Mirror* of a protester lying prostrate on the ground, her face covered in fear as a police constable stood over her, was a highlight of the media scrutiny. The day would soon gain infamy as 'Black Friday'.

Herbert Asquith's mulishness and political trickery had paved the way for the violence that would follow.

22.

FLESH AND BLOOD, BRICKS AND MORTAR

Miss Muriel Matters writes to me from London. She has resigned from the National Executive of the Women's Freedom League and, with Miss Tillard, is taking up slum work in Lambeth.

The announcement in the February 1911 edition of the *Westralian Worker*, a trade union news sheet, was as sudden as it was surprising. Barely five months after a spectacularly successful tour of Australia, the suffrage campaign's best orator was gone, not just from the leadership of the WFL but, it appeared, from the organisation itself.

Behind the flamboyant lectures and town hall speeches, Muriel was beginning to have doubts about the tactics being used in increasingly desperate attempts by suffragette protesters for attention. The more the WSPU pushed toward violence, the more senior politicians resisted negotiating a solution. To do so, they said, would be akin to yielding to terrorism.

The newspaper photographs of police violence on Black Friday had won the movement some public sympathy, but Emmeline Pankhurst wasted the opportunity by refusing to accept government assurances that the Conciliation Bill would be back on the agenda in the new parliament, causing many MPs, previously sympathetic to her demands, to reconsider their support.

And it wasn't just the WSPU. The only time Muriel felt defensive during the tour of Australia was when questions arose about a protest at a by-election for the seat of Bermondsey in October 1909 when two WFL members decided by themselves to throw dye into the ballot box and ruin the votes. The stunt, born out of frustration that Asquith had managed to avoid the four-month picket outside parliament, had backfired, because an attendant claimed – wrongly as it turned out – that the liquid was acid and he had been blinded. The media and public responded angrily, as did Millicent Fawcett, the sage-like suffragist leader who had been a quiet supporter of the WFL's activities until then.

Muriel was conflicted. Unlike the carefully planned protests in which she played a leading role, the Bermondsey stunt was off the cuff, not unlike the increasingly confronting Pankhurst activities, and when Teresa Billington-Greig, the calming influence and measured guile inside the leadership group, resigned, disillusioned that the greater emancipation of women was being sacrificed in the haste to win enfranchisement, Muriel followed suit, quietly disappearing from the scene.

'The vote was but a tool in my eyes,' Billington-Greig would write in her resignation letter printed in the WFL organ, *The Vote*. 'The movement has allowed itself to be narrowed, lowered and exploited; dragged down to the same level as that set by men politicians ... It has ceased to be governed by reason and conviction and has yielded itself up to emotion.'

Muriel had the same concerns as Teresa Billington-Greig, who planned to devote her energies to wider social issues. Prison reform, sweatshops, marriage equality and the protection of children were firmly on the agenda of both women. In the weeks before her decision to step down, Muriel had made an impassioned speech about 'fallen children' at a WFL branch meeting held inside the Bijou Theatre. Her concern, raised because of an appeal for funds by Canon Newbolt at St Paul's, was not just that there were 1500 children who had received help in a home at the cathedral but that nothing was being done to address the problem of broken homes and parents incapable of bringing up children.[1]

'The very title, "Fallen Children", is one which, as a woman, I resent very much,' she told the seven hundred members. 'Everyone presupposes that, if a person falls, they had been in a position to stand or fall. Canon Newbolt does not suggest any remedy; he simply calls upon people to keep this home going. I say we are done with charity, we want justice. We ask, as practical women, how are we to find a remedy?

'It would be better, and cheaper, to deal with the children now than to deal with them later, when we shall have to, in the reformatory. By dealing with the child, we fit that child to take care of himself or herself. It is a remarkable thing that in this human race of ours there is not the feeling for the future that there is among the ants and the bees; they work as a community. And so, we say that for these moral lepers you should have your colony. In order to do this, we have got to mould public opinion.'[2]

As much as she loved the stage and the spotlight, and rode the bumps and grinds of public speaking with the skill of a rodeo rider, Muriel was increasingly frustrated at debating a hypothetical. If she truly believed her own rhetoric, that the vote was a means to an end, then there were real people already suffering who could be helped. Her heart lay not in the beautiful streets of Westminster but the slums of the east and south-east of the city, particularly Lambeth on the southern bank of the Thames which had been largely built on reclaimed marshes.

It was the same conviction that had driven her desire to help young chorus girls with the short-lived League of Light, to fight for the reprieve of Daisy Lord and to stand by the waitresses of Piccadilly. She also had Violet Tillard, now partners – the performer and the sidekick. A team, prompting one social columnist under the name Pomona in Melbourne's *The Weekly Times* to hint at something more to their relationship, observing: 'Miss Tillard, who accompanied Miss Matters on her Australian tour, is still her guide, philosopher and friend'.[3]

Their plan was to establish a 'women's settlement', an education and workplace sanctuary for destitute women where practical skills could be taught, almost certainly modelled on the work of Alys Pearsall Smith, a friend and the wife of British philosopher Bertrand Russell who had created an innovative school for mothers in St Pancras to teach them how to care for their babies. They would enlist the support of the Salvation Army, founded in East London by the Methodist preacher William Booth and his wife, Catherine, which had acquired property in the area. She discussed her plans in an interview as she stepped down from the WFL:

> The women's suffrage movement has a recognized hold with
> educated and middle-class women. We have yet to deal
> with those women who, owing to adverse conditions under
> which they exist, are not able to help themselves. To this end,
> therefore, I am forming a women's settlement with other
> women workers, to carry on educational work in many forms
> in the slums of Lambeth.[4]

It would mean tackling the slum lords, beginning with the royal family. The Duchy of Cornwall Estate, a treasure chest held for the benefit of the seventeen-year-old Edward, Prince of Wales, owned a significant slice of an area called Kennington Park, which yielded the prince's coffers an astonishing £82,000 a year. King George had recently announced plans to clear and remodel the slums, based on the redevelopment of homes at Golders Green, near Hampstead.

Muriel wrote: 'An announcement in the press spoke of King George as the model landlord and stated that the whole of the Duchy of Cornwall estate was to be reconstructed, old slums were to be demolished and in their places "Englishmen's homes" erected. If this promise is to be fulfilled, well and good. And when it is an accomplished fact, let us not forget the small beginnings that led to this result.'[5] (The remodelling would begin two years later, but it would be another twenty years before the slum was finally cleared.)

As Muriel and Violet began their work, focusing on teaching mothers homemaking and health skills from simple personal hygiene and cooking to basic nursing, the socialist democratic Fabian Society was in the midst of a four-year study of the poor of Lambeth. The report, called 'Round About a Pound a Week', to reflect general wage levels in the area, would become an important social document, mapping the lives of the 'respectable poor' of the district around Vauxhall. Even here, in families where the husband had employment, the infant mortality rate was 20 per cent and the third biggest budget item, behind rent and firewood, was burial insurance. Food ranked a poor fourth.

* * *

The *Christian Commonwealth*, a weekly paper printed in London's East End, billed itself as 'The Organ of the Progressive Movement in Religion and Social Ethics'. As well as trying to bring the message of the pulpit out of emptying churches and into homes, the editor, Albert Dawson, together with several correspondents, had

helped establish a suffrage society called the Free Church League
for Women's Suffrage, a non-denominational advocacy group with
the rather sanguine motto *It is the Dawn*.

The appearance of Muriel Matters on his doorstep in early 1911
was a blessing for Albert Dawson in more ways than one. Not only
had the Free Church League scored one of London's best-known
suffragists, but he recognised her literary potential and hired her
as a contributing writer for his pages. Muriel felt equally fortunate
because it meant a return to the church roots she had largely ignored
since arriving in London, it would replace the income she had lost
by leaving the WFL and, most importantly, give her a public outlet
for her Lambeth campaign.

While other journalists wrote of statistics and regulation, and
parliament considered an overhaul of its Poor Laws, Muriel decided
to tell the stories of the people she met each day in the streets of
Lambeth, desperate and beautiful in her telling, like Liz, a nine-
year-old school girl, 'pale, patient and wistful with fragile limbs
and a humpy back', whose malnourished childhood had led to
consumption, a disease likely to kill her.

Muriel and Violet had met the family when a care worker
pointed out the child who should be 'put on dinners' and sent to
recover outside the toxic city, such was her wasted condition.
But Liz's father, a casual labourer who eschewed charity – 'not a
cadger' – could barely earn enough to feed his family that seemed to
grow each year, let alone send his eldest to the country in the hope
that clean air might save her.

Muriel paid for the train ticket and hoped she would live: 'Later
we pictured Liz in her new surroundings. In a room decked around
with dimity she will sleep. In a room and a bed of her very own
her tired little limbs will stretch in snowy, sweet-scented lavender
sheets, dreaming the dreams known only to childhood. She will

wake in the morning to fields of buttercups, "the little children's dower", and daisies.'[6]

They met a woodcutter who had fallen on hard times and struggled to somehow find the rent for a house that was unfit for animals, let alone a family: I can see him now, disabled by rheumatism, his whole body aflame. For years he had paid his rent regularly – the books were there to show – and with his wife he had helped to bring up four orphaned child relations. The two elder ones, girls, were now working in a factory and a cook-shop nearby, and after their labour they returned to sleep in a room with walls not water-tight and the contents covered with mildew. It didn't need much imagination to read into the old man's words a fear for the future – 'this is no fit place for them two girls to come back a' nights' – but an awful fate awaited those who wouldn't or couldn't pay.[7]

Across from the woodcutter, a family of five had been turned out into the street on a day's notice, only saved from destitution by a chemist who gave them a room above his modest shop. Muriel called him the 'Old Saint', who, more often than not, dispensed medicine free of charge: 'To him, young and old come for treatment. If they can pay they do, and if they can't afford to, "Well, that's all right." But for that other medicine he dispenses, balm for the broken-hearted and soothing syrup for the tired of soul, they can never pay. What a wealth of love and philosophy in that old grey head.'

On a warm autumn day, she found a tramp camping in a Kennington park with a half-starved cat in his arms. The man had been a soldier and was now a forgotten invalid, an outcast with a paralysed hand. She watched as he hobbled across the park to buy a tumbler of milk, handing over his only penny, then returning to the cat waiting on the grass: 'At last the tumbler was emptied, the cat had taken all, and the two friends turned to gaze inquiringly around. Joy and satisfaction was on the tramp's face, but the cat, sphinx-like, sat and waited. "Your cat?" said I. "No lady," the man replied. "She came crying to me now, and being often hungry myself I thought I'd give her a feed, poor little thing." What love, what faith, what understanding of the source of all supply that gift entailed.'[8]

But the column that had most impact was an achingly sad story of a woman who had lived in the same cottage for forty years:

> Results of the wear and tear, alike of flesh and blood and bricks and mortar, are obvious, but the effects upon mind and soul are hidden from human eyes. No.1 [Blank] Street, on the estate of the Duchy of Cornwall, in the borough of Lambeth, was once a pleasant little cottage from whose back window she, then a young woman, could look to the park beyond. With a manageable rent, things went well enough with husband and wife and six children.
>
> But changes came. The husband sickened, became a confirmed invalid and finally died. Yet she 'managed quite well for a time', she assures one with a quavering voice. 'I was able to work very hard,' she states with pride, and the light brightens the faded eyes, and one gets the impression of past energy and capacity. One after another, four of her children in their growing years are 'taken away', leaving a daughter and a son. The former – sickly and subject at times to something in the nature of fits – remained with the mother.
>
> The latter on reaching manhood married, and now has a wife and seven children dependent on him. 'He would help, you know,' says the old optimist, 'if he possibly could; he's been a good son, but the wife and children need all he can

Muriel was known to draw crowds in their thousands – supporters and foes alike – when she spoke outside at public meetings, dodging missiles and insults. This photo shows her addressing a crowd in the Welsh town of Caernarfon in late 1909. *Muriel Matters Society*

THEATRE ROYAL.

---o---

EVERY SUNDAY NIGHT.

---o---

SELECT KINEMATOGRAPH ENTERTAINMENT.

TOWN HALL.

DIRECTION ... ... BEAUMONT SMITH.

THE MOST NOTABLE ENGAGEMENT OF THE YEAR.

TO-NIGHT (SATURDAY), TO-NIGHT.

First of the only three appearances in Adelaide during her brief Australian tour of
THE RENOWNED SUFFRAGETTE,

MURIEL MATTERS,

Whose remarkable and thrilling career as a worker in one of the most intensely
interesting periods in modern history have made her

FAMOUS IN TWO HEMISPHERES.

To-night, Miss Matters will introduce her Fascinating Lecture,

"THE WOMEN'S WAR."

Brimful of Incident and Anecdote of the Great Non-Party Political Movement.

VIVIDLY ILLUSTRATED WITH PICTURES,

Including "Bernard Shaw Listening to Suffragist Speeches," "Suffragist Prisoners in Gaol
Dress," "Downing street, showing the Cordon of Police."
THE AIRSHIP ASCENT—RISING TO 3,000 FEET,
illustrating Miss Matters's Sensational Attempt to Present a Petition to King Edward from
the Women of England, and many other interesting Episodes of this Picturesque Period.

FASCINATING AND RICH IN HUMOUR.

Brimful of Anecdote and Interesting Stories of the Great Personalities with whom Miss Matters
has come in contact.
BERNARD SHAW—LORD CHIEF JUSTICE OF IRELAND—FORBES ROBERTSON—MR. AS-
QUITH—MR. LLOYD-GEORGE—MARIE CORELLI—MRS AND MISS PANKHURST—BEATRICE
HARRIDEN—WINSTON CHURCHILL—LORD CREWE—LORD MORLEY—ELLEN TERRY.
Miss Matters's Remarkable Speech to the House of Commons earned for her the title, given by
The Daily Mail, of

THAT DARING AUSTRALIAN GIRL.

She is regarded as the Foremost Woman Orator in Britain.

PRICES,   PRICES,

3/, 2/, 1/.   BOXPLAN—HOWELLS, YOUNG, till   **3/, 2/, 1/.**
1 o'clock; afterwards at Duhst and
Biven's,
Book Seats Early.
Doors open 7 o'clock.   Commence 8 o'clock.

MONDAY NIGHT, JUNE 13,

"INSIDE HOLLOWAY PRISON."

Miss Matters will Lecture in Prison Dress, telling of her Experiences as a Prisoner on behalf
of the Cause.
TUESDAY—"THE TORCH OF FEMINISM," in which Miss Matters will reply to local criticism.
A. E. MARTIN, Representative.

Muriel's return to Australia in 1910 was greeted with great fanfare and packed theatres, including the Royal in Adelaide, as 'that daring Australian girl' told her stories of derring-do. *Muriel Matters Society*

VOTES FOR WOMEN.

MISS MURIEL MATTERS,
WOMEN'S FREEDOM LEAGUE.
1 ROBERT STREET, ADELPHI, LONDON, W.C.

PHOTO. LENA CONNELL,
90, GROVE END ROAD, N.W.

Trail-blazing female
photographer Lena Connell
captured Muriel's serene
composure and presence in this
1910 portrait.
Mary Evans Picture Library

Plays by groups such as the
WFL and the Actresses Franchise
League became important fund-
raising and propaganda tools
during the suffrage battles. In
November 1909, Muriel acted in
and helped produce one of the
more famous, *How the Vote was
Won*, in Cardiff. The play tells of
the day women across England,
from workers to housewives,
go on strike, highlighting their
importance to the nation.
Mary Evans Picture Library

WOMEN'S FREEDOM LEAGUE.

C. CORN.

CARDIFF.

"HOW THE VOTE WAS WON."
CHARACTERS BY MISSES VALDEMAR, PORTER, YATES AND HOPE.
MESDAMES WOOLF, HOPE AND BARNARD,
MESSRS. SASSOON AND PHELPS. DOG. WALTER WOOLF.
STAGE MANAGERESS: MISS MURIEL MATTERS.

"WHEN YOU WANT A THING DONE, ASK A MAN TO DO IT."

Muriel, her scarf wrapped around her head to hold her hat in place, puts on a brave face as she waits for the airship pilot to start the faulty engine. *Getty Images*

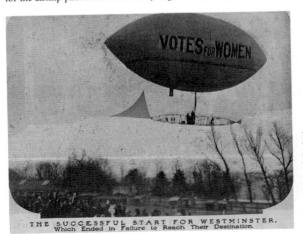

A newspaper photograph of Muriel's airship as it set sail from Hendon towards Westminster. Unfavourable winds would blow the airship off course but the protest would make headlines around the world. *Muriel Matters Society*

Muriel discusses tactics with fellow WFL member Edith Craig as they walk down Whitehall toward Downing Street, probably in 1909, to make yet another attempt to be seen by the Prime Minister Herbert Asquith. *Muriel Matters Society*

The children at the Mother's Arms school in East London, probably the first attempt to bring Montessori teaching principles to Britain. *Muriel Matters Society*

Muriel's pragmatic teaching methods engaged children not only in the classroom but also their everyday life, from helping in the kitchen to table manners. *Muriel Matters Society*

Muriel, with her wide blue eyes, golden hair and engaging presence, was the antithesis of the mainstream media's caricature of suffrage protesters as ugly spinsters with no hope of finding a husband. *Muriel Matters Society*

Muriel pets a family dog, most likely during her 1922 visit to Australia. *Muriel Matters Society*

A reunion in 1928 of prominent suffragists and suffragettes on the tenth anniversary of the passing of the Representation of the People Act, which enfranchised women over the age of 30 who met minimum property qualifications. Muriel is at the centre of the back row, with Teresa Billington-Greig to her right. Emmeline Pethick-Lawrence is second from left in the front row, next to Sylvia Pankhurst. *Muriel Matters Society*

Although she faded from view during her later years, Muriel's deeds in the suffrage movement were never forgotten and on occasions like this in the 1950s, journalists would visit her in Hastings to hear her recount her adventures. *Muriel Matters Society*

Muriel's house (right) overlooking the seafront at Hastings where she lived for the last two decades of her life. *Alamy*

earn.' As time passed builders grew busy in the locality and no.1 [Blank] Street now has no outlook. Stables block the park view, and the alley from the front window is narrow and dim.

The only heartening, though perhaps not altogether healthy, sign is the tiny window sill, where an ivy plant grows bravely from its earthen pot. Pinned to the stiffly starched, clean, tightly drawn curtains, a card announces *Mangling Done*. This is the sole source of income, amounting to never more than three shillings a week and sometimes not so much.

The daughter – the sickly one of forty-odd years – remarks: 'We does our best, but work has fallen off. People don't like sending work here.' It is not difficult to understand why. In the adjoining room stands a mangle. The walls ooze with damp and mildew. The door, under which the cold winds blow on the old woman, now crippled with rheumatism, is studded with rat-gnawed holes, through which the pests run riot in the cottage.

At the old woman's bidding, the daughter goes to the top room, and from the right-hand corner of the chest of drawers in brown paper fetches rent books back to 1869, and testifying to the regularity of the rental payments. The rent of the cottage is no longer 4s 6d, as in the days of its decency, but for this dark, damp, unhealthy and rat-eaten habitation the sum of 6s 3d weekly is charged.

'Mother's pension goes toward the rent,' explains the daughter, 'and the further 1s 3d comes out of the mangling profits, leaving exactly 1s 9d a week to budget with. 'For aye, the poor are piteous to the poor,' and from the comparatively poor brethren in the neighbourhood come the clothes worn by mother and daughter.

There has just arrived by post from an old school fellow
of the daughter, 'in service' in the country, a starch box of
flowers; and as the aged widow offers me a tiny crocus it
seems to open its golden heart in prophecy of coming spring.
Perhaps some of our readers would like to help to bring spring
to the winter of this withered Englishwoman.[9]

The publication of Muriel's column brought an instant response, the
office of the *Christian Commonwealth* inundated with donations of
money, enough to pay the widow's rent for the rest of the year, and
clothing. It would be more than enough as Muriel would discover
two months later: 'On my usual round I call at no.1 [Blank] Street,
and learn that the widow of whom I wrote recently has "moved".
This Saturday noon the married son, hurrying from work, arrived
to inquire after his mother, and was met by the daughter, whose
parched throat failed to voice what the silence told. He passed
quickly to his mother's side, and Death the Messenger spoke.'[10]

* * *

Bryceson Treharne, the Adelaide Conservatorium maestro, had
not given up on Muriel Matters. In early April 1911, as she and
Violet concentrated on the poor of Lambeth, a small item appeared
in the columns of the *Bulletin* back in Australia and was then
repeated in newspapers across the country: 'The spinster days
of little suffragette, Miss Muriel Matters are numbered, as her
betrothal to Mr Bryceson Treharne, director of the Adelaide Music
Conservatorium, is announced. Mr Treharne has put in some
very good work in the musical world in Adelaide, but is of a very
unassuming and retiring nature, and the women's vote will interest
him but little.'[11]

Muriel must have accepted that the brooding musician had mended his misogynistic ways, and put aside her own concerns about marriage to accept his proposal. Clearly they had rekindled their friendship during her stopovers in Adelaide as she criss-crossed Australia during her lecture tour, and it seemed she had boarded the mail boat bound for Perth and then London promising to consider his proposal.

It would take five months for Muriel to say 'yes', a decision perhaps driven not by love so much, given that they'd rarely spent time together, as her obvious care for the children she had seen in the slums of Lambeth and a hankering, now she was in her mid thirties, for children of her own. It may also have been a submission to the taunts she had endured over the years from suffrage opponents about her unmarried status and the unspoken allusions to her being a lesbian, a word that rarely found its way into public discourse.

Whatever her reasons, Muriel's affirmative answer was delivered by sea back to Adelaide where, excited at the news, Treharne promptly announced it to the press.

Two months later, another newspaper snippet would report that Treharne intended to travel back to Britain 'to wed that clever and enthusiastic little suffragette and then return to settle in South Australia'.[12]

Apparently no one had checked with the bride who was now mixing her slum work with a return to the stage as a public speaker, appearing at functions for the Actresses' Franchise League and the Free Church League for Women's Suffrage, among others. For several weeks she and Violet led a caravan tour around Buckinghamshire for the Tax Resistance League, which meant she was absent from London in June when, in a rare show of solidarity, the three main suffrage groups combined their resources

to organise a grand suffrage parade to coincide with the coronation
of King George V and Queen Mary. The march was attended by
an Australian contingent including Vida Goldstein, who later wrote
that she holidayed with Muriel, and Margaret Fisher, wife of the
Australian Prime Minister Andrew Fisher.

It seemed that her days with the Women's Freedom League
were over, although she was a willing participant in its April protest
when thousands of suffragettes and suffragists alike boycotted
the 1911 Census. Hundreds spent the night at Trafalgar Square,
members of the Actresses' Franchise League chose the Aldwych
skating rink, while others held an all-night picnic on Wimbledon
Common. In the country, women even hid in haystacks to avoid
being served with census forms.

Muriel and Violet stayed home in their rented rooms in the
terraced townhouse at 9 Fentiman Road, Lambeth, a short stroll
to the hovels of Lower Marsh where they spent most of their
days. Instead of hiding, Muriel accepted the form which she then
ruined, scrubbing out the declaration that she had filled in the form
'correctly and to the best of my ability', and instead scrawling in a
bold, upright hand:

No Vote, No Census.
    As I am not a person under the franchise laws, I am not a
person for census purposes.[13]

Her enthusiasm for protest was far from quelled, and she joined her
Australian compatriot, the author Stella 'Miles' Franklin (then a
leading trade union leader in America) and Charlotte Despard in
helping to organise one of the most important strikes by women
workers the city had seen. The Bermondsey Women's Uprising of
1911 ranks alongside the 1888 match girls' strike as an important

moment in the battle for decent working conditions and wages for women. More than twenty thousand factory workers downed tools on August 15. The owner of the jam manufacturer Pink's could not believe it when his entire workforce walked out and carried placards around the building, bearing the slogan *We are not White Slaves – We are Pink*. Of the twenty-one factories on strike, nineteen won substantial wage increases, Pink's among them.

* * *

On December 15, Bryceson Treharne boarded the steamship *Otranto* for the six-week voyage to London. His plans had changed somewhat in the five months since he announced he would be bringing his bride back to Australia to live. Instead, Treharne had resigned from his post at the conservatorium, as he told the *Register* two days before he departed after eleven years in the city: 'Mr Treharne is to marry Muriel Matters and they will probably settle in England.'

23.

THE FIANCE

The Position of Women as the New Year Dawns

It was a unique front page headline in the *Christian Commonwealth* on January 3, 1912. Never before had a London newspaper devoted such prominence to the coverage of women's affairs. The paper ran a 2500-word assessment of women's suffrage, not merely as a political campaign for a democratic voice but for a woman's place in society as a whole. The article, which read like an editorial, did not carry a byline but its author had been touted in a few lines on the back page of the previous edition – Muriel Matters.

Although still a passionate advocate for suffrage, and a fearsome public speaker who would continue to be heard on the stage across all parts of the United Kingdom, Muriel had made the transition from a frontline militant agitator who drove caravans, made speeches to howling mobs, invaded the House of Commons and flew in rickety airships, to a freelance suffragist who campaigned for equality and a radical overhaul of social and economic policy.

Albert Dawson and the editorial board of the *Christian Commonwealth* had given their new recruit free rein in her revealing snapshot of the state of feminism. 'Although the new year finds women still unacknowledged citizens, a glance at the events of the past twelve months shows that we are entering with amazing rapidity upon a life of larger opportunities, privileges and responsibilities,' she began with guarded optimism, before unveiling her vision:

> All the forces of reaction, tradition and prejudice are still
> directed to hold women within the four walls of the home,
> to force her to stay there because she has no vocation, no
> money, no education, no opportunity to enter other spheres;
> to limit her interests to the German Emperor's 'K's – '*Kinder,
> Küche, Kirche*' [children, kitchen, church]. But that regime
> belongs to an age past and gone. A nobler conception of the
> wife, the mother and the woman is throbbing in human souls
> and wrestling for expression in our customs, laws and social
> institutions. Woman must marry, not for a living, not because
> she has no other alternative, but because, with the world
> before her, love divinely compels. The home must hold her,
> not as a four-walled fortress from which there is no escape,
> but as the centre of her universe, through which she can take
> a full and responsible share in the nation's life. It is only from
> this standpoint that we can fully appreciate the events of the
> past year, and measure their significance.

Muriel argued that one of the biggest anomalies was inequality in the workplace – 'A woman teacher, equally qualified and doing the same work as a man teacher, draws lower wages simply because she is a woman' – although there had been some limited progress. In the medical profession: the appointment of a woman to a senior management position, on the same salary as her male counterparts, to administer the National Insurance Act; and breakthrough legislation that allowed workers to insure against sickness and unemployment. 'We are indeed moving!'

But artificial, conventional and conservative restrictions still hampered women, particularly in the professional, educational and artistic worlds: 'The universities of Oxford and Cambridge, while opening their examinations to women, refuse them the degrees that are the symbols to the world at large that those examinations have been passed. The Royal Academy has never yet conferred the RA on any but members of the male sex. Women are allowed to qualify as barristers, but forbidden to practise. Among churches, the Society of Friends and the Unitarians alone ordain women to the ministry. A large number of public bodies still grow pale at the mere suggestion that a woman should serve as chairman.'

Despite this, there had been achievements over the previous twelve months that earlier generations would not have imagined:

One after another the barriers go down before them. A fortnight ago the Royal Academy School of Art awarded its blue riband to Miss Margaret Lindsay Williams. The previous winner was also a woman. Out of the fourteen prizes awarded this year ten were carried off by women. These arresting triumphs of the 'weaker sex' have raised again the question of whether the academy has the power to make a woman an 'ARA'. The French Académie des Beaux-Arts, confronted by a similar issue in the sculpture section, decided in the affirmative, and in spite of a tradition of nearly two hundred years, has awarded the Grand Prix de Rome to Mlle Heuvelmans. It is not a novelty for a woman to carry off the Nobel Prize. This year the Swedish Academy has awarded the prize to Mme Curie who, with her husband, discovered radium.

In the educational world there had also been advances. The National Union of Teachers had elected a woman president, there was a movement to provide higher education for working women, and a Central Labour College for Working Women was proposed in London. More and more women were joining trade unions, with 160,000 members across the kingdom, and there were two unions for women's interests, the National Federation of Women Workers and the Women's Trade Union League.

The ecclesiastical world was also shifting its attitudes, albeit slowly. The Wesleyan conference which met in 1911 at Cardiff had allowed women members into its sessions, and the Lutheran and Reformed Churches had given women a vote in church affairs: 'The Bishop of Iceland has supported a bill to make women eligible to hold ecclesiastical office, and declared St Paul himself would have favoured the change were he here.'

The struggle for democratic acknowledgment continued, while around the world countries and states followed the leads of New Zealand and Muriel's native Australia, including six American states and the Scandinavian nations. There were advanced agitations in France, Germany, Italy, Russia, Portugal, Spain, Bohemia and the Netherlands, while women in India, China, Turkey and Japan were staking a claim for improved education:

The writing is on the wall of Belshazzar's Palace: 'Mene Mene Tekel Upharsin'. The doom of masculine exclusiveness is sounded. The vote, which is the key to all other closed doors, must shortly be granted to some women. The immediate political issue is how many women can be included in the first posse to be enfranchised.

If Muriel's bubbling passions for feminism, social welfare and now journalism weren't enough, she had also enrolled in a law course at

the London School of Economics.[1] There seemed to be little time
for a fiancé and marriage.

* * *

Bryceson Treharne arrived in London in early February and
immediately immersed himself in the music and art scene, studiously
avoiding his fiancée's slum work in Lambeth. In a letter to a friend
in Adelaide he at first bemoaned being back in London: 'This old
place has not changed much; neither have its people. They are still
violently reactionary, but in many ways it is good to mix with them
once more. The old tendency to laugh scornfully at anything unusual
still exists. This was very evident at the Futurist Exhibition which,
by the way, had some very wild work in it, notably a picture entitled
The Rising City which, I hear, Rusoni has bought.'

But he then softened, his love of music and the culture of Europe
obvious – as was the reality that he had very little in common with
the woman with whom he was clearly infatuated and yet did not
even mention in his letter. 'There is a lot of activity among some
of the younger bloods – musical ones in England I refer to,' he
wrote. I have heard quite clever stuff by Balfour Gardiner, Arnold
Bax, Bainton and Percy Grainger whose work is very fresh. Elgar's
Second Symphony I do not care for, except its cleverness. The only
Debussy works done here have been two things at the Royal College
of Music and conducted by Stanford. Can you imagine him? They
were quite well done, but coldly received, which shows how the
wind blows in academic places. I heard some remarkable playing by
Godowsky's pupils the other day, but the press was mostly sparing
in its eulogy, which is its wont.[2]

While her husband-to-be enjoyed the artistic delights of
London, Muriel was again on the speaking circuit, her lot now

thrown in firmly with Millicent Fawcett's suffragists. She travelled across the country, her bookings managed by the International Suffrage office in Adelphi, just around the corner from the Women's Freedom League headquarters.

Muriel bore no animosity towards the WFL or the WSPU – after all, they were fighting for the same result – but the now violent protests of Emmeline Pankhurst's suffragettes, including breaking windows en masse, had driven her further and further from militant action.

Toward the end of April, Muriel attended a clutch of meetings of NUWSS sub-branches across the Midlands. In the cathedral city of Lichfield, north of Birmingham, she told members that although they might disagree with the tactics of the suffragettes, 'they did it through great devotion':

It is contended that women should not have the vote because our point of view and outlook is different to that of men. I believe that this constitutes the greatest reason why we should have the vote. Men are educated to believe that amassing wealth is the criterion of success, but it is we women who have to come to grips with life itself.[3]

In Stafford she said the issue was about human rights rather than women's rights: 'There has been an artificial meaning built around the word "womanly". Purity is not merely a feminine virtue but a human virtue; just as bravery is not just a masculine virtue. It is only when we learn to remove these sex distinctions that we will be able to move forward.'

In Chesham she predicted that their efforts were just the beginning of a global push for equal rights:

I have felt for a long time that in this country the average
woman has been content that the average man should take
the gifts which have been won for them and pay for them,
sometimes with life itself. The right of free speech, the right to
express religious convictions, the right to education, the right
to a free press have all been paid for in the past and women
of the twentieth century owe a special debt of gratitude to
the women who have gone before us. It is sometimes thought
that the women's movement of today is a new thing, and an
ephemeral thing that will pass away, leaving no trace behind
it. I do not take that view.[4]

In the first weeks of May she headed back to London to prepare for
her wedding and to greet her brother Len, who had gone to Canada
and the United States for his own wedding. Their mother, Emma,
was also due to arrive from Perth, although she was travelling
alone. Mother and daughter had stayed in contact over the years,
the release of snippets from her letters to newspaper columnists
making it clear that Emma was proud of Muriel's accomplishments.

Len and his new wife, the social columnist Emilie Domela,
would find themselves on a liner heading across the Atlantic with
many of the women and children who had survived the April
15 sinking of the liner *Titanic*. The tragedy would have special
significance for Muriel because one of the men who drowned was
William Stead, the newspaper icon who had helped her when
she arrived in London and with whom she had maintained a
friendship over the years, even working with him on the *Christian
Commonwealth* to which he had occasionally contributed.

Muriel penned an obituary in which she wrote of their first
meeting, how she hesitantly entered his cramped office at the *Pall
Mall Gazette*, and noticed a sign above his desk, which read: 'As

time is short and callers are many, the latter are requested not to waste the former.'

Instead of presenting as a grim and impatient figure, Stead, shaggy haired with piercing eyes, took Muriel to lunch, listened to her story and offered help. 'There was an element of greatness in his character,' she wrote, 'a greatness that came from a kaleidoscopic nature which responded to every one of its kind in the world. This at-one-ness with his kin, his capacity for belief in the goodness of human nature, was the keynote to his power and achievements. He once told me: "I have put the same amount of work into my failures as my successes. For one the world has naught but praise, for the other naught but blame. Meantime, I and my motives remain the same. They judge not the motive, but solely the result."'

* * *

On May 25, the *Mail* in Adelaide reported the happy event:

News has been received from London of the marriage of Miss Muriel Matters and Mr Bryceson Treharne, formerly of the Adelaide Conservatorium of Music. Miss Matters is an Adelaide lady who moved to the Golden West a few years ago, and subsequently went to England. There she has taken a prominent part in the suffragette movement, and was one of those ladies who chained themselves to the Grille in front of their seats in the House of Commons, so that they could not be forcibly removed. A year or two ago Miss Matters toured Australia lecturing about women's rights.

There was nothing more, no mention of a honeymoon nor Muriel's plans as the new Mrs Treharne. Instead, Muriel was back on the speaking trail, appearing at events in Urmston and Flixton, towns near Manchester, to talk about the Conciliation Bill which was still stuttering its way through the House of Commons.

It would be two months later before the *Mail* had another story: 'We regret that the announcement which was made in the *Mail* several weeks ago that Mr Bryceson Treharne had married Miss Muriel Matters in London was incorrect. We add that this information was accepted from an apparently authoritative source.'

A week later the *Sunday Times* in Perth confirmed that Muriel had changed her mind: 'In reply to a letter from a friend on the happy event, Mr Treharne replied: "Your congratulations are wasted. I was not married."'[5]

There had been hints, of course, that the union was not going to work, particularly during Muriel's 1910 tour when Australian newspapers picked up and republished a *Daily Mirror* interview with leading suffragists about their views on love and marriage. Muriel had shared two succinct thoughts: 'I hold the view that wooing should not end with matrimony,' and 'A little lightness, a little gaiety in married life – provided there is equality – are bound to make for happiness.'[6]

24.

PILGRIMS AND
GUERRILLISTS

Muriel's new sister-in-law, Emilie Domela, had been a social columnist for the *Daily Mirror* in Perth for many years, confined to the 'women's pages' and quarantined from serious news, as was typical of the limitations placed on women at the time, even in her enlightened home state that had granted women the vote soon after South Australia.

She wrote under the pseudonym 'Egeria', after an early female Christian pilgrim, and addressed her columns, which included accounts of her own travels, to her 'Dear Ladies'. Muriel Matters had featured on several occasions, particularly after she joined her family in Perth and then in the early years of her sojourn in London. No doubt Len – a decade younger than Emilie but clearly wanting to impress her – had dropped pieces of information about his sister's adventures.

In 1912 in London, where she was studying the harp at the Royal College of Music, Emilie was witnessing first-hand not only the contribution of her sister-in-law but the prominence of other Australians in the world's biggest city. When Len took a job writing for an American newspaper and later with the Australian High Commission on the Strand, she decided to pen a book to correct 'the wrong idea that Australians are without honour in England', echoing Henry Lawson's words of advice in his poem 'From the Bush':

> *Hold up your head in England,*
> *Tread firm in London streets;*
> *We come from where the strong heart*
> *Of all Australia beats!*
> *Hold up your head in England*
> *However poor you roam!*
> *For no men are your betters*
> *Who never sailed from home.*

Two women headed Emilie Domela's list, the diva Dame Nellie Melba and the 'champion lady swimmer of the world' Annette Kellerman, but there were many others such as the Shakespearean actor Oscar Asche, the musical comedy specialist Claude Flemming, the composer Percy Grainger, artists Arthur Streeton and Rupert Bunny, and writers Barbara Baynton and Mary Gaunt. It wasn't just the arts world that interested Domela. There were also prominent academics like Gilbert Murray, Regius Professor of Greek at Oxford, and Professor Grafton Elliot Smith, a renowned anatomist and Egyptologist, as well as several leading journalists on Fleet Street.

And there was Muriel Matters, the Heroine of the Grille and, lately, mistress of the poor of whom Domela wrote in part:

> First of all she is Australian, with all the Australian incapacity
> for understanding why the people of England should not do
> as the Australians do in matters political. The very sanctity
> of the silence maintained behind the Grille at Westminster

would irritate her. Australians in England have become red revolutionists in the face of manners and customs they hold to be bad, and yet are reverenced by the English people, apparently, solely because of their moth-eaten antiquity.

Miss Matters went into the suffrage movement with her heart. She walked in it with her head and became one of its chief exponents. Then, as the radical of today becomes the Tory of tomorrow, she became in one sense a Tory among suffragists when violent militancy took the place of appeals from the heart and brain. Today Miss Matters is counted one of the best speakers among the women of England and one of the sober educationists of the cause of votes for women. Her voice is heard on platforms throughout the country. In many a by-election she has been a striking personality, with strange inconsistency helping Conservatives, the avowed upholders of the established order of things which she detests, but always against the party which has the power to grant the vote, and ameliorate social evils, but does not do so fast enough for the Australian revolutionist.[1]

Muriel also contributed to the book by not only taking the reader through her personal journey as an agitator and social reformer, but by declaring her belief that the battle would be won:

It is a hackneyed phrase – England is Conservative – yet coming from a younger country where the tides of life run high and the pulses beat more strenuously, one can testify to the profundity of such a statement. Into the very bones and marrow of this sea-girt people has entered that insularity which, although the cause of so much that is admirable, breeds likewise the sincere belief that what is, must continue

to be. Every fresh idea, whether it be in the world of thought,
or made manifest, say, in the world of machinery, is met
with a resistance worthy of their best naval traditions. It is
interesting to be an onlooker but to be a combatant proves
more interesting still. I had to cross the line to discover myself
as an active agitator in this movement. Everything in this
country conspired towards this discovery. A mighty leverage
is at work, a new spirit which will ultimately transform the
face of this country. Old landmarks are passing. It means
the break-up of a social and economic order based upon the
privileges of the few. A new order is being evolved, a new
aristocracy will be raised; not one founded on birth, nor on
money, nor even on intellect, but on character.

She was right. The Western world was about to be torn apart,
economically and socially, although not by a political revolution as
she expected and hoped, but by war.

* * *

Early in 1913 Muriel was back on the road – 'rejoined the
suffragettes', as one newspaper back home reported without detail
(and misunderstanding the difference between violent militancy and
political agitation). Once again it was under the NUWSS mantle
rather than the WFL's, her task not to create branches but to keep
them open and their members hopeful and engaged at a time when
the goal seemed further away than ever before. The bloody battle of
the suffragettes had taken its toll on confidence, particularly away
from the epicentre of the London war zone. Country folk were wary
of reports of violence in the big city, but Muriel did not change her
rousing verbal delivery:

'English people are too much in the habit of subletting their brains', she told a crowd at the Northampton Co-operative Hall in February. 'I desire above all else to see in England a growing body of really thoughtful and intelligent young people. When speaking to Australian women I had often been asked, "What is wrong with English women? They must be a very unsatisfactory lot of people if men are so afraid to trust them with the vote." But of course English women are just as good as Australian women; what is wrong in England is not the women but the way in which they are regarded.'[2]

The tour went on through March, from town to village, from school houses to industrial halls: Muriel spoke at Newbottle Council School, Seaham Colliery, Murton Miners' Hall, Hylton Shipwrights, Shiney Row Primary, and Ryhope, Fulwell, Houghton, Easington, Philadelphia and Hetton in the north, then she travelled west into Wales where, for the first time in two years, she appeared under the banner of the Women's Freedom League, but only to merge the Swansea branch with the NUWSS members.

In April she ventured into Scotland. There were two hundred at Earlsferry, 'an audience of farmers' listened to her at Cupar Cross and at the Ladybank Masonic Hall she digressed from her speech to announce that Emmeline Pankhurst was deemed too ill to be returned to prison. On some days she spoke twice: Elie at 3.00 pm and Kennoway at 8.00 pm on April 28; likewise on April 30 at Guardbridge she gave a lunchtime speech at the mill gates followed by an evening meeting ten kilometres away in the Wormit Town Hall. When the skies lifted at Tayport she stood outside and drew the townspeople before scampering inside the Newburgh Linoleum Works when the rains came.

The violence she had experienced at rallies during her caravan tour and then later in Wales had mostly subsided, or so it seemed, but there were occasional flare-ups. In Perth, the fear of a suffragette uprising permeated the meeting on the banks of the River Tay. As Muriel spoke, missiles were hurled, including a ham bone that landed at her feet. She continued without pause. The next day the ham bone was presented to her, polished and set with a silver plate bearing the inscription *NUWSS Perth 20/6/1913* as a souvenir of the most successful open-air meeting ever held in the city.[3]

Back in London, the NUWSS had announced a great pilgrimage of suffragists in which thousands of members from four hundred societies and seventeen federations across the country would march to London in mid July and meet at Hyde Park for a mass rally. It was a statement directed partly at Herbert Asquith as he continued to demand to be shown that women wanted the vote, but more so at the public, to demonstrate the power of a law-abiding protest and counteract the common belief that all suffrage sympathisers were violent militants.

There would be four main routes to the city and some participants would be on the road for more than a month, particularly the women travelling the Great North Road which connected England to its cities nearest the Scottish border. Those coming from the west would use the Bath Road, a track carved in stages over several centuries and funded by turnpike tax. The biggest group would come from the south: along the Portsmouth Road that linked London to its navy, and also along Watling Street, an ancient track that ran from the south-east, on which the warrior queen Boadicea fought the Romans.

Muriel's role would be to lead the march from the latter two sections, the south and south-east, decked in the scarlet, green and white of the NUWSS. It was a return to the towns of the caravan tour of five years before, the counties of Kent, Surrey and Sussex. She travelled down to Hastings and across to the east coast haven of Whitstable where she was welcomed by a fuselage of missiles before delivering a powerful speech that honed in on the plight of the 'sweats', describing the case of a widow charged with attempted suicide rather than helped when she could no longer see a future in sewing uniforms for a penny an hour. Others toiled in stinking factories, carefully stitching shirts and embroidering beautiful handkerchiefs and tea towels that sold for twenty times what they were paid. Finally, she told of watching a woman fall and die, waiting for food relief during a strike. The inquest revealed that she was starved; her small rations of bread and milk had been shared among her four children, who were now motherless.

'Certain legislation has helped a little but no measure has touched the root of the trouble,' she told the now silent crowd. 'I and others believe that with the help of women they would get better results in the great national home than they got without them, just as in private homes they do not attempt to run them without some woman – a wife, a mother, a sister or a daughter. I believe that that if a woman throws her weight, her knowledge and her womanly intuition to bear she will bring about as good a result in parliament as she does in the private home. I ask the men to trust their womenfolk as they have already been trusted as wives and mothers.'[4]

Some women began marching on June 18, starting from northern cities such as Newcastle and Carlisle, and from towns across Yorkshire and Lancashire, most walking but others riding bicycles and horses along what was still largely a dusty track. At the other end of the country, four women set off from Land's End in Cornwall for the 430-kilometre walk to the capital. More than six hundred set out from Manchester on July 5 and three hundred from Liverpool. The procession grew larger as they approached London, collecting old members and new, the road clogged with marchers and banners, even horse-drawn vans set up as mobile changing rooms, as heavy dresses were unsuited to a long hike. At night they slept in billeted homes and were welcomed with meals cooked by those who supported the pilgrimage but couldn't make the journey themselves.

As the days grew warmer, the crowds following the pilgrims grew bigger, police estimating there were more than 15,000 at one afternoon meeting in Kent.

By the time the various groups converged on the outskirts of London on July 25 they numbered more than 50,000. More importantly, they had already achieved their goal as the press coverage had largely dropped its initial cynicism and embraced the protest as peaceful, colourful and legitimate.

The next day they brought London to a standstill as the crowd, now swelled to over 100,000,[5] entered Hyde Park through four gates. Muriel entered through Hyde Park Corner in front of the Kentish Federation and the East Coast and Brighton pilgrims, while others came through Marble Arch and the Alexandra and Victoria Gates. All assembled near the Reformers' Tree, the charred stump of an oak tree that had become the focus of the men's suffrage battle half a century before.

There were twenty wooden platforms spread across Speakers' Corner in the north-east corner of the park, some occupied by political supporters but most representing a federation. All were there to support the same resolution: 'That this meeting demands a government measure for the enfranchisement of women.' It was moved by Millicent Fawcett, the long-time NUWSS leader who was making her first public speech in forty years. Muriel Matters sat on platform 18, for once part of the support team rather than the focus of the afternoon.

The Times, so often a critic of suffrage protest, praised the event: The demonstration of the non-militant women was chiefly notable for the insistent emphasis which the 'pilgrims' from every part of the country laid upon the law-abiding character of their movement and the respectful attention which was shown to them by the crowds on their processional routes and in the park. The two tendencies may be fairly regarded as being virtually cause and effect. The proceedings, indeed, were as much a demonstration against militancy as one in favour of women's suffrage. The entire absence of disorder and the unquestioned success of the demonstration are the reward of the great body of women suffragists who seek to convince the country that the taint of militancy is not upon them.

The rally was in complete contrast to a WSPU protest the next day when 15,000 crowded into Trafalgar Square to hear Sylvia Pankhurst declare: 'We have come here to hold a council of war. The time for argument is passed. Our motto is *Deeds Not Words* and we are going to act.'[6] Surrounded by a bodyguard of East London dock workers, she then walked through the crowd and down Whitehall toward Downing Street with the intention of confronting Herbert Asquith. Behind her, police closed ranks and stopped the crowd from following, then arrested Pankhurst and twenty-four men and women as a melee threatened to explode.

* * *

Despite her provocative behaviour, Sylvia Pankhurst, with her mother and sister, had been living an increasingly uncomfortable existence as the war between the WSPU and the government descended into chaos. As the protests became more violent, the Asquith Cabinet introduced the cruel Prisoners (Temporary Discharge for Ill Health) Act, otherwise known as the Cat and

Mouse Act, which enabled prisons to release women hunger strikers when they became ill and then have police re-arrest them after they had recovered to continue their sentence.

In some cases, women were rearrested several times, forcing them into hiding as police pursued suffragettes as fiercely as they rooted out German spies, as fears of war grew. The suffragettes had also lost the broad support of MPs as the Conciliation Bill, which had drawn the overwhelming support of MPs in 1911, was resubmitted and voted down by the same politicians.

Breaking windows had given way to far more destructive protests, the WSPU abandoning any desire to court public sympathy. Acid, ink, lampblack and tar were poured into pillar boxes in the dead of night to destroy mail; telegraph and telephone lines were cut; a glasshouse at Kew Gardens was smashed; an axe was thrown at a carriage carrying Herbert Asquith; and a railway carriage set ablaze.

As with previous WSPU protest tactics, arson grew from an isolated event and was adopted on a grander scale. In March 1912 a woman entered a post office and set alight a basket of wood shavings. Three months later, two women tried to burn down a Dublin theatre in which Asquith was watching a performance.

By late January 1913, Emmeline Pankhurst had declared 'guerilla warfare'[7] on the government, labelling her supporters 'guerrillists', in the campaign. Human life was sacred, she said, but they were going to do as much damage to property as they could until the vote was won: 'War is to be declared. The sword is to be drawn and never sheathed again. We are going to make life intolerable to the citizens.'[8] The battle for the hearts and minds of the public was long gone. All that remained was the confrontation.

On June 4 tragedy struck when a teacher, Emily Wilding Davison, one of the WSPU's most prominent protesters, crept under a railing at the Epsom Racecourse and stood in front of the

King's horse, Anmer, as it thundered down the track in the Epsom Derby. She died four days later from her injuries, the mystery of her protest never fully resolved, although martyrdom was thought unlikely. A young woman had been sacrificed unnecessarily and because of ill-disciplined leadership.

Adela Pankhurst, the youngest of the three sisters, had already left the organisation, later telling another member: 'I knew all too well after 1910 we were rapidly losing ground. I even tried to tell Christabel this was the case, but unfortunately she took it amiss.'[9] Adela would not only leave the WSPU but England as well. She sailed to Australia in 1914 and worked as a peace activist with Vida Goldstein.

Despite misgivings, Sylvia had stayed with the WSPU although her relationship with her sister Christabel had soured badly. She was arrested three times early in 1913 for protesting, but on the first two occasions had been bailed out of prison against her wishes. At her third court appearance she received a two-month sentence and promptly went on a hunger strike, only to be released on Good Friday, so weak that she was unable to walk. Over the next year she escaped eight attempts by police to have her rearrested under the Cat and Mouse legislation.

But it was her battle with Christabel that attracted most attention, bubbling over in late 1913 when Sylvia attended a meeting at the Albert Hall in support of the Irish trade union leaders Jim Larkin and James Connolly, key figures in the infamous Dublin Lockout Strike that would cripple Ireland for five months as workers demanded the right to unionise and for improved working conditions. Not only did Sylvia attend the meeting alongside Charlotte Despard and others, but she spoke to the cheering mob on the theme that her mother used to relate, that 'behind every poor man there stands a poor woman'.

Christabel was livid, insisting Sylvia had gone against WSPU policy, compounding her insubordination in opening WSPU branches in the working-class areas of the East End of London. Membership of them had swelled with Sylvia's jailing and hunger strike, sparked by 'a tremendous flame of enthusiasm' generated when she threw a rock that broke a window in an undertaker's shopfront in Bow.

There were several thousand new members by the time Sylvia was released from prison, much to the annoyance of her older sister who regarded working women as a liability to the cause: 'Working women are the weakest portion of the sex,' Christabel told Sylvia. 'How could it be otherwise? Their lives are too hard, their education too meagre to equip them for the contest. Surely it is a mistake to use the weakest for the struggle. We want picked women, the very strongest and most intelligent.'[10]

Their final confrontation would occur early in 1914 when Sylvia was summoned to Paris where Christabel lived in virtual exile from police. Sylvia agreed to travel, despite being ill and fearing she was going to be pushed out of the WSPU, 'given the conge' as she would later write in her autobiography, *The Suffragette Movement: An Intimate Account of Persons and Ideals*. 'She [Christabel] turned on me. "You have your own ideas. We do not want that; we want all our women to take their instructions and walk in step like an army." Too tired, too ill to argue, I made no reply. I was oppressed by a sense of tragedy, aggrieved by her ruthlessness. Her glorification of autocracy seemed to me remote indeed from the struggle we were waging.'

Sylvia was left with the choice of closing the East London branches or leaving the WSPU. She chose the latter and the branches reformed under the banner of the East London Federation of Suffragettes. Two months later they launched their

own newspaper, the *Women's Dreadnought*, with a terse message for
Emmeline and Christabel Pankhurst:

> Some people say that the lives of working women are too hard
> and their education too small for them to become powerful
> voices in winning the vote. Such people have forgotten their
> history.[11]

25.

A HUSBAND

ENGAGEMENTS
MATTERS—PORTER: Miss Muriel Matters, formerly
of Adelaide, elocutionist and suffragette, and Dr William
Porter, late of New York, and now of Welbeck Street,
London.

The announcement on September 6, 1913, in Adelaide's newest newspaper, the *Mail*, formalised a news item reported in its rival, the *Chronicle*, the week before and highlighted what had been missing in the strange engagement to Bryceson Treharne – acknowledgment by the bride-to-be.

Barely fifteen months after rejecting Treharne, Muriel had agreed to marry another man.

The *Bulletin*, unfailingly dismissive of Muriel's suffrage deeds, weighed in a week later with a snippy mention in its social columns: 'From London comes word that Muriel Matters, the Adelaide reciter, who went to London and turned militant suffragette, has also agreed to plunge into matrimony with Dr William Porter, of New York, now curing the ills of the Great Fog. This must be Muriel's severalth engagement. She was once engaged to a member of the London *Daily News* staff, and afterwards to a prominent

Australian musician, but in each case returned the ring because, as she explained, the feminist cause had more charms for her than matrimony.'[1]

Who was this mysterious man who had stolen the heart of the beautiful but seemingly unattainable feminist iconoclast?

William Arnold Porter turned forty-two a few days after the engagement announcement appeared in the paper. He was born in Delaware, Ohio, to English parents, William and Teresa, and was raised in an artistic family, even if his own professional life drifted toward the sciences.

Both his parents were artists. William senior, in particular, was well known, acknowledged in the publication *Who's Who of American Art* for his landscapes and lithographs and for having decorated a china tea service for the eighteenth president of the United States, Ulysses S. Grant. He and his wife were both born in the West Midlands cathedral city of Worcester and studied at the Royal College of Art in Kensington. After graduating in 1869, they married and promptly emigrated, settling in Philadelphia where William junior and his younger sister, Gertrude, were raised in middle-class surroundings while their father took a post as principal of a prominent technical college.

His parents' homeland beckoned and in 1897 William junior sailed for London, eager to carve out his own life. Four years later, when he was thirty, the British census recorded that William was boarding with a single mother and her child, and working as a dental assistant in the Midlands city of Leicester, not far from his parents' birthplace. But by 1903 William was not only back in the United States but had married and settled in Ohio with his new wife, Mabel.

And so began a rather confusing trail of cross-Atlantic travels, some with Mabel and some without, over the next decade.[2]

Government records can reveal the travels and, to a certain extent, the achievements of a person, but they don't disclose his or her travails, only hint that life is often a series of new directions and even U-turns. Such was the case with William Porter.

Mabel sailed between America and England on at least two occasions while her husband appeared to have moved permanently to London in 1907, at least according to a document signed by the United States consul, Robert J. Wynn, which recorded that he was practising 'American dentistry' in the famous medical neighbourhood of Harley Street, Mayfair, and living in Bloomsbury.[3] In the meantime, Mabel continued to live in the family home 5000 kilometres away in the city of Wilmington.

It was inevitable, perhaps, that the marriage would not last, given that Mabel was ensconced across the Atlantic with a younger sister and her mother. And so it was, the divorce registered in 1912. The following year, William obtained a fresh certificate of registration declaring that he was an American citizen, permanently living in London, and operating a dental surgery at 11 Welbeck Street in Marylebone, the street that was home to the Bechstein Hall where Muriel Matters had made such an impact when she first arrived in London. Possibly that is how they met.

Another, more likely, explanation is that they were introduced by Octavia Lewin, one of the founders of the Women's Freedom League and a homoeopathist and assistant physician who lived at 25 Wimpole Street, which runs parallel to Welbeck Street. Dr Lewin had trained in America for some years and Muriel knew her well, having attended a number of 'At Homes' she had hosted, including an event in February 1910 of 'nurses and their friends.'[4] However they happened to meet, it was clear that William Porter was besotted, with Muriel revealing later that he had proposed three times before she finally accepted.

Porter was a good-looking man, at five feet ten inches a good four inches taller than the average British male, with piercing blue eyes and brown hair that would remain thick as it turned grey. He seemed in many ways the antithesis of the brooding but brilliant Bryceson Treharne, although neither of them was enamoured with Muriel's choice of career. Unlike Treharne, though, William Porter had no desire to take Muriel away from London. And the time for motherhood, if that's what Muriel desired when the rough and tumble of activism was over, was fast running out.

William's persistence had paid off, or so it appeared given the engagement announcement, but by December, with his mother and sister on their way to London for the wedding, a number of items concerning the couple appeared in newspapers which appeared to contradict one another. The first reported that Muriel had been travelling in Switzerland for a couple of months and was about to return to London,[5] while another stated that the pair had told friends by letter that they would be married before Christmas and planned to spend their honeymoon travelling in the same country.[6]

Neither report was true, as it turned out. Christmas 1913 came and went, as did Teresa and Gertrude Porter who returned to the United States with their son and brother still a divorcee. It seemed that Muriel had changed her mind once again and eschewed her latest suitor.

* * *

Dublin in January 1914 was freezing. In tenements inhabited by striking workers and their families along Henrietta Street, on the northern fringe of the city centre, 835 people crowded into fifteen houses, the heating non-existent, their clothing threadbare and food scarce. The Dublin Lockout was taking its toll and soon desperate men would bow to the inevitable and end their five-month strike or face starvation. Muriel Matters had joined the fray, leaving her fiancé and his wedding and honeymoon plans behind in London to join the effort to feed, clothe and house the vulnerable. She also penned a letter to the *Daily Herald*, issuing an appeal focusing on the plight of children.

In doing so, she took a political stance for the first time in her career. While campaigning for the Women's Freedom League she had assiduously steered clear of party politics, at times confusing those closest to her when she campaigned against sitting Liberal members, aiding their Tory opponents, on the basis that the battle for suffrage was apolitical.

But this was different. Just as Sylvia Pankhurst had done the previous summer when the strike began, Muriel took a position and sided with the striking workers and their controversial leaders, Jim Larkin and James Connolly. Mostly, she was worried about conditions for the families of striking workers, and found their stoicism and unwavering support for the union leadership inspiring. 'Nearly 20,000 children of the locked-out workers of Dublin have yet to be clothed,' she wrote:

> Despite the bitter biting winds that meet them at every corner
> of the streets, the brave men and women of Dublin are still
> full of courage and hope. It is the most wonderful mental
> atmosphere that the writer has ever known. Weeks of strain
> have passed over these people, leaving them with a spirit
> within their starved forms still unquenchable. We appeal to
> all your readers to help us to keep life within their forms,
> food and clothing for their embodied spirits, that Dublin may
> be compassed and in time transformed into a fit habitation

for these Irish rebels. Help us at once and send your gifts of money and clothes straight to Liberty Hall.[7]

It was the beginning of a shift in her attentions, subtle as it might be, toward addressing the social problems associated with deprived children. Muriel had campaigned in Lambeth largely on improving the living and working conditions for women, and thereby for their children, but now she had begun to speak more about the children themselves. The theme would continue, and strengthen, in the coming years.

Back in England a few weeks later, Muriel took part in a conference on 'The Child and the State', applauding the work of a Colorado judge named Ben Lindsey, a social reformer and pioneer of the juvenile court system: 'In the state of Colorado, one of the states where women are enfranchised, the principle underlying the treatment of the delinquent child is the recognition of the children's innocence for their own misdeeds and the responsibility of the parents, who more justly should bear the punishment. A child of thirteen is allowed no control over property or money; surely he should not be entrusted with the sole responsibility for his own character, the sole care of his own mental and moral equipment.'

Muriel wanted to take things one step further, and urged the appointment in Britain of women magistrates to handle juvenile delinquency cases: 'It is most desirable that the child who falls into the hands of the law should not be introduced into the ordinary police court and its surroundings. The better method is that of allowing the children's cases to be heard in the magistrate's room … women would be desirable as magistrates to deal with cases of child delinquency.'

It was a prescient suggestion that would be adopted five years later when London's first woman magistrate, Gertrude Tuckwell, was appointed and immediately advocated that specially selected magistrates be employed to deal with young people. Muriel's belief was that punishment was not the answer to addressing the problem of delinquency:

> The causes of child delinquency must be sought for elsewhere than in the unformed child. They will be found in unhealthy surroundings and environment, and in vicious example. Often the surroundings of the child and its physical conditions are alone sufficient to account for its delinquency. What is needed for the child is not reformation but formation, training and the opportunity to develop. Ours is the responsibility, if we withdraw what child life needs – healthy surroundings, pure influences in the home, harmless amusement and play. The desire for play is as much a human instinct as it is an instinct in the young of animals, and should be recognised.

Muriel feared that probation as an option to harsh sentencing was being ignored by courts in Britain, despite successes in reducing reoffending rates, and warned that juvenile reformatories were too harsh and needed 'humanising' including by way of involving women staff and visitors. She pointed to the experimental George Junior Republic institution in Pennsylvania, established for boys from troubled homes who lived in a village environment where they learned responsibility by administering their own form of government and laws: 'There is a value of social influences and the power of love and beauty and music to build up the human soul.'[8]

These concepts were not new to Muriel; she had been considering them since her own prison experience in 1908, firstly railing against the 'vindictiveness' of an adult prison system intent on time-serving and punishment rather than reform aimed at 'rousing self-respect' then, by logical extension, to childhood prevention – free kindergartens, a children's court and health inspections of schools among her proposals.[9] A century later, many of these ideas are the norm but in the first decades of the 20th century, they would have been regarded in many quarters as radical.

* * *

The success of the NUWSS summertime pilgrimage and the peaceful Hyde Park rally appeared to have added some zest to the suffragist campaign, not only at a membership level but also in the tone of the press coverage as Muriel resumed her speaking circuit travels. Like the WFL before them, the elders of the NUWSS recognised her value as a speaker who attracted large crowds. There was also a growing range of male supporters willing to stand beside her onstage, like Sir Victor Horsley, an eminent surgeon and scientist who was the first physician to remove a spinal tumour. He watched in awe as the petite figure held an audience of several hundred captivated at the Coventry Corn Exchange.

'In the past, the attitude has been that a woman is just a piece of blotting paper to receive a man's impression,' Muriel said, adding that there were still some prominent men who believed that God had created men to govern. But democracy, the 'spirit of the age' had changed everything:

> We aim for a higher ideal than the vote, and that is the freedom without which there can be no real development. People do not like anything new. A new insect appears on the scene and the cry is 'Kill it, kill it'. A new type of woman has arrived, and the cry is the same … as it cried out against women riding bicycles. Now we are not only astride

these infernal machines, as the cycle was called when women
wanted to ride it, but we are astride those infernal machines
that soar in the air. All the stupid twaddle with which our
male opponents meet us about women being sweet, innocent
things must be stopped, because what is meant is that women
are sweet, ignorant things. We as individuals must learn to
know ourselves and have a conception of what is due to us as
individuals, because only when we have that conception will
we know what is due to others.[10]

Muriel changed her subject matter and themes from night to
night: in Tadworth on February 17 she spoke 'with rare charm
and ability',[11] according to Sir Victor, about the international
women's movement and the first international congress of suffrage
organisations held in Budapest; at Newgate on March 3 she talked
about the spiritual side of the women's movement. The *Chester
Chronicle* marvelled at her theatrical performance the following
week at the Barnstaple Parish Room while standing on a chair: The
platform was too low for her liking and remarking, 'I hate being
unable to see the faces of my audience,' she promptly mounted a
chair. If one occasionally trembled for the lady's safety as she became
animated with enthusiasm, one must confess that she occupied
her precarious position with graceful ease, an accomplishment
that would have been impossible for a mere man. Miss Matters
told the crowd: 'In the twentieth century women are claiming the
right to share in commercial and industrial greatness. There is no
intellectual test that has been applied to woman which she cannot
stand. She is making her mark even in the scientific realm and
she not only asks to share in the administration of the law but to
come right in by the side of man as a political factor, to have direct
political representation and not be regarded as the echo of a man.'

She finished by predicting the vote would be granted within five years.[12]

By March there was a new term to describe Muriel's place in the suffrage ranks. On the eve of a speech in Berwickshire she was referred to in the local press as a constitutional suffragist: 'For elections she is greatly sought after as one of the most attractive and magnetic orators. Her sympathy and interest in problems of poverty and labour is very deep as is also her realisation of the importance of the spiritual side of the women's movement.'[13]

As Muriel continued to appear for suffrage groups attached to the NUWSS, her former colleagues at the Women's Freedom League were finding it increasingly difficult to occupy a niche of any credibility. The loss of their strategist Teresa Billington-Greig and their speech-maker Muriel had left a hole that had become impossible to fill. In a major change of direction, the WFL joined the annual Pankhurst rally in Hyde Park, but other than that they were engaged in few high-profile protests other than the continuing campaign of tax resistance, with those participating risking jail terms for their beliefs.

The WSPU, now free of Sylvia Pankhurst who had rebranded the East London branches, was struggling to maintain control of its members, partly because its leaders were dodging police. Christabel Pankhurst was still in Paris and her mother had been convicted of inciting violence by condoning the planting of a bomb in the half-built home of David Lloyd George. She had been jailed, then released under the Cat and Mouse Act and was trying to avoid being rearrested.

With their leaders in hiding, WSPU members were running amok through London and beyond, opening new lines of protest from the relatively harmless act of hurling eggs and flour from the public galleries of courtrooms to more serious physical assaults on public figures and vandalism of artworks at the National Gallery, the Royal Academy, the British Museum and the Tate Gallery.

Muriel, in the meantime, travelled the country through spring and into the summer, speaking at a garden fête in Newcastle, at a miners' gala in Durham, where she gave a speech alongside the Labour leader and future prime minister Ramsay MacDonald, and moving on to Liverpool, where the *Echo* delighted in publishing several of her best lines as 'wisps of wisdom'. She then moved south to Wanderwell in Dorset where she dressed down the suffragette movement, insisting that 'they must do their work without violating the rights of other people'.

At an open-air meeting in Brenchley, Kent, in early July she declared that the denial of a vote for women was 'a clear violation of Christian principle'. In Leeds a week later she faced a Uniting Church minister angry that militants had been 'utterly ruinous' to the cause, reminding him that despite their differences, suffragists and suffragettes ultimately stood together: 'One must read into the union that it is one of spirit. The movement among women is only a part of an age-long, worldwide, never-dying struggle of the human soul, whether male or female, for freedom. The women are asking for human rights for human beings.'[14]

What would turn out to be one of her last speeches for the suffrage cause was delivered in the city of Exeter, in Devon, just sixty kilometres from Plymouth, where her grandparents, Thomas and Mary, had set sail more than half a century before to begin a new life in Australia.

Muriel was probably not thinking of familial links that night, although her speech was predicated on history. It concerned the evolution of thought and attitudes toward women, beginning with the Dutch Renaissance scholar Desiderius Erasmus, who said a woman was 'an absurd and ridiculous thing but pleasant and entertaining' and the seventeenth-century English poet John Milton who referred to Adam as 'standing for God only and Eve for God through Adam'. Muriel's references went on: Samuel Johnson, creator of the *Dictionary of the English Language*, when asked about women studying art, responded, 'Women study art? My dear ladies, back to your toilet.' In the following century, the Romantic poet John Keats wrote, 'Woman is a milk white lamb needing man's protection.' The crudest was, perhaps unsurprisingly, the French emperor Napoleon Bonaparte who declared, 'Woman is given to man to produce children. She is our property and belongs to man as the tree belongs to the garden.'

Then Muriel switched to present-day critics:

Will these people, these cynics hanging in the background of intellect, never realise that mere physical strength is not the only kind of strength? Will they always persist, in face of historical facts, in face of woman's place in the mental and spiritual atmosphere of the present day, that women were in all things, and necessarily, the weaker sex? Will they never learn from the case of Florence Nightingale the capacity of women – a capacity for organisation and furthering national welfare, to say nothing of a capacity for alleviating human suffering? Will they not realise that this capacity must be recognised in the natural course of human evolution?

When votes for women come it is not the end of the fight. It is only the beginning. The pioneer must always be in front because night is still ahead. There are people who say, 'It is all very well to give women the vote, but where is it going to stop?' We must reply that it is not going to stop. There is no end to progress. Man has made his discoveries in the last century and must now stand by and see women make hers in her realm. They cannot stop it. It is an evolution and when the first moments of freedom come, the feelings might almost be volcanic.

Courage is the first essential for women in this age; next to honour, the greatest of womanly virtues is courage. Why courage? Well, because women have to fight that spirit of monopoly which has always been at the bottom of man's attitude toward what he was pleased to call the weaker sex. Monopoly, no matter in what degree and character they find it, is the animal element in human nature, and never more than in man's persistence when dealing with womankind – his holding on to something which does not belong to him alone, and therefore his shutting out of common justice and liberty in the highest sense.[15]

On July 9 Emmeline Pankhurst was discovered by police and rearrested, only to be released two days later, weak and ill after going on a hunger strike. On July 16 she reappeared at a rally to celebrate her fifty-sixth birthday, only to be arrested again. It would be the last major gathering of the militant suffragettes. On August 4, Britain declared war against Germany. The angry fight for the democratic vote had been overtaken by a desperate fight for freedom.

26.

WAR AND PEACE

Friends in Perth heard by last week's mail from London of the marriage of Miss Muriel Matters to Doctor Porter. The marriage was very quiet, only a few friends being aware of it, among others Mrs and Miss Annette Scammell, formerly of Fremantle.

Daily News, Perth, November 21, 1914

The deed was done. Muriel Matters had finally been encouraged down the aisle, even if it was in the Kensington Registry Office on a gritty October day in front of a handful of friends, including the young woman pianist who had performed with her in Perth a decade before. None of her family were there this time. Len and Emilie, now with a child, had left for Argentina where he would manage a newspaper.

Muriel was a war bride, wedded under the cloud of conflict that would last four long, terrible years. She was now Mrs Muriel Matters-Porter, having insisted on retaining her name, as had Teresa Billington-Greig and several other of her former suffrage colleagues. The couple would settle in a quaint mews house in the cobbled streets of Kensington, a stroll across Hyde Park to William's surgery which seems to have been thriving. He didn't qualify for war service on three counts – his age (forty-three), his profession and his citizenship.

William described himself as a dental surgeon on his marriage certificate (Muriel left the 'occupation' section blank), but at other times, particularly when travelling, he used the term 'physician'. In fact, William Porter was not qualified as either, his only professional training the 'apprenticeship' he had undertaken in Leicester more than a decade before. There are no records in either the United Kingdom or the United States to indicate that he attended any dental school, and he only registered as a dentist when laws tightened in 1921, qualifying because of his practical experience. This was entirely legal, although his choice of title was pushing the boundaries, especially as he was running his business in such an exclusive area.

There were no plans for a honeymoon as the outbreak of war changed everything, although for some others the consequences were far more serious, Bryceson Treharne among them. Muriel's jilted fiancé had stayed in Britain and ultimately found a woman who made him happy. He had married Maud Thackeray, a promising soprano and former student of his in Adelaide, in the summer of 1914. The two were on their honeymoon in Germany when the war broke out.[1] Treharne, on a British passport, was promptly arrested and put in a civil prison camp with four thousand others outside the town of Lindau where he would spend the fifteen months on threadbare rations and sleeping in a tent before being released. Ever the musician, Treharne spent most of his time composing, sometimes turning the words of the great poets into lyrics, including a poem by Lord Byron, 'When We Two Parted', released in 1918 as the war ended,[2] which contained a verse that might well have described his own parting with Muriel:

When we two parted
In silence and tears,
Half broken-hearted
To sever for years,
Pale grew thy cheek and cold,
Colder thy kiss;
Truly that hour foretold
Sorrow to this.

* * *

The war sliced through life. Muriel had been due to speak in the Lincolnshire town of Grantham, alongside Millicent Fawcett, just a week after her nuptials but the event was cancelled. Instead, the NUWSS branch members offered their organisation to 'help our fellow citizens who may be thrown into distress by the present terrible crisis'.[3]

After nine years, beginning with the brave defiance of Christabel Pankhurst and Annie Kenney at the Manchester rally in October 1905, the fight for the vote had ebbed and flowed between hope and bloody defiance. But as Europe descended into chaos it seemed to be further away than ever.

The great body of political patronage that had seen a dozen or so conciliation bills passed by the House of Commons only to be stymied by Cabinet was in reverse and growing levels of public and press support that at one stage had made the legislation seem an inevitability had evaporated. The last formal meeting of the WSPU was held in Holland Park Town Hall less than three weeks before the declaration of war. 'Very little interest has been taken in the press,' one member lamented in a letter.

The initial blame for the failure to achieve the vote could quite rightly be placed at the door of Herbert Asquith and Winston Churchill and, to a lesser extent, to Cabinet members like David Lloyd George, for being obstinate in the face of logic and fairness. But the unharnessed suffragette violence, particularly from 1912 to 1914, had given those same men political sanctuary. In the end it was political expediency that defeated the suffrage movement, leaving not just women but men, more than 40 per cent of whom were not eligible to vote, disenfranchised. The biggest roadblock was not an extreme misogynistic view of the world, but the fear of the political elite that they might lose power if they yielded to an unknown.

A quandary now faced suffragettes and suffragists alike. With their campaigns suspended until the end of the war – whenever that might be – what could be done with their significant and passionate resources? And where did Muriel Matters, who had been a prominent and eloquent suffragist, stand?

Emmeline Pankhurst happened to be penning an autobiography when war was declared. She had been writing it as events unfolded and the conflict provided a convenient ending, which she grabbed eagerly, concluding her book with this prophetic paragraph:

Our battles are practically over, we confidently believe. For the present at least our arms are grounded, for directly the threat of foreign war descended on our nation we declared a complete truce from militancy. What will come out of this European war – so terrible on its effects on the women who had no voice in averting it – so baneful in the suffering it must necessarily bring on innocent children – no human being can calculate. But one thing is reasonably certain, and that is that the Cabinet changes which will necessarily result from

warfare will make future militancy on the part of women
unnecessary. No future government will repeat the mistakes
of the Asquith Ministry. None will be willing to undertake
the impossible task of crushing or even delaying the march of
women toward their rightful heritage of political liberty and
social and industrial freedom.

For once, Herbert Asquith and Emmeline Pankhurst found
common ground. Holloway Prison was cleared of WSPU members,
the Cat and Mouse Act was suspended and Christabel was back in
London after more than two years in self-imposed exile. In return,
Mrs Pankhurst agreed to call off her hordes and reassigned her
army to help the war effort. The women of the WSPU would no
longer break windows and set fire to public buildings but instead
would drive their menfolk to war.

But not everyone agreed. Elements of the WSPU split off and
created two new organisations, one adding the word suffragettes to
the WSPU name and the other the word independent. A number
of the trade union and politically based societies were also keen to
continue the campaign for voting equality. So too was the Women's
Freedom League which saw an opportunity to step into the breach
left by the collapse of the WSPU. Charlotte Despard, aged seventy,
declared: 'The great discovery of the war is that the government
can force upon the capitalistic world the superlative claims of the
common cause. The Board of Education has concluded that one in
six children is so physically and mentally defective as to be unable
to derive reasonable benefit from the education which the state
provides. My message to the government is: "Take over the milk as
you have taken over the munitions."'[4]

NUWSS members and branches were torn, although not
about whether to continue the suffrage campaign which Millicent

Fawcett called off within forty-eight hours of the declaration of war. The question for the suffragists was whether to support the war effort – siding with the Pankhursts – or to raise their voices in another capacity, this time as pacifists.

While Millicent Fawcett refused to speak out against the war, Muriel Matters-Porter fell firmly on the side of the pacifists, driven by her Wesleyan roots. However she was also keen to explore the potential for women's employment in backing up the men who had gone to fight. In January 1915 she took centre stage at a NUWSS conference in south London as the attention swung to raising funds and providing aid to Belgian refugees, the victims of the early exchanges of the war.

Muriel hated the notion of war and the sacrifices that inevitably lay ahead, but thought that if the conflict offered anything it would be to show the capacity of women, as history had already demonstrated time and time again: 'Whilst the men were roamers and away killing, women were building for themselves and their children.'[5]

* * *

On April 14, 1915, Muriel hosted a peace conference in London. It was held in the Central Hall in Westminster, the huge domed structure completed just three years earlier in the heart of the world's most important city.

Muriel had helped form the organisation called Women Mobilising for Peace (WMP), and had been appointed its secretary, and it was in that capacity that she fronted the filled-to-capacity hall, buoyed by messages from comrades in Iceland, Sweden, Italy, Holland and South Africa. Delegates from those and other countries, together with women from WMP, would travel to the

Dutch political capital, The Hague, a fortnight later to attend an international peace conference as the groundswell against the horror began to take shape.

After a day's discussion the WMP released a six-point declaration, focused not on ending the war but on post-war development; it covered the terms of a peace settlement and the reformation of the Foreign Office and the diplomatic service to ensure the involvement of women and transparency of discussions. The WMP wanted Belgium restored and the rights of small territories acknowledged and in the future a reduction in armaments. Perhaps most prescient was the call for an 'international council' through which the balance of power would be guided and controlled. Three decades later, the United Nations would be formally launched in the same auditorium.

Muriel wrote home to a family friend the next day, and a section of her letter would find its way into an Australian suffrage newspaper:

> The conference and the public meeting which followed were most successful. I believe you have had a trying time; it is bad enough here to have to deal with a nation of almost mad people, but it must be worse in Australia because our people are cruder than the English – at least I think so. We are in a very unsettled state here over The Hague conference. The government has picked out twenty women from one hundred and eighty to go. They state there are no boats, and give other excuses. We know them of old; but some of the women's societies are innocent lambs, and are swallowing the excuses whole. There is no doubt that the experience in the early days of the suffrage militancy has proved invaluable for some of us.[6]

The Foreign Office was indeed standing in the way of the British delegation, refusing to provide passports because, it insisted, 'there is much inconvenience in holding large meetings of a political character so close to the seat of war'. In the end, twenty-four 'peacettes' would make the hazardous journey across the English Channel in a boat that had to navigate a sea of minefields.

Muriel was determined to attend and decided to ensure her passage by skirting the Foreign Office and secretly obtaining an American passport, courtesy of her marriage to William Porter. On April 16 she made an application at the United States embassy, completing a standard form in which she gave her name as Muriel Lilah Porter, declaring that she had had never been to the United States and needed the passport to attend a women's conference in Holland. The document noted that she was five foot three and a half inches tall, of fair complexion with light brown hair and grey-blue eyes, although some other details were dubious, including her date and place of birth – listed as November 2, 1880, in Perth – probably to avoid the problem of holding dual citizenship, which was banned at the time. She was told the passport would be issued four weeks later, on May 13, which was too late for the conference, so she made a second, emergency application and took an oath of allegiance on the spot. The application was ticked off by a senior embassy official.[7]

The International Congress of Women would run over four days, attended by more than 1100 delegates from countries including Britain, Denmark, Spain, Norway, Sweden, Switzerland, Belgium, Austria, Hungary and Italy. There were thirty delegates from Germany and representation from the United States, which had not yet entered the war. Two participants would later receive the Nobel Peace Prize and the Women's International League for Peace and Freedom would emerge from its discussions. The resolutions were broad, from a general call for peace, disarmament and the development of a Society of Nations to the enfranchisement and involvement of women, education for children and the opening up of free trade.

The program of events would record some well-known names among the British contingent, including Sylvia Pankhurst, the WSPU stalwart Emmeline Pethick-Lawrence and Charlotte Despard. Muriel was also listed, representing the Union of Democratic Control, a non-partisan group formed the year before because of concerns that foreign policy was being made in secret and beyond parliamentary overview.

As Muriel threw herself into her new role as a pacifist, her younger brother Charles, a 28-year-old veterinary surgeon, was leaving Australia, a member of the 6th Battalion bound for Gallipoli.

* * *

On June 30 Muriel delivered one of her most important speeches. At least, that's the way she must have felt because unlike the hundreds she had delivered from the back of horse drays, from stools and statue plinths, *The False Mysticism of War* was typed and kept for posterity. It was delivered to an audience of one hundred or so inside Devonshire House in Bishopsgate, a fitting venue given that not only had it been one of the first private houses rebuilt after the Great Fire of London under new planning laws that strove to find stability for a city destroyed by its own haphazard construction, but it would also be destroyed in 1941 by a Luftwaffe bomb.

Muriel, who published the speech under her maiden name, set out to argue the case for pacifism, a near impossible task in the face of a war that was now in its tenth month and had already claimed tens of thousands of lives. Her purpose was not to magically end the conflict but to lay the foundations for society beyond its bloody conclusion. Society itself had to change. War could not simply be blamed on systems and forms of government, secret diplomacy, vested interests or armament trusts.

'At the back of all these manifestations is the thought that produces them,' she began

> Some of us believe with [prominent left-wing journalist]
> H.N. Brailsford that 'Armies may destroy armies but no army
> ever destroyed militarism because it is a state of mind.' In
> recognising this we must track to its lair that false teaching
> which I label 'The False Mysticism of War'.
>
> In the case of war I use the term not as applicable to any
> particular system but to the pernicious, although vague, mass
> of talk, the outcome of many different modes of thought and
> sentiment in which we indulge. In some cases, it is articulately
> definite. But mostly it is the vague feeling that war has some
> hidden meaning based upon some spiritual truth; that war
> is an expression of some inner, inevitable, divine need; an
> unfolding of God's divine purpose for men and nations.

For an hour she spoke and held the audience rapt, her speech a lesson of history's failings and the Western world's insistence on misinterpreting, indeed perverting the teachings of Christianity to justify armed conflict: 'The Western world in espousing Christianity found that the faith made no appeal to armed force ... The result was that converts to Christianity wishing to indulge in warfare had to search in their minds for justification. Like the ancient ones, the modern authorities pass on their justification of war to the masses, full of ignorance, fear and superstition. The same old questions and doubts on the part of the mob have to be answered. "Failure and bankruptcy of Christianity"... have to be met and dealt with ...'

The doctrine that war was a necessity, 'human nature being what it is', had to be resisted:

> Whatever else it may be, human nature is not static, it is dynamic. If the world is being rid of slavery ... of the plague, duelling and other evils, all at one time considered inevitable and part of God's divine purpose, why cannot we rid the earth of this hellish war? For war is hell. The sterner militarists, devoid of sickly sentimentality, have always told us so, and we know it. Then why entertain the idea, why prepare for it, why live in it? Have we not been told to pray 'Thy kingdom come, Thy will be done on earth as in Heaven', and does not prayer involve faith and works?

Muriel railed against children's books that reserved the word 'patriot' for soldiers but ignored the contribution to society of inventors, scientists, philanthropists and others:

> Why? Because being great humanists their works are not solely for, not in the interests of, their own particular country alone. Their thoughts and discoveries benefit the whole of humanity – therefore they are not patriots. Patriotism is love for one's own country alone, and that same limiting thought prompted the idea of the picture published in a child's paper of an old man showing a gun to a small child as 'His First Lesson in Patriotism'. And when the children leave the nursery and go to school, what is the dominant thought? 'The rough corners of the individual are abraded' ... The sanctity of the individual is neither recognised nor respected. What

wonder that later on the child violates the sanctity and the
rights of other individuals, and he and others ... 'are rendered
susceptible to the dominant thought' of someone stronger in
will than themselves whose tool they become.

A truer patriotism was much broader than any single
country. Humanity should be placed above nationality: 'Love
of humanity at large does not involve a denial of love to those
nearest to us. Love international does not involve a denial of
patriotism but really secures it. Nationality is colour in life,
but humanity is the music of life – the rhythm and harmony
in which the pulses of the whole human family beat. Love of
our own nation, like love of our own family, should be but the
gateway through which we pass into a larger consciousness ...
We must think of the soul of our nation and people as well as
their material life.'

She ridiculed the notion that only war called out the best
in people. 'So do any great crises,' she said. 'Colliery disasters
and shipwrecks call forth much beauty in action. But this is
not a proof that war and the disasters mentioned are good, but
that the capacity for sacrifice of self is one of the beautiful,
indestructible elements within the human soul. If we would
but trust our life to spiritual force, holding the material life as
nought ... we [might] learn to die to self in daily life for our
ideals.'

Ultimately, it was women who might be the solution:

Woman will best act as man's 'valuable coadjutor' by realising
that as the builder of human life she builds something greater
than 'all the rows of buildings ever built – a tenement for a
soul'. When that full realisation comes to woman, will she

approve the violation of the sanctity of that soul in times of peace through wrong education and the destruction of that temple in times of war through wrong education and the destruction of that temple by the blast of the cannon? ...

We have got to build a new order, to rebuild life on higher levels. It is not enough to abhor war; we have got to believe in harmony. So we must bring our beliefs in love, beauty, human nature, colour, music and joy, and weave them together into a new social fabric.

In another place or another time her words might have been seen as dramatic or even flowery, but the speech was delivered as Herbert Asquith appealed for 'national thrift' in the face of the realisation that the war would not be over swiftly. When it was published some months later, Muriel's speech was picked up and discussed by several newspapers including the *Daily Herald*.

Its politics were left-wing and anti-war; it was against conscription and even supportive of conscientious objectors. One of its younger stars, the poet and journalist Gerald Gould, reviewed the speech, describing its call to transform society as an idea 'justly and beautifully developed'. He went on: 'But where is the line to be drawn between right force and wrong force? Miss Matters does not concern herself with this dilemma. Her subject is narrower than that, and within its due limits is treated eloquently and nobly.'

Just five weeks later Muriel would receive news that her brother Charles had been killed in action at Gallipoli, shot as the Australians attacked Turkish trenches at Lone Pine in an infamous diversionary assault intended to allow the advance of other units at Chunuk Bair.

His war records show a soldier who had made an impression in the few months he fought. Enlisting as a private, he was promoted to corporal and then sergeant by the time he reached the Dardanelles on June 25, a few days before his sister's peace speech in London.

The file includes a sad letter, written fifty years after his death by his oldest sister, Elsie, seeking to have his medals awarded posthumously. Charles had joined up within weeks of war being declared and travelled to Victoria for training. But he had fallen ill, been discharged and then rejoined. In doing so he had become 'lost' in the chaotic recruitment system and was attached to a Victorian battalion when he left Australia in April 1915: 'I trust the information is sufficient for the issue of his veteran's medallion to me,' she wrote. It would take five years for it to be issued.

More disturbing was the eye-witness account of his death by another soldier, a Private Crichton, who watched Sergeant Matters, a man easily identified by his heavy black moustache, gunned down, shot through the head as he reached the Turkish lines on the first of two attacks on August 7. Both attacks failed and the survivors retreated. Later they watched the Turkish soldiers throw bodies out of their trenches into no-man's-land where they couldn't be retrieved. 'Matters, being picked out owing to his heavy moustache appeared to have been stripped,' Crichton reported. 'The witness did not observe the Turks burying the bodies.'

Like hundreds of other young men who died in four days of blood-letting, the body of Charles Matters was left to rot on the battlefield, his name inscribed on the Lone Pine memorial.

27.

MOTHER'S ARMS

Even before she became a revolutionary of early childhood education, Maria Montessori was doing things that most women of her time and place would not have dreamed of. Despite the protestations of her father, a Ministry of Finance official, she eschewed the traditional role of an Italian woman of the late nineteenth century and pursued an education beyond the first years of primary school.

Instead of pursuing *lavori donneschi* – women's work – the free-spirited young woman chose mathematics, history, geography and the sciences, declaring she wanted to be an engineer before changing her mind and, much to the consternation of male classmates and professors, enrolling at the University of Rome to study natural sciences and medicine. Such was the animosity that she was forced to study dissection techniques alone with a cadaver, warding off offensive odours by smoking tobacco inside a mask.

When she graduated in 1896, the first Italian woman to earn a medical degree, Maria found a job as an assistant in the university's psychiatric clinic, followed by an appointment to run the city's school for 'hopelessly deficient and idiot' children, where she began experimenting with teaching techniques.

It was the beginning of a fascination with early childhood education and development that really took root in 1906 when she was invited to oversee a state-funded school for the children of low-income working parents. There were sixty children aged from three to seven in *Casa dei Bambini*, where she replaced the heavy tables and chairs with child-sized furniture and concentrated initially on the practical, teaching the children how to dress and care for themselves and how to care for their surroundings. They learned to sweep, clean, cook and even how to arrange flowers.

She watched their play and designed equipment to turn the play into lessons, creating simple tools to teach children how to read and write and count: tracing letters and numbers with their fingers in a wooden box filled with sand, using cut-out letters around a board to make words, and tiny coloured blocks to learn basic arithmetic. Children were encouraged to explore and learn at their own pace, driven by curiosity and a quest for independence.

Recognition inside Italy and beyond into Europe followed. As the number of Montessori schools expanded and her efforts produced stunning results, transforming not only schools but orphanages, Maria began running teacher training courses and international interest took hold. In Britain a few publications began to discuss the new educational philosophy, including the *Christian Commonwealth*, the paper Muriel wrote for, which published a feature on Montessori's work in 1912.

'It is morning everywhere in the world of education,' it began. 'New knowledge of physiology ... may be applied not only with a new freedom, but with the conscious co-operation of a great number of persons who were formerly strangers in primary schools. The isolated pedagogue disappears. Dr Montessori perceives the immense significance of the co-operation of doctor and teacher, and the closeness and intimacy of the new association with parents which these may together establish.'

Maria Montessori's vision tucked snugly into Muriel's concerns and ideas about remedies for childhood delinquency and the need for individual attention in children's education. She had become aware of Montessori's work after returning from Australia, where she had seen the influence of Froebel, and had even discussed the possibility of opening a Montessori school in Dublin with the union leader Jim Larkin during the Lockout in the winter of 1913–14. The problem was finding trained teachers who could staff the facility.

The speeches Muriel continued to make around the country were always predicated on a call for peace, but also engaged in the practical, and particularly focused on how women could play a role by stepping into many of the industries normally the preserve of men. If there was a silver lining to the war it was that it opened up the workforce to women in a way that none would have envisaged. Women filled factories, drove buses and tilled fields. The changes would largely remain post-war.

In December 1915, Muriel was in the city of Coventry, seeking funds for women's hospitals in France and Serbia. There were six complete hospital units already, entirely staffed and run by women, with 1300 beds. More than £70,000 had been raised to run them, but more units were needed, particularly field hospitals as the casualties continued to grow on the battlefields of France.

Muriel spoke eloquently and inspirationally on the theme of 'New Ideals for Old': 'It is not for us to Anglicise or the Russians to Russianise or the Prussians to Prussianise any portion of the world. It is our mission to try and humanise the nations,' she implored. 'We cannot have peace until we make peace more important than it has ever been in the past. There is no such thing as an "outbreak" of war. War was thought for, worked for and lived for. We can never get a state of harmony on earth until we prepare for it, work for it, live for it ... and dream of it.'

Invariably, her subject matter would drift toward children and shortcomings in education: 'We have been wrong when we have consciously or unconsciously asked that the child or the adult should be successful in life – the "get on or get out" idea. Children have not been regarded as individuals at all. Every child born into the world is a new thing; it is quite different from anything else that has been before it. Yet in education we ask that they should all grow to be the same standard, while the competitive system has taught each to regard the other as a rival. Competition is the unnatural theory, co-operation and unity in service is natural.'[1]

As the war dragged into 1916 she decided to shift focus once again. Arguing for peace embodied the same dilemma as the suffrage debate; it was an aspiration based on sound arguments but was almost impossible to achieve because of the brick wall of politics and men. Just as she had stepped aside from the Freedom League to take on practical work in the Lambeth slums, Muriel decided that *doing* was better than theorising. The 'thing' in her life, as she would later remark, was to get as close to the human element of a problem as possible. Find the source to discover the solution.

She had tried to find Montessori teachers for Jim Larkin, but it had proved impossible. The solution to the shortage in Britain seemed simple enough; she would be trained herself, particularly when she discovered that Maria Montessori had moved to the Catalan capital of Barcelona where she had opened another school. More importantly, she was also running an intensive teacher training course. Muriel enrolled, one of the few from outside Spain.

There were 185 students who took the three-month course from a building in the heart of the old city, mostly local teachers but with a smattering from Portugal, Canada, the United States, Britain and Australia. Each day, the *dottoressa* would deliver lessons from a blue-and-orange armchair which were then translated first into Catalan, then Spanish and finally English.

One of the British students – unidentified, but probably Muriel – wrote back to London enthusiastically: 'The claim of Dr Montessori that the truest system of education of children is through the senses seemed to me to be entirely vindicated by actual results and, moreover, that the principle could be applied much further than to infancy. I had ample opportunity of observing the startling results of touch as an aid to learning both in the schools of Barcelona and at a very remarkable school in Palma, Majorca, and that the whole system has a wonderful way of turning rampageous little urchins into cheerfully diligent little students, whose pleasure it is to be quiet, industrious and well behaved.'[2] In May 1916, enthused by what she had seen and learned, Muriel headed back to London. All she needed was a sponsor and a classroom.

* * *

Sylvia Pankhurst had achieved what her mother and sister had not – arranged a meeting with Herbert Asquith. On June 20, 1914, as the government held its breath at the growing European crisis, Asquith allowed six women to put forward their argument for getting the vote. Sylvia did not attend the meeting: 'I did not care to go. Let these working mothers speak for themselves; it was for this that I had struggled,' she wrote in her 1931 autobiography.

The tactic appeared to work. Asquith listened: 'I tell you quite frankly that I have listened with the greatest interest ... [to] ... the special, individual experience of the various members of the deputation. It has been a very moderate and well-reasoned presentation of your case, and I assure you that I will give it careful and mature consideration … If the change has to come, it must be democratic in its basis.'[3]

It fell short of a promise but it was clear that Herbert Asquith could see the inevitable moment was ahead. Sylvia read it as 'an unmistakable softening in his long hostility', later observing: 'Everyone felt this an omen of the turning of the tide.'

This was the first move of Sylvia's ambitious and often overwhelming plan to tackle what she called the 'abyss of poverty' in the East End. When war was declared she opened three cost-price restaurants to combat profiteering, drawing on free labour and goodwill to build and stock the premises. Within a year they were serving more than four hundred meals a day, with two-course lunches provided to adults for two pennies and to children for one penny. Evening meals were simple: a pint of hot soup and a chunk of bread for one penny, eaten on the premises or taken home.

The Australian novelist Miles Franklin, who was working in London at the time as a journalist, observed: 'Dear me, what courage, industry and sheer grit to keep clean these ramshackle, mouldy places with tin-pot means of accomplishment at hand.'[4]

While Emmeline, Christabel and the rest of the WSPU were marching in favour of conscription for women as well as men, Sylvia was organising the distribution of food to mothers for their starving babies. The packages not only included rations of milk, barley, eggs and a bone marrow concoction called Virol, but leaflets and feeding charts on the nourishment of infants. She opened a toy factory with the dual purpose of providing employment for women who had lost work when factories closed because of the war and also providing a source of simple wooden children's toys now that trade with Europe had been closed.

In 1915 Sylvia found a disused pub at the corner of Old Ford
Road and St Stephen's Road. It was across the road from a weapons
factory and called, appropriately, the Gunmaker's Arms. Using
volunteer labour she had it converted into a mother-and-baby drop-
in centre, delightfully renaming it the Mother's Arms. It became
the centre of her work, and incorporated a free medical clinic and
a nursery where mothers could leave their children while they went
looking for work.

It was the children who worried Sylvia most. Not only were they
affected physically by a conflict that left them hungry, but many
would lose their fathers and any sense of direction and discipline in
their lives, as she explained in her 1932 book *The Home Front*:

I was worried about the toddlers. They grew chubby and rosy;
they acquired cleanly habits; voluntary workers came to pet
and play with them; toys poured into the Mother's Arms
without stint, but as soon as they came they were broken and
thrown away. Sybil Smith sent a big rocking horse as large
as a Shetland pony, used for years by her children, but in
perfect condition still. Within a month of its arrival, it was
no more. Every hair on the tail and mane was gone; the eyes
gouged out, every joint in the wood severed; the remnants
had been torn from their stand. To me it was amazing that
young children under five years of age could have done it.
To the busy staff at the nursery it was all a matter of course;
one could not even get the horse repaired, for half the almost
unrecognisable pieces of battered wood had been thrown in
the fire or the dustbin before I knew it. To me this meant
more than the wrecking of a costly toy. It impressed on me
that the toddlers had learned only one sort of game; to pound
and break, to wreck and destroy. That must be altered.

She found the answer one morning as she scoured the morning newspapers, looking for items to write about in her newspaper, the *Women's Dreadnought*: 'My eye caught a tiny paragraph: Muriel Matters had returned from studying under Maria Montessori in Barcelona. I telephoned here and there until I got in touch with her. She responded with zealous understanding.'

Although they had represented opposing sides of the suffragette movement, the two women were like-minded: both were against violent militancy and in favour of a broad concept of universal suffrage, one not defined by sex or class or financial means.

Sylvia had the second floor of the Mother's Arms converted into a schoolroom with low tables and walls lined with shelves that could be reached by young children. Child-sized artefacts like hair brushes and brooms were made by a local volunteer while Muriel and an assistant 'with admirable good taste, economy and expedition, had run about procuring all else that was appropriate'.

The school opened with just seven children aged between three and five years, as an experiment to test what Sylvia and Muriel called 'the Method'. Not everyone was as convinced as Muriel about the Montessori technique, as Sylvia reminisced:

> The commencement was slyly reported to me as utter chaos. Nurse Hebbes, who won children's affection by romping with them, wore the enigmatic smile of a sphinx, Lucy Burgis, who had been Norland trained, talked fast with ardent approval of the intention. Nurse Clarke was aloof in manner, and obviously sceptical.
>
> The devotees of Montessori, with Pleasance Napier as musician and pupil, held on bravely. Muriel Matters would have no compromise; there must be no physical compulsion, no 'violence' as she termed it, even of the mildest; yet there

must be ordered activity. Any child who was 'disorderly' was banished from the sanctuary; condemned to be returned to the babies, if only for an hour or two, as 'not yet old enough' to remain. At a certain stage there was one child only in the Montessori room, many times but two; yet in some brief days the children had been completely won.

Now with what grave delight they handled the apparatus, swept and dusted their room, washed their hands and faces, changed bibs and pinafores, waited on each other at meals. With care they handled dainty china – Muriel Matters would permit no coarse unbreakable stuff. Instead of the old clump, clump, clump on the flat of stamping little feet, they went lightly on their toes, acquiring grace and balance by stepping to music on a white line painted on the floor. They learned the magic of quiet in the silence game.

My hope was fulfilled. Yet always there was a sorrowful thought: We are building only a little oasis there. Around us was the vast misery of the lack of far-extending slums.

The problem, as usual, was lack of resources, which in this case meant a lack of teachers. Three women, young factory workers, had stepped forward, eager to be trained, but it was neither practical nor possible financially to send them to Barcelona when Sylvia could barely feed the masses on their doorstep. When Charlotte Payne-Townshend, the wife of George Bernard Shaw, offered to pay the women's wages, Muriel agreed to become their teacher.

What had begun as an experiment to find a practical solution to the problem of what she had described as the 'fallen children' had become a focal point of Muriel's personal campaign for social justice. Muriel Matters-Porter had evolved from an agitator to a facilitator.

28.

A MEASURE OF JUSTICE

By most accounts, Francis Sheehy Skeffington was a good man, gentle and kind, who strived for fairness in a harsh world. He was certainly not threatening physically, his flourishing beard offset by a slight physique and smiling Irish eyes. 'Skeffy' was a well-known writer and activist, who added his wife Hanna's name to his own and was the inspiration for the character McCann in his friend's James Joyce's first novel, *A Portrait of the Artist as a Young Man*.

Yet Skeffy was murdered, 'shot like a dog' during the Easter Uprising of 1916 when Irish republicans tried to end British rule. He had been trying to keep Dublin's poor from looting when he was arrested by soldiers on the night of April 16, lined up and shot along with two journalists in a muddy back yard by a kangaroo court firing squad under the command of a panicked and arrogant British army officer, Captain John Bowen-Colthurst, who then tried to cover up his crime.

Muriel Matters was in Barcelona with Maria Montessori when the murder occurred. She had known Francis and Hanna from her days in Dublin during the industrial turmoil of the Lockout. She and Violet Tillard, who had remained in Dublin after Muriel left, had mixed with the couple and various union leaders, although they were there not to take a political stance but to draw attention to the plight of starving women and children.

Hanna, who helped establish the Irish Women's Franchise League, was more militant than Muriel, having been sent to prison for breaking windows and, more seriously, for throwing a hatchet at the head of Prime Minister Herbert Asquith. But there was a comradeship and bond between the two women that went beyond political tactics, particularly when Francis attempted to broker a peace deal between unions and employers.

Two months after his death, Hanna was struggling to win any sort of government acknowledgment and investigation of her husband's senseless murder. The British parliament was doing its best to ignore the incident, fearful of the impact an inquiry would have on the minds of the public who were happy to see the republican rebels as the enemy.

On June 27, Muriel, who had remained in contact with Hanna, stepped into the fray. At the same time as she was establishing the Mother's Arms school in the East End, Muriel wrote to her friend and offered to help, imploring Hanna to leave Dublin and come to London:

> Dear Mrs Sheehy Skeffington,
>
> I understand Tillie has written too. Have just come from Mr Pethick-Lawrence. Is it possible for you to come over? We feel strongly that your presence in our midst will do more than anything. The question has got to be brought up again with all the pressure possible to bring. They will ignore us in our attempts. They will not be able to ignore your presence. Tillie and I both ask you to let us know how we can help you coming over in any way. The Lawrences will do anything also. But he does feel that very little can be

> done with members unless you come over. Have talked to
> Mr Ponsonby. We want more publicity for your solicitor's
> letter. Can you send or bring copies and let us know the cost?
> We have a tiny, quiet flat in among the mews at the back
> of Kensington Square. Will you stay with me? We shall try
> and help you in any way possible. With affectionate regards,
> yours sincerely, Muriel Matters[1]

Hanna heeded the advice and three weeks later she was sitting with Muriel, whom she had taken as a witness, in the front parlour of no.10 Downing Street, opposite the man she hated and had once attacked with a hatchet. Now, she needed him if she was going to get justice.

Herbert Asquith was clearly nervous, drumming his fingers on the green baize table, his private secretary by his side. He began by apologising, not for the murder directly but because he believed the House of Commons would not support a full inquiry. The best he could offer was what he described as an 'inadequate inquiry': 'I told him I should not be satisfied with an inquiry that he told me in advance would be inadequate,' Hanna later wrote. 'If I were not satisfied I should take further action.'[2]

It was then that the prime minister made an offer of compensation, in lieu of an inquiry – a bribe to make it go away. Hanna was not surprised, having already been sounded out unofficially, the proposal couched in terms of securing the financial future of her son, Owen:

> Mr Asquith put the proposition ever so delicately, but it was
> obviously his only object in sending for me. He was mellow
> and hale with a rosy, chubby face and silver hair, suggesting a
> Father Christmas. But he never looked me straight in the face
> once during the interview.

I listened to his persuasive talk about compensation and finally told him the only compensation I would consider was a full, public inquiry into my husband's murder. Our interview ended.

Hanna, supported by Muriel, would stand by her decision and resist the Asquith pay-off. He was forced to agree to an inquiry, but narrowed its terms of reference to try and eliminate embarrassment for the government and the army. Hanna's lawyer was not entitled to cross-examine witnesses. Bowen-Colthurst meanwhile had been found 'guilty but insane' by a court martial, and spent a few years at Broadmoor Hospital before emigrating to Canada, a free man.

Muriel Matters had yet another reason to despise Herbert Asquith.

* * *

In the end the question of women's suffrage would be won, it seemed, like so many other questions of moral value – in the pursuit and defence of power. The various suffrage bodies, splintered by war and infighting, had reformed in different guises by 1916, some under the name of peace. But now there was an added issue: the tens of thousands of men who were fighting at the front for their country who had no say in its political future, as the vote was restricted to males who met certain property qualifications. Human suffrage became the new catch-cry. War, in all its bastardry, had illuminated the hypocrisy of the political class.

Lord Northcliffe, owner of *The Times* and the *Daily Mail*, who had been a strident opponent of women's suffrage, had ballot boxes taken to the Front to illustrate the point, and agreed to meet Sylvia Pankhurst, who, despite detesting his politics, saw the opportunity to wrap the two issues together, as adult suffrage, in a single piece of legislation.[3]

Northcliffe's actions were not driven by a sudden belief in women's rights but by the baser instincts of a businessman and politician; he wished to unsettle his opponents, in particular Herbert Asquith whose grip on power was increasingly fragile. Whatever his motives, they had the desired effect of helping to place women's suffrage back on the political agenda.

In August 1916, Herbert Asquith told the House:

> The moment you begin a general enfranchisement on these
> lines of state service you are brought face to face with another
> most formidable proposition. What are you going to do with
> the women? I have received a great many representations from
> those who are authorised to speak for them, and I am bound
> to say that they have presented to me not only a reasonable,
> but I think, from their point of view, an unanswerable
> case. They say … if we are going to bring in a new class of
> electors … we cannot possibly deny their claim. What is
> more … they say when the war comes to an end, when the
> process of industrial reconstruction has to be set on foot,
> have not the women a special claim to be heard on the many
> questions which will arise directly affecting their interest, and
> possibly meaning for them large displacement of labour? I say
> quite frankly that I cannot deny that claim.[4]

It was a stunning turnaround after so many years of obstruction, but the fight was not yet over. Far from it. To Sylvia's dismay, her mother and sister immediately opposed Asquith, insisting that muddying the waters with women's suffrage might prevent soldiers from getting the vote. From her perspective it was a sell-out for the sake of political expediency and to cosy up to David Lloyd George who would soon replace Asquith as prime minister.[5] Muriel, who was working at the Mother's Arms and sat on the Women's International League for Peace and Freedom committee with Sylvia, agreed.

Muriel seemed to be everywhere, presenting Montessori workshops in Hastings one week, fronting peace protests in Glasgow the next and making suffrage speeches in between. She was also penning articles for the *Christian Commonwealth* as well as the *Women's Dreadnought* on the progress of her Montessori experiment at the Mother's Arms, and making the daily trip across London from the calm affluence of South Kensington to the angry poverty of Bow.

It was there that her real passion lay, where politics played no role. Her belief and commitment were clear as she wrote about 'A', a troubled three-year-old girl:

> When she came to us from the nursery she was described as
> a child with a violent temper, but within three weeks a great
> change came into her life. It was really 'into her life', for it was
> a case of inner growth, and the external appearance changed
> also. She grew plump and the little face that looked white,
> at times drawn with hard lines, changed in colour. All that
> energy which hitherto had not found adequate expression
> became ordered and directed in the varied activities of the
> classroom, so that her life, too, was ordered and enlarged.
> From an inharmonious, undirected force she became
> harmonised and directed.[6]

Muriel's timing was impeccable. 'Montessorianism' captured the imagination of mainstream education. Teachers and bureaucrats flocked to Muriel's lectures to hear the theories behind the processes, and parents filled town halls to hear her insist that their children should be understood as individuals who developed at different paces to one another. The current system's focus was too narrow and its dependence on punishment counter-productive, she maintained.

Muriel's enthusiasm for the Mother's Arms school meant her frontline role with suffrage groups was diminishing, but she still spoke at meetings and was a prominent fixture at conferences, which were frequent as it appeared more and more likely that parliament might agree to at least partial recognition for women. In June 1917, the Australian prime minister issued an instruction that Muriel and Miles Franklin, who was living in London, were to be invited to attend quarterly luncheon meetings of the high commissioner and state agent-generals to 'express the women's point of view' and to 'report as to whether any useful public service is to be served by the luncheons'.[7]

* * *

March 28, 1917, was a busy day in the House of Commons, dominated as expected by war issues, from shipping losses, mine sweepers and aerial defence to munitions, food shortages for prisoners and an outbreak of smallpox among the troops. There was a sense, though, that the war might be coming to an end, either through negotiation or, more likely, with the defeat of the German forces. The United States had signalled its entry by providing raw materials, supplies and money and would soon commit troops.

But the real business of the day was left to its end, when discussion, adjourned earlier, returned just after 5.00 pm to the thorny issue of electoral reform. Colonel Richard Godolphin Walmesley Chaloner rose to speak, the member for Liverpool Abercromby and Boer War veteran declaring himself to have been a supporter of women's suffrage in his first years as an MP but stating that he was now decidedly against the proposition because by numbers alone, due to the war dead, women would dominate at the ballot box.

'No nation has ever been ruled by women and that is the state to which this country would be reduced,' he argued. 'We all admire women, but, after all, I like to see them on a pedestal and not on the footing of equality. If you bring them down off the pedestal and put them on an equality with men, you will kill the best spirit of chivalry which exists today and put the government of the country into the hands of women who are not fitted for it by nature and temperament. It would be the most destructive and dangerous thing ever done by this House of Commons.'[8]

John Clynes, the member for Manchester North East and a future Home Secretary, disagreed, arguing that thousands of women were already voting in municipal elections and local government had not suffered:

> It is a delusion, for which men should be ashamed, for them to conclude that if we give votes to these millions of women it is certain they will act and vote alike as women and that there will be no difference of opinion on the great and varied questions with which they would have to concern themselves. History, experience and the general working of politics and political parties show that women are no more likely to be agreed upon such questions than men.

It was clear that the parliament remained divided about women's voting rights, although the tide had turned. And Herbert Asquith, the man who had so long stood as the bulwark against women's rights, was at the heart of the change. The previous October, as his tenure at no.10 Downing Street was becoming perilous, Asquith

had called an all-party conference to thrash out a position on
electoral reform, including the end of plural voting, the widening
of the franchise for men, and the introduction of voting for women.

The resolution of what became known as the Speaker's
Conference on Parliamentary Representation was overwhelming,
although initially the details were undecided. Women should have
the vote, but should it be given to all those aged thirty and over
or only those aged thirty-five and over who were local government
electors or wives of local government electors (owners and tenant
householders) or university graduates?

An age restriction, vehemently opposed by suffragists like
Sylvia Pankhurst and Muriel but supported by Emmeline and
Christabel Pankhurst, was designed to allay fears of opponents
such as Colonel Chaloner that women would simply overrun men
by sheer numbers. So instead of almost 2.7 million women aged
over twenty-one being given the vote, it was eventually agreed that
their numbers would be cut to barely 700,000 aged over thirty-five.
And the poor would remain disenfranchised.

These were the resolutions accepted by the Cabinet of David
Lloyd George and now before the House. This night would not
create a new law, but it would ensure that it would happen.

Herbert Asquith had been the first speaker in a debate when
it began in the morning that would take several hours, likening
himself to an ancient Greek poet named Stesichorus who was
struck blind after ill-advisedly lampooning Helen of Troy, but had
his sight restored when he wrote a palinode, a poem that retracts
the sentiments expressed in a former poem:

Some of my friends may think that, like him, my eyes, which
for years in this matter have been clouded by fallacies, and
sealed by illusions, at last have been opened to the truth.

Some years ago I ventured to use the expression, 'Let the women work out their own salvation.' Well, Sir, they have worked it out during this war. How could we have carried on the war without them? Short of actually bearing arms in the field, there is hardly a service which has contributed, or is contributing, to the maintenance of our cause in which women have not been at least as active and as efficient as men, and wherever we turn we see them doing, with zeal and success, and without any detriment to the prerogatives of their sex, work which three years ago would have been regarded as falling exclusively within the province of men. This is not a merely sentimental argument, though it appeals to our feelings as well as our judgment. But what I confess moves me still more in this matter is the problem of reconstruction when the war is over. The questions which will then necessarily arise in regard to women's labour and women's functions and activities in the new ordering of things – for, do not doubt it, the old order will be changed – are questions in regard to which I, for my part, feel it impossible, consistently either with justice or with expediency, to withhold from women the power and the right of making their voice directly heard. And let me add that, since the war began, now nearly three years ago, we have had no recurrence of that detestable campaign which disfigured the annals of political agitation in this country, and no one can now contend that we are yielding to violence what we refused to concede to argument.[9]

It was just after 11.00 pm when the vote was called. The division was emphatic – 341 to 62 in favour of adopting the conference resolution and agreeing that legislation should be introduced promptly 'along the lines' of its findings.

The victory celebrations may have been slightly muted that night, given the age restrictions that would take another decade to remove, but the vote's significance was underlined the next morning when David Lloyd George hosted at no.10 Downing Street a deputation of women, including the three main suffrage leaders – Emmeline Pankhurst, Millicent Fawcett and Charlotte Despard. Mrs Pankhurst described the vote as 'a measure of justice', to which Mrs Fawcett, in a rare moment of agreement, nodded: 'I would rather have a proposal that is not so good and gets through than one that is better and does not.'

29.

A FINAL JOURNEY HOME

The Ladies' Grille came down quietly and permanently in September 1917, the panels unbolted and carried away as the House of Commons slumbered below in its autumn hibernation. The removal of two panels almost a decade before during the protest led by Muriel Matters had been a stirring symbol for the suffrage movement, just as the decision to replace them months later had been indicative of the government's refusal to bend to such audacity.

That barrier had now been broken down, although not before a three month debate on the cost of the removal – '£5 and should require two men of various trades for three to four days'.[1] It was enough at least to acknowledge that women – or some of them – should be treated equally in the democratic process, so it was deemed right that the symbol of that barrier should go permanently. It was an offering of sorts, a recognition not only of the negotiated changes to electoral laws but of the hugely significant role of women during the war.

The discarded panels would be stored in a backroom for years, staff uncertain what to do with the symbol of misogyny erected because men couldn't abide the notion of being overlooked by women. Eventually fourteen were used in the Members' Lobby to be used as window decoration, beneath statues of past prime ministers, including Margaret Thatcher, the Iron Lady and first woman PM. They remain there today. Of the others, two remain in storage, one was given to the Museum of London and another loaned to Parliament House in Adelaide. No one is quite sure to which panel Muriel was chained.

When the parliament resumed in October, a few women climbed the two flights of stairs to sit once more in the room that had cut them off from democracy, not just from its construction in 1834 but since a rowdy night in 1778 when women, from the Strangers' Gallery, had the temerity to heckle MPs for their miserable handling of the country and its economy. Even without the bars the space was dark and claustrophobic, and the view below remained distant and obscure, which only emphasised the senseless futility of shutting away half the population from coherent discussion and law-making.

The Representation of the People Bill had been presented to the parliament in May 1917, and in a rare, free vote in the Commons on June 19 was passed by 385 votes to 55. It would become law on February 6, 1918, giving women over the age of thirty the vote provided they lived in a house with a rent of over £5 a year or had earned a university degree. These were largely married women and mothers, the millions of younger women who had contributed to the war still disenfranchised, meaning that women would make up just over 40 per cent of the voting public at an election held in December, a month after the bells of armistice rang out across London.

Still, it was a huge leap forward, enough to convince the WSPU to disband. Emmeline and Christabel Pankhurst had formed the Women's Party at the end of 1917 and would stand Christabel in the 1918 election, only for her to lose by a few hundred votes to the Labour candidate. The party would fizzle out the following year.

When Millicent Fawcett stood down in 1919 the NUWSS also folded but then reformed, swapping the word 'suffrage' in its title for 'equal citizenship'. It became the NUWEC, its agitation program focusing on equality in issues such as pay rates, sex morals and divorce laws, pensions for widows and children, guardianship, women entering the law and widening the voting franchise.

The WFL, headed emotionally, even if not formally, by Charlotte Despard, who was now in her seventies, would continue for another decade, evolving into an activist group for equality. Three members would stand in the 1918 election, among the nineteen women who would contest seats. Only one of the nineteen, the Sinn Fein candidate Constance Markievicz, was elected, but she did not take her seat in the parliament in line with her party's abstentionist policy.

The following year the socialite Nancy Astor would become the first woman in England to take her seat in the House when she won the seat of Plymouth Sutton in a by-election caused by the elevation of her husband to the House of Lords. It was not a fitting scenario, given that Lady Astor was not only American but had never been associated with the suffrage movement, but a giant breakthrough nonetheless.

* * *

Muriel celebrated her forty-first birthday on November 12, 1918, the day after the war officially ended. The unbridled joy that spread across the city hid the struggle ahead to rebuild a shattered nation, just as Muriel's personal celebrations were tempered by the reality that she was at a crossroads in her life. There was relief that peace had returned and the satisfaction that women would soon be voting and standing in an election – 'progress', as she would describe it –

but there was also the realisation that it was unlikely that she would ever be a mother. For a woman so dedicated to the education of the young, it seemed an unfair outcome.

Her marriage to William Porter remained something of a mystery. Muriel joked on more than one occasion that she only married because of Porter's persistence and because the war had effectively shut down the suffrage movement. They lived together for the next three decades until his death, moving house every few years, but never closer to the East End than Bloomsbury, and eventually out into the Berkshire countryside.

By day at least they lived separate lives as couples often do, neither with any meaningful interest in the other's work and both too devoted to their craft to develop a shared interest. For Muriel, it seemed to be a union of convenience which developed into loyalty and friendship over the years, but short of the true love that might have given her cause to pause occasionally from her good works on behalf of society.

William took on a business partner and pursued a successful career while his wife, who would continue to call herself Miss Muriel Matters in affirmation of her professional identity, ran her school and toured the country, not as a suffrage agitator or a pacifist but as an expert in early childhood education and a member of the Women's Education Union which championed equal pay for women teachers.

'Bill never stood in the way,' Muriel would say simply in a letter to a friend years later.

Muriel helped welcome Maria Montessori to London in 1919, when the Mother's Arms school, now greatly expanded, became one of the showpieces for the Montessori system, but it was her fearlessness in speaking out for a revolution in education that would resonate. Education was, or should be, a science, she argued. Young children needed to be given the freedom to study rather than sit in rows to be crammed with information in silence.

'A great change has taken place in the practices of the teaching profession,' she told a crowd of five hundred in Dundee, which included the city's director of education. 'If you, as teachers, follow the example and principles of other branches of science in the application of your work, the profession will be able to claim for once that it is in some way measuring up to the standard of the general scientist. Teachers must demand the right conditions under which to make their advance in the system of education. Scientific methods should be used not merely for the defence of society but for its development, and the study of children demands a fusion of modern science.'

One of the great fallacies for Muriel was the idea that children could all arrive at the same standard of knowledge at the same time. The reality was that young children developed at different rates and the education system needed to adapt, particularly when teaching children aged between two and five, which were the formative years in their development. Even understanding a child's home environment was important and could affect teaching techniques and help young delinquents learn to 'harmonise' with others. Simply punishing them by whipping was cruel and counterproductive.

Traditional classrooms and equipment were an impediment to learning, Muriel said:

Imagine if we grown-ups found ourselves in an environment
so disproportionate to our size, as children do, or if we
found ourselves among people, giants in comparison to us,
who snatched things away to do them themselves, instead
of leaving us to puzzle out our own problems? Instead of

developing our capacities, we would find our energy spent in
defending ourselves. That's what happens in classrooms.

Ordinary school desks are dark, so as not to show the dirt,
but it's the wrong principle. The child should have a table,
small to fit his size, and white so that his imperfections in
inking or otherwise dirtying it offend him. In the same way,
if he constantly uses china, instead of an enamel mug, he soon
learns that the frailer article does not stand the banging about
he could give with impunity to the metal vessel.[2]

Her talks quickly developed into a program of six lectures, dealing
with the psychology of education and bringing her into contact
with leading educationists of the day, including the headmaster
of Rugby School, Albert David, the philosopher and principal of
University College, Exeter, Professor Hector Hetherington, and
the headmaster of Westminster School, Harold Costley-White.

They also took her home to Australia in 1922, when she repeated
her trail from twelve years earlier, landing in Perth and travelling
first to Adelaide and then Melbourne, delivering lectures on child
psychology before adding Sydney and Brisbane to the lecture tour.

In the twelve years since her last visit, the fortunes of her
parents, Emma and John Matters, had changed markedly. John had
left the department store, apparently far too much of a perfectionist
for the management, and set up business as a tea merchant, mixing
a special blend he named Amber Tips in a room at the back of the
house.

Now aged sixty-nine and his rebellious days far behind, John
would be remembered by his grandchildren as a dignified man,
content with a nightly bottle of beer and a wedge of cheese which,
to their delight, he shared with a pet bull ant that often ventured
onto the dining table.

His wife Emma was a tiny, bent and buoyant woman, forever singing hymns as she busied herself around the house and always with a hot pot of soup on the stove or freshly made apricot tart. Emma would make more than one trip to London to spend time with her daughter, once coming home brandishing a pair of hiking boots bought during a side trip to Switzerland.

If there had been any doubts about Muriel's path in life, they were doused by Emma Matters' delight in annoying her husband by loudly voting Labor, knowing that he was a dyed-in-the-wool conservative.[3]

* * *

Muriel's onstage presence and oratorical flair was still evident as she began her second national tour of her homeland: 'It is a radical defect in our treatment of young lives that we have no science of the care and nourishment of psychic life. Freud, Jung and others following them are endeavouring to repair the scars of life; the Montessori system prevents those scars. Hence it provides a path for the redemption of humanity. The first essential in a true educator is a wide self-culture. Only by self-discipline and self-analysis might a person hope to obtain that knowledge of his own soul, which would enable him to enter sympathetically into the lives of others.'[4]

Invited to pen an article for the Sydney *Sunday Times*, Muriel revealed that her commitment to children's education went far beyond being a devotee of Maria Montessori. She had investigated experiments by the American educator Homer Lane on the behaviour of delinquent children, the work of British author Norman MacMunn who ran a war orphanage in which he gave children freedom of expression, and the practices of Emile Jaques-Dalcroze, a Swiss composer who developed a system of learning and experiencing music through movement. Just before leaving for Australia she had spent time with the Austrian portrait painter Franz Cizek, the founder of the Child Art Movement in Vienna, who opened up his studio and allowed children to use his art supplies to express themselves.[5]

Although her tour was focused on education, Muriel would invariably be asked about her days as a suffrage campaigner: 'We carried our lives in our hands,' she told one interviewer, relating how one night she and Violet had been trapped in the centre of the Common at Tunbridge Wells, sheltering in their van as thugs bombarded it with missiles. And in Wales an angry man confronted her as she prepared for a speech: 'Do you know what I would have done with the woman who struck Winston Churchill if she had struck me?' he asked, eyes ablaze. Muriel shook her head. The man glared: 'I would have struck her dead.' The threat hung in the air as he walked away.

'Our invariable program was: first night a riot; second night a meeting for women and accredited men; third night an enthusiastic public meeting,' Muriel reminisced. 'We got everything in the way of tributes, from the jawbone of a sheep to bouquets, both floral and verbal.'[6]

Muriel's message of change wasn't always greeted positively in Australia. In Perth, the *Daily News* published a letter under the dubious heading 'Old Maid's Children', from Elizabeth Granton, a mother of five, who took issue with the fact that Muriel had no children of her own:

> I cannot understand any woman having the audacity to attempt to lay down the law concerning the upbringing of little ones when she herself has had no means of proving her words. This talk about a child's soul and the physiology of

childhood sounds very pleasant and uplifting in theory, but put into practice is a different business. I hope to look after my children's well-being, both from a material and a practical point of view, but I certainly have no desire to learn how to do either from a woman who cannot enter into the true spirit of real motherhood.[7]

Muriel did not demand the right of reply, as she had previously when faced with letters with which she did not agree. The ignorant rebuke clearly had found its mark in her personal regrets about not having children. It may have accounted for her strange request when she went to see her youngest sister, Isabel, who had recently had her first baby.

Jocelyn Davis was that baby. She is now ninety-four and says her mother told her years later that Muriel stood at the crib admiring her niece, commenting that Bridget would be a nice name. It was the suggestion of a woman who had picked out the name of her first daughter, but never had the chance to use it.

'Then she asked my mother if she could adopt me,' says Jocelyn. 'It was the strangest request but she was apparently serious. Of course my mother said no, but it shows how much Muriel wanted children of her own.'

'We were always told that it was Uncle Bill who didn't want to have children. It makes me wonder how such a strong woman seemed unable to convince her husband of her right to have children.'

One explanation could be that however much she longed for them, Muriel Matters decided against having children of her own. It would have suited her marriage, one of companionship and loyalty rather than passion and, having witnessed the pressures faced by feminist colleagues with children, allowed her to devote her time and energy to the well-being of the thousands for whom she despaired.

Although she would never again meet her famous aunt, Jocelyn maintained a relationship, if distant, with the woman who wanted to adopt her. As a child, Jocelyn would send cards and letters and Muriel, in turn, posted gifts for birthdays and Christmases, the occasional dress and books, including a copy of *Princess Mary's Gift Book*, a collection of short stories, essays and illustrations published in 1915 under the name of the then eighteen-year-old princess to raise money for the war effort through the Queen's Work for Women Fund.

During the Depression years, Muriel would also keep Jocelyn's mother in nice clothes: 'Uncle Bill would attend medical conferences which meant Aunt Muriel needed a new dress which she would send to my mother afterwards. The Depression years were hard but my mother was always well dressed.'[8]

* * *

Violet Tillard was dead, one of the thousands of victims of a typhus epidemic that raced through Russia where she was living as a relief worker in the isolated town of Buzuluk, near the border with Kazakhstan.

Muriel received word as she prepared for her journey to Australia. They hadn't seen each other for several years, and only occasionally after parting company in Ireland back in 1914. Muriel had returned to London after the Dublin Lockout ended, but Violet stayed and continued working with strike-affected families. She was a conscientious objector during the war and in 1919 went first to Germany, to help in the fight against tuberculosis in Berlin, and then on to Russia where she encountered mass starvation.

Violet, who had joined the Quakers by this time, was horrified by what she found in Russia. 'One feels horrible in such good conditions when the people are literally starving at our doors,' she would write. 'A boy of sixteen lies dead a few yards away ... It isn't so harrowing to see them lying dead. They suffer no more. It is the doomed shadows one sees around the streets and in the homes which are so horrible.'[9]

In late 1921 she turned her attention to three of her fellow workers who had contracted typhus and nursed them back to health. In doing so, she fell ill herself. She died on February 19, 1922, aged just forty-seven.

Her heroism was captured by the Marxist revolutionary Leon Trotsky who mentioned Violet in his writing: 'In our bloodstained and at the same time heroic epoch, there are people who, regardless of their class position, are guided exclusively by the promptings of humanity and inner nobility. I read a brief obituary of this Anglo-Saxon woman, Violet Tillard; a delicate, frail creature, she worked here, at Buzuluk, under the most frightful conditions, fell at her post, and was buried there ... Probably she was no different from those others who also fell at their posts, serving their fellow human beings.'[10]

It would take eight years for Muriel to collect and write her thoughts about her friend, in an obituary that would remain unpublished. Even after eight years, the tears were close to the surface:

She set one a standard to live by. Certain qualities were
obvious to all. Courage, sympathy, generosity, selflessness. All
her fellow workers had proof of these. But there were reaches
in the mind and spirit of Violet Tillard that only the intimacy
of deep friendship could reach, if indeed even the love of a

friend could fathom. Shy, elusive qualities accompanying the
grimmest kind of determination and will, perhaps brought
only from her Huguenot ancestry, shot through an almost
dare-devil gaiety when faced with situations requiring nerve
and set purpose. We women saw this in the suffrage campaign
cause when in prison in 1908 ... or later when the men found
a doughty champion in their fight as conscientious objectors
during the war. No wonder the British public was puzzled
by the personnel of the suffragette movement! Could anyone
look less like the *Punch* type of new woman than did Violet
Tillard? Tall, slender, delicate, reticent. No wonder the anti-
suffragists when, seeking their literature, she dared them in
their own den at Westminster, invited her to join, saying, 'For
a nice woman like you it is quite safe to join us, there will be
no processing or anything unladylike like that.' It was the
only time I knew her to sneak away from foes. The horror of
being mistaken for 'a really nice woman' almost vanquished
her. And yet could the 'Antis' be blamed for seeking her
membership? Even in prison clothes – I see her now that
first awful day in Holloway, October 30, 1908 – with the
rough boots, long unshapely dress, check apron and harshly
pointed prison cap – yet Till managed to look so graceful.
How cheerful she was, how philosophic when many others
were either edgy, weepy with strain or rebellion. But that
imprisonment left its mark ... on a system not too strong by
nature.'[11]

30.

AN UNCONVENTIONAL CANDIDATE

The first public hint of a role in politics for Muriel came in late November 1923 with an advertisement for a Labour Party meeting in the Market Hall at Hastings. It read: 'Miss Muriel Matters will speak on the subject of "Labour aims and education" at 8.00 pm.'

Clearly, the party believed her to be a drawcard, and so it proved as a large crowd grew to hear her. Muriel didn't disappoint with a typically strident cry and rebellious catchphrases that focused on women in the workforce, as reported briefly by local press: 'Where are the women?' she called out, stirring up the crowd. 'Can we say that anyone has put forward a constructive program with regard to the woman worker? We are still cavewomen in this country, and years behind our American sisters.'[1]

Party officials liked what they saw, and a week later she was addressing another branch meeting, seemingly establishing her credentials (and still using her maiden name) as she talked about her experiences in the district fifteen years earlier, when she arrived driving a horse and van, making suffrage speeches by the seaside and dodging rotten fish.[2]

She reiterated her point about women workers in a letter published in the *Hastings & St Leonards Observer*, in which she lamented the demise of the women's movement in the post-war years: 'The militant suffragists were not only genuinely democratic but altruistic ... united in their desire to promote better conditions for women workers. I now find that the interests of professional women are given the first place. There is very little to enlist the sympathy of, or on behalf of, the woman in the street.'[3]

Since returning from Australia via America, where she had made a series of speeches on early education and visited her husband's family, Muriel had broadened her crusading interests yet again, this time turning to the post-war housing crisis, joining the National Housing Council and working with Miles Franklin who was on the housing committee of the London City Council.

Muriel took an interest not just in the agitation for reform but in the practicalities of surveying suitable land and designing housing as slum clearances gathered pace across the country. She had long been connected with inner-city slums such as Lambeth, and now other cities in England and Scotland were facing the same problems.

In Dundee she was welcomed as a 'famous social champion and one of England's leading reformers'. She praised Scotland's first public housing estate, built over a demolished poorhouse and slum, that set a standard in social housing, incorporating one of Europe's first district heating schemes as well as green space and allotments for each maisonette house, 'It is a dream of mine come true,' she told the gathering of residents and public officials.[4]

Until this point, beyond dalliances with trade unions and involvement in some industrial disputes, Muriel had largely kept away from mainstream politics. In particular, the suffrage campaign had been apolitical, but this was different. It came as no surprise that her natural political home would be on the left of the political spectrum, but until now it had been a private matter.

When she began making stump speeches for the Labour Party, it was a conscious decision to join the political fray itself.

There was an early election in December, soon after Muriel's maiden 'political' speech, as the Conservative prime minister, Stanley Baldwin, sought a mandate to shore up his leadership. The move backfired when he lost office to a coalition of Labour and the Liberals, making Ramsay MacDonald Britain's first Labour Prime Minister.

But MacDonald's numbers were shaky and the coalition would last only ten months as Britain went to the polls for the fourth time in as many years. Muriel had resisted three earlier approaches to stand as a Labour Party candidate, but this time agreed for the seat of Hastings because of her close friendship with MacDonald and his late wife, Margaret, both of whom had appeared onstage with her numerous times over the years. Her candidacy was made public in late August 1924, making her one of twenty-seven women, representing all political parties, who would stand for seats across the country.

The newspapers gave her little chance – she was a socialist in a Conservative constituency – and the local coverage of her announcement was brief, almost dismissive. It attracted generous coverage in Australia, though, and some interest in American papers because of her colourful past and her recent visit. 'She is an emotional speaker and scarcely in the colloquial unpretentious House of Commons style, but the Labourites expect her campaign to attract attention,' the *Evening News* in Pennsylvania offered.

There was one exception in England. The *Observer* published a glowing tribute to her work over the years, under the heading 'A Distinguished Women's Leader', beginning with her role as a suffrage agitator:

Though not a member of the extreme militant party, she
was prepared if needs be to suffer for her convictions and to
sacrifice all things for the cause. Northing daunted her; the
injustice inflicted on her fellow women by the withholding of
the parliamentary vote, and the consequent neglect by each
succeeding government of their interests and those of their
children burnt into her soul and she never rested until victory
was won.

It went on to discuss her other passions: 'Many other interests
come into her life: welfare work, penal reform, internationalism
and peace. All these she advocates with forceful and persuasive
arguments and, moreover, with a clarity of vision which is at once
arresting and convincing.'[5]

Muriel wasn't disputing the fact that she had little chance of
winning the seat, at least not privately: 'It's a forlorn hope, but I rather
like hopeless situations,' she told an old Adelaide friend. 'I have been
in many, as you know, the suffrage and the like, and laughed to see
the cause win through at long last. An election campaign provides
the most fruitful field for propaganda. It is the only time men will
consent to be educated. Other meetings attract only the converted.'

She was just as keen to tell her friend, a Mrs Wholohan, about
her work since returning to England:

Back again and committed to more strenuous work than ever.
America was wonderful but I could have knelt down and
kissed the soil of England on my return.

We have been concentrating on the housing question, and
have succeeded in bringing off the first International Congress
of Women on Housing. Lady Aberdeen presided and I opened
the congress – July 16, 17 and 18 – with a bold speech on

'The Duty of the State'. We also had a public demonstration at the Queen's Hall at which other speakers were Lady Astor, Miss Margaret Bondfield [a future Cabinet minister], Mrs Wintringham [the second woman after Lady Astor to take up a parliamentary seat] and Mrs Pethick-Lawrence.

She had also rediscovered her enjoyment of agitation, revealing that she had made a typically vocal protest at a meeting in Drury Lane at which Neville Chamberlain, the Cabinet minister and future prime minister, addressed hundreds of women.

He exhorted them to 'keep the home fires burning'. I stood up in the front row of the dress circle and exclaimed: 'Give us the homes first to burn them in'. All the commissionaires in the huge theatre surrounded me and threatened my ejection, but I held my own.

Then I rushed off to Leicester where I helped support Frederick Pethick-Lawrence against the arch-militarist Winston Churchill, who was defeated by 4000 votes.

After attending a congress in Scotland – the only woman among some hundreds of men, mainly local – I decided to stump the country and finished up consenting to stand for Labour at Hastings – this after refusing in the past to stand for three 'safe' seats.

Muriel's brother Len was on his way to England and would help her with the campaign, and William would take time away from his dental practice:

My brother Len and my husband are keen on my candidature. The former will be my agent and the latter will look on and approve quietly.

Many of my old suffrage friends will rally to my
assistance, but we shall lose the seat. Not that that will
depress me. The good work will go on. My opponent is
the House of Northumberland – England's most feudal
dukedom. However, I like a fight and am not to be put down
by the insolent attitude of Lord Eustace Percy, who tells the
women that all they need do is plant hollyhocks outside their
insanitary dwellings. So shall I come out with the slogan
Hollyhocks or Homes? Personally I love hollyhocks; they are so
gay but we need homes first.

Above everything else, I want a fair deal for the woman in
the home. I want modern lighting and heating and appliances
for her. But how can she do her job with weapons as
antiquated as those of the stone age and in the surroundings
as innocent of sanitation as then?

Your heart would ache if you could see the wretched
tenement rooms – two, often only one, for the whole family.
Not even the semblance of ordinary decency. Is it a wonder
that there is drunkenness and vice? So my theme is and ever
will be 'Home and Mother'.[6]

Her last comment was another illustration of her personal regret
about motherhood.

* * *

Lord Eustace Percy, the first (and last) Baron Percy of Newcastle,
represented everything that Muriel detested in British society.
A son of the Duke of Northumberland, Lord Percy was a man
born to privilege. He had been elected comfortably to the seat of
Hastings in 1921 after a career in the diplomatic service and had

been returned twice already, in 1922 and 1923, amid the flurry of elections caused by post-war political instability.

To make matters worse, he had opposed her personal causes, moving against a motion in the Commons to extend voting to men and women at the age of twenty-one and voting against a housing bill that would erect more than 500,000 homes for low-paid workers at minimal rents, insisting it was a 'rotten' idea. Muriel's disdain for his arrogance was borne out when the election campaign proper began in October. Such was his confidence that Lord Percy announced only five public appearances, adding that he would be away from the electorate for much of the campaign which, he said, boiled down to a choice between the stability of a Conservative government and the Bolshevik-loving 'wild men' of Labour.

In his last speech before leaving town, Lord Percy warned of a 'gloves off' fight. Although not mentioning her by name, he said of Muriel: 'She is a wily socialist canvasser who calls and makes alluring promises as to what condition of affairs will be in this country if only a socialist government is returned to power. Already we have been informed of several cases in Hastings where this shameful attempt to mislead housewives has been made.'[7]

Muriel couldn't care less. With her opponent gone and her brother and husband due in town any day, she was in her element – on the stage delivering a message that was passionate and articulate. 'I am no politician,' she declared at a rally by the seashore, saying it gave her licence to speak her mind, adding that she wanted to be known henceforth as Muriel Porter, or 'MP'.[8]

She was wary of making political promises because it was impossible for her, as an individual, to guarantee they would be kept. Neither would she be bound by party loyalties, she told one meeting: 'I do not claim for my party any monopoly of truth. We should be able to free ourselves from party bias and develop as detached an attitude as possible towards current issues.'[9]

'I have made it clear that I am no mere cipher on the division list, but if I go into the House it is to urge and vote upon issues the furtherance of which is more to me than party,' she told *The Vote*, the magazine of the Women's Freedom League, which acknowledged its former champion.

When pushed, Muriel identified good housing and a decent rail network as priorities for the electorate on a practical level, but insisted that the broader principles of government were more important, like the distribution of wealth: 'Everything has been in the hands of a selected few,' she railed. 'I believe in the workers' movement because it enriches people. From early infancy children must have a chance they are not getting now. The housing bill is a gesture to the class who have never been provided for, but left to live in filth and dilapidated houses. The bill might cost money but the people with a heritage of good living are those who should pay for it. It is not the fittest in the physical or intellectual but in the spiritual sense who can survive in the end.'

As the weeks went on the crowds continued to come to listen to the 'Little Blue Lady', as she became known while door-knocking the city in her blue coat and hat as the autumn cold set in. She was refreshingly different, a would-be MP who would much rather talk about the philosophy of life and how political leadership could make a difference. The *Observer* watched in amused admiration:

> Small though the chances of a Labour candidate in Hastings may be, Mrs Muriel Matters-Porter and her supporters will lose no votes for lack of energetic campaigning. Meetings have been held every night this week and large audiences have been addressed by the candidate, whose charm of manner captivates

even those who are a little bewildered by her visionary and idealistic political philosophy. Her wide experience of other lands, her experience in the feminist movement and in education, and her reminiscences of famous men and women attract many who would be the last to support the Labour Party.[10]

Len had arrived in Hastings and settled into the party rooms in the middle of the town. He had the same adventurous spirit as his older sister, only he expressed it through journalism rather than activism. He'd travelled through Japan and Russia on his way to England and had just finished an article on Argentinean farmers and their fight against locusts. For the moment, though, Muriel was his priority, and he was bothered by some of the 'gross and utterly unwarranted attacks on my sister'.

Len was responding to a letter campaign that had begun against Muriel, accusing her wrongly of being involved in acts of violence in the suffrage movement, and tagging her socialism as bordering on communism. He was also angry that the *Observer* would print what he regarded as libellous and anonymous letters.

Muriel was, as usual, quite capable of defending herself, firing back at one accuser, who'd hidden behind the pseudonym 'Anti-Socialist':

I was never a member of any group responsible for acts of violence. You may or may not agree with socialism, but it cannot be denied that it is, fundamentally, an attempt to apply the principles of Christianity to public life ... Who is it that is obscuring a clear issue by filling the minds of working people with lies? Clearly they all come from a group of wealthy people who believe that the present method of life by which

they live at the top in wealth and comfort while millions live
substantially under their rule in misery and poverty is the
best method. History and modern knowledge show they are
mistaken – there are other better ways, for which I stand.[11]

* * *

The election ended predictably, but without regret. A nationwide
tide against Labour's unstable coalition and fears over the party's
'Red' ties swept MacDonald from no.10 and ensured Muriel would
be beaten comfortably by Lord Percy who would hold the seat for
another thirteen years. Labour would not win Hastings until 1997.

Undaunted by the experience, Muriel resumed her campaigning
soon afterwards. 'Our Muriel', as she was sometimes introduced,
had become a permanent fixture of the Labour Party in southern
England and seemed destined to stand in the 1929 election – the
first in which women had the same voting rights as men – but
withdrew from the ballot before campaigning got under way.

She had turned fifty by then and was no longer interested in the
rigours of a political career, preferring instead to join a peace march
in London, to stand with the novelist Thomas Hardy against blood
sports, to speak out against vivisection and to continue to fight for
better housing conditions for women and their children.

Feminism remained a great and enduring passion, as did
children's education. 'No civilisation has yet revealed the rhythm
of woman,' she told a feminist conference in 1926. 'Every time the
world has been faced by crisis they find the women falling into the
masculine rhythm and flocking to the banner of man. Woman has
not found her own rhythm ... Men like to pose as sturdy oaks and
look upon women as the clinging ivy, but some of the oaks appear to
be tottering on their trunks and only the ivy keeps them in place.'[12]

In 1928 she attended a gathering in London to celebrate the voting enfranchisement legislation which finally gave women electoral equality with men, one of forty leading suffragists and suffragettes, among them Sylvia and Christabel Pankhurst, Millicent Fawcett and Teresa Billington-Greig.

The same year, William Porter, now aged fifty-seven, sold out of his business partnership and the couple moved out of the city to live in the village of Hazlemere in Buckinghamshire. By the 1930s Muriel had also begun to withdraw from public life, making the odd appearance and delivering speeches when early education was an issue, and always eager to point out the evils of hunting. She wrote the occasional, typically spirited letter to the editor, ranging from praise of libraries to an expression of hope that disarmament might lead to a harmonious, united world.

Every few years there would be an anniversary celebrating the achievements of the suffrage movement. In 1939, for example, Muriel was interviewed by BBC Radio on the thirtieth anniversary of her audacious flight over London's rooftops. The interview was recorded and her voice is clear and rich as she responds to the journalist asking if her stunt was daring.

'Daring? Yes, well I suppose it was daring as one looks back from the point of view of age and perhaps wisdom, but at the time I didn't stop to think of what a risky venture it was. I was young and the experiences of the suffragettes soon taught one to be tough,' she answered.

'Sometimes the chances of success for our cause seemed very small but we went on ... the flight achieved all we wanted. It got our movement a great deal of publicity, as you can imagine, for in those days the sight of an airship was enough to make people run for miles.'[13]

31.

OLIVER

On an early winter's evening in 1947 the film director Anthony Asquith hosted a genteel party of theatre and film types at a grand house in Cadogan Square, Knightsbridge, on the privileged western fringe of London.

Among the guests was Oliver Waldren, a 26-year-old fighter pilot fresh from the war. Now out of uniform, he was a budding BBC radio journalist and amateur actor who relished the company, conversation and creative energy of such occasions.

Decades later he could recall the room and the crowd of mainly young lively and eager people, the tinkle of laughter, the clink of crystal. He could sense the mood of the city, struggling to emerge from the pall of war, still under the yoke of rationing but taking its first tentative steps toward a brighter future.

Clutching his favoured glass of red wine, the young man circled the cavernous room, an ode to splendor from its grand chandelier to its stern family portraits, looking for someone different and interesting to meet, to strike up new acquaintanceships and exchange ideas.

Finally he spied his host, a man whom until recently he had only known by sight and reputation. They had struck up a pleasant conversation at another function a few weeks earlier; hence Oliver's invitation on this evening. Asquith was the son of a former prime minister, Herbert Asquith, whose family owned the great house through which he was wandering.

Asquith junior, or Puffin as he was called rather unkindly by his mother because of his sharp features, was a film director known not just for his movies but his eccentric dress. He had confided in Oliver that his chosen career was an attempt to flee the stuffiness of his family. Asquith was aged in his mid forties and was already celebrated for movies such as the film adaptation of the George Bernard Shaw play *Pygmalion* and the wartime drama *The Way to the Stars* among others, and would soon embark on possibly his most famous movie, *The Importance of Being Earnest*.

In spite of his imposing presence, it was clear that Asquith was not in command of the conversation in which he was engaged. As harmless as the mature woman guest appeared, demure alongside the evening glamour of the younger females in the room, she had cornered the host and backed him up against the great fireplace.

Oliver couldn't hear what was being said above the chatter of the room but her manner and Asquith's eyes pleading that he, Oliver, intervene were enough to confirm that a man used to being in charge was at the end of a tongue-lashing – 'a right belting', as Asquith would later tell Oliver, without further elaboration.

Intrigued, Oliver approached the pair and stood to one side, close enough for Asquith to grasp the opportunity and turn toward the interloper, breaking the magnetic hold of the woman who was clearly unhappy, her blue-grey eyes flashing as they locked on the young man. Asquith made his excuses and withdrew to mingle with his other guests, relief etched on his face. Oliver was left to face the consequences of his audacity alone.

'She was not happy that I had intervened and let her prey get away,' he chuckled. 'I thought at that moment that I had done

my dash with this lady.' But rather than flee like the man he had
rescued, Oliver stayed. He had found someone new and interesting.

Her name was Muriel Matters-Porter, an alluring figure whose
character dwarfed most of the others in the room. It was difficult
to assess her age, although Oliver would have scoffed if he'd been
told that she had just turned seventy. She spoke with an eagerness
he could still sense years later: 'There was something about her
that made me want to stay and talk. It was her spark, I think; you
could see it in her eyes – a mind open and alive. Her age was made
irrelevant by her attitude.'

The pair chatted about education and politics, as best as he could
remember. Her political views were very much of the left, verging
on socialism, he guessed, and yet her intellect was supple enough
for her to listen with interest when he digressed at one point to raise
his theories about the lost city of Atlantis.

He could sense there was more to Muriel than she was prepared
to reveal, but she was happy to keep the focus on him and keen
to hear of his ideas, dreams and fears. It was as if she lived in the
present, and that what had come before was irrelevant. All that
seemed to matter to her was the conversation in hand. And the
future.[1]

* * *

The chance meeting had left an indelible mark on the psyche of
a young man who was struggling with his own sense of identity.
Like Asquith, with whom he would enjoy a close friendship, Oliver
had grown up cowed by an overbearing father who eventually left
his mother for a younger woman, a navy man who commanded a
destroyer in the Great War and was disappointed when his only son
chose not to follow in his footsteps.

Instead, Oliver tried to carve a career as a broadcaster with the BBC before the war intervened. With the conflict finally over he had rejoined the corporation but, like many young men who had witnessed the worst of humanity, was finding it difficult to settle into normal life.

The culture of the BBC seemed to have been changed by war, somehow less tolerant and prescriptive. He loved the idea of writing and broadcasting but the atmosphere was claustrophobic. In the months before the Asquith party he had quit and found a job driving expensive cars – Bentleys and Aston Martins – from the factories to their new, wealthy owners. It was fun but he knew it wouldn't last.

Around the time he met Muriel, Oliver was considering striking out on his own, to travel and write for a living. Their discussion that night at the Asquith's and her interest in his dreams would help give him the confidence to chase them, and he would spend much of the next two decades travelling through India and the Middle East. Perhaps that was why he could recall the details so vividly.

Oliver had not expected to see Muriel again but fate conjured another meeting, this time at the country home of a feisty businesswoman named Mabel Wilson. 'Willo' was a 45-year-old Irish spinster and teacher who ran a preparatory school from her red Georgian home in Great Missenden Buckinghamshire, outside London. The school, one of several she would manage over the years, was especially popular among actors, producers and diplomats as a place to send their children. But on weekends, when the children went home, Willo opened the building up to friends seeking a quiet escape from city life.

Oliver had met Willo while on leave during the war and they had stayed in contact. A few weeks after the Asquith party, Oliver accepted an invitation from her to stay at Great Missenden for the weekend, arriving late on the Friday night. The following morning, he went downstairs to greet his hostess only to find her deep in conversation with Muriel – the woman from the party – who happened to live nearby and also had a connection with Willo through their joint interest in education. The weekend cemented the friendship between Oliver and the two matronly women, mother figures to whom he gravitated over the next two decades when not travelling.[2]

32.

A WINDOW BY THE SEA

For as long as anyone can remember Hastings has been a place of neglected promise, the site of a battle that defined the course of British history and embedded its modern culture, yet a community whose citizens have long complained about being ignored by London politicians and where inattention has allowed decay to spread its sordid hand.

Pelham Crescent, the town's best-known street, stands as testament to its rise and fall, a curve of residential splendour constructed in the early years of the nineteenth century and designed, as one observer noted, to face the spectacle of the sea like a theatre balcony.

The crescent was the vision of the Earl of Chichester, Sir Thomas Pelham, whose family had owned the old Norman castle at the top of the cliff for more than four hundred years. The town's fortunes had surged in the wake of the Napoleonic Wars. The population trebled as it became a popular seaside resort, prompting the earl to include in the design of the crescent a glass-fronted shopping arcade, inspired by Trajan's Markets in Rome, the world's oldest shopping mall.

Above the arcade, linked by a ramp, stands a row of fourteen four-storey houses with commanding views across the English

Channel, but it is the centrepiece – a church – which is most striking. St Mary in the Castle was built in the middle of the arc, its yawning entrance of pillars set against the towering cliffs. It is strangely, although probably unintentionally, reminiscent of the rock architecture of Petra in Jordan.

St Mary's was designed to embrace a large congregation with seating for 1500 worshippers in a horseshoe-shaped theatre. Such was its impact that it became a dominant place of worship in Hastings for the next century; in it the wealthy paid for the best seats and others queued for the benches behind them.

But fortunes changed and the population began to retreat from the seafront and the town's boundaries spread into the hills behind. Services at St Mary's became fewer as the congregation thinned, the church began sharing its clergy with others in the town centre and eventually ceased altogether. But the splendid building remained, forgotten much like the woman next door who, in her heyday, was a figure of admiration and infamy in equal measure with a congregation of loyal followers.

In late 1949 Muriel Matters-Porter, now aged seventy-two, moved into no.7 Pelham Crescent, which hugs the right-hand side of the church when viewed from the beach. By then the buildings had started to tire and fade, much like Muriel's own existence. Although she remained a notable local, sometimes invited to present trophies at schools, her real fame had ended long before and life had begun its inevitable descent.

She had lived on the Hastings beachfront before, moving into no.6 Beach Terrace, at the foot of Pelham Crescent, during the 1924 election campaign. She and William had lived there until 1928 when the council bought the street to resurrect the storm-damaged seafront. Beach Terrace was now a car park.

Complicating the move was the recent death of William who had passed away from pneumonia in a hospital in the neighbouring town of St Leonards-on-Sea. Theirs had been a marriage of mystery, a union that to Muriel's obvious regret never produced children but had, nonetheless, lasted thirty-five years. Unlike his wife, William Porter had lived life without any public fanfare. His dental business had been dissolved in 1928 and the couple had shifted to a house in the town of Hazlemere, halfway between London and Oxford. Probate records would show that he left his modest assets – valued at £2,726 pounds 19 shillings and 5 pence, worth around £100,000 in today's terms – to his wife, who would continue to use her married name after his death.

A clue to the strange but loyal relationship is contained in two letters penned by Muriel, the first in 1956 to Clarice Hatherleigh, wife of her cousin Frank who had just passed away. Muriel was glad that Clarice had her two sons to dull the loss of Frank. She knew how it felt: 'Bill and my brother Leonard, both so very dear, went – and I was left – but my mind realises well that life at this level is only possible when our container is sufficient unto the day ... So on you go.'[1]

She wished she could see Clarice one last time – 'Australia is never far from my heart' – but it did not seem possible: 'I am becoming very aware of a thinning of the veil ... The subtle, other realms of consciousness are very near.'

There was clearly great sadness behind her missive. All but one of her siblings and their spouses had gone, even Len, the closest, who had died in 1951 having entered parliament himself as the member for Kennington, the electorate encompassing the old Lambeth slums. He served two years but would be best remembered for writing the first full-length book on Jack the Ripper, in which he identified a mysterious 'Dr Stanley', who had fled to Argentina, as the murderer. The theory was later discredited, although it inspired a play and a movie.

Muriel felt alone now, at least in terms of those from her past. The three great figureheads of the suffrage movement were long dead: Emmeline Pankhurst in 1928, Millicent Fawcett the following year and Charlotte Despard in 1939 at the age of ninety-five. Most of her contemporaries had also gone: Vida Goldstein in 1949, Miles Franklin and Emmeline Pethick-Lawrence in 1954 and she would also outlive Christabel and Sylvia Pankhurst and Teresa Billington-Greig. She was left clinging to memories in a town that had accepted, rejected, embraced and then largely forgotten her; she realised that there would soon be an end to the adventure of life – a 'vivid jaunt' and 'gay-glad days'.

Muriel was more buoyant three years later when she wrote again to Clarice in the last days of a glorious summer, with the sun streaming through her bay-front window: 'Am on my divan gazing at the sixty-mile horizon facing my rooms (Alas! No room to entertain boyfriends!!)', she began, now aged eighty-two and lamenting the fact that she wasn't with friends that day. 'It's a lovely summer day so doubtless they are all capering in their "Greek"-style dresses on the big lawn under beech trees and surrounded by evergreen bushes and roses.'

There were also events planned in London for the late summer to which she had been invited: 'Alas! Hastings is sixty miles from the capital – distance and fares eat time and money – we shall see.'

Her musings then drifted to the esoteric, and she voiced her frustration that 'the masculine principle' was still driving life at the expense of women: 'So pray for the operative maternalistic-centripetalism to hold the centre. Yeats, who was very perceptive, said (I knew him long ago) the centre falls apart. That is, alas, too true.'

She was watching life change about her, 'new forms' being shaped and institutions evolving, and in the midst of transformation she couldn't help but look back: 'At times I see too clearly. It is an ache, distressing to head, heart, eye of the mind. I miss Bill and Len. They knew I was "queer" but let it be! Am aware of them often.'[2]

Was Muriel admitting that she was gay, a lesbian who had struggled with identity all her life, admired by men and chased by them, and unable to declare her true feelings because of the expectations of society and the desire to be a mother? Had she loved Violet Tillard passionately but married William Porter, and lost the love of her life in the process? Had she and Tillie parted badly in Dublin, encouraging her to seek love elsewhere?

The words could certainly be interpreted that way, the word used widely to describe homosexual relationships since the late nineteenth century, although it seemed strange that she would suddenly reveal herself at the bottom of a letter to a distant relative. Niece Jocelyn thinks not, her aunt a strong-willed woman who would have been refused to be cowed by convention and been unafraid to follow her heart if that were true.

Maybe she was using the word 'queer' to describe something different, perhaps in the sense that she was idiosyncratic in her pursuit of social causes, and that her husband and brother had patiently accepted her zealousness over the years.

For a woman of such profound and clearly stated opinions, she would remain an enigma.

* * *

April, 2015

The spring sunshine, still low and angled in the sky, is shining through the bay windows of Muriel's old home. She would have looked out each morning to judge what time to make her daily tiptoe across the pebbled beach to swim in the ice-cold waters, a reminder of her homeland on the opposite side of the world.

Like many people alone in their old age Muriel had thrived on ritual; a morning walk to the town library to read the newspapers and afternoons visiting friends or writing – by hand, never typewriter – from a table beside the window, watching the muted blue of the Channel turn grey and then black as the sun faded and winds stirred.

Then there was Oliver Waldren. In 1960, finding city life in London claustrophobic, he accepted an invitation from Willo to visit her in Hastings where, following Muriel's lead, she had bought a large house which she was running partly as a school and also as a bed and breakfast. Would he like to rent a room? Yes, he would. The friendship between the trio had been rekindled.

Oliver was one of the few who visited Muriel in these rooms during her final years. And he was here again, forty-five years after her death and now a spritely ninety-three years old, to talk about their friendship which spanned the last two decades of her rich life.

The interview is with Frances Bedford, a long-serving politician and member of the South Australian Parliament's ruling Labor Party who had stumbled onto Muriel's story several years before, condensed into a handful of sentences in a research monologue on the involvement of Australian women in the Women's Suffrage Coronation Procession in 1911 that hinted at an intriguing life fallen through the cracks of history.

The desire to know more about the woman mentioned in the document had become something of an obsession. Documents piled up in Frances' office: newspaper clippings, photographs, maps, books, land titles, death certificates – all filed diligently, lovingly in fact, as the story grew and a heroine began to emerge. Helpers were sought, admirers found and the Muriel Matters Society formed. Frances even had a costume made to replicate the modest dress and hat she wore on the caravan tour of 1908.

But it wasn't enough. Surely there was someone alive who knew Muriel, even fleetingly. That's why she was here in this room. The discovery of this delightful old man, eager to please and thankful to still be relevant, was heartening. It had been a mixture of luck and diligence on the part of her stalwart group of enthusiasts and now he sat, ready to tell his story and, hopefully, shed more light on the life of the woman they sought to understand.

Muriel had lived here for twenty years with her cats and her books and her writing; thoughts, letters, theories, passions. It wasn't hard to imagine walls lined with crammed bookshelves and piles of papers stacked against the walls in ordered chaos. There were simple furnishings – a couch and a desk and chair, from Oliver's memory – for someone comfortable in spare surroundings, curtains pulled back and open to the sounds and smells of the ocean below.

It was all gone now, swept away by an anonymous hand and dumped without care or thought in the days after her death, the brazen energy and deeds of her youth forgotten by a world that somehow passed her by. The room was empty, a first-floor space for community meetings, washed cream and stripped of its past other than a blue plaque glued to the front wall of the house – *Muriel Matters-Porter, Adelaide-born activist. First woman to 'speak' in the House of Commons. Lived here 1949-1969* – a minor triumph of recognition organised by Frances on a previous visit.

Muriel had never lived in the past, Oliver insisted. If she was proud of her achievements, he never knew because they weren't mentioned. Even when another friend whispered of her past adventures he thought it intrusive to ask because what mattered to her were the present and the future.

He would often drive her home after she had spent the day with Willo. Sometimes Muriel would burst into song, usually an aria from an opera like Richard Strauss' *Salome* or *Ariadne auf Naxos*: 'She was very good. I assumed that her reason for leaving Australia was to come and sing opera in London.'

But most of the time they just talked. She was forever quoting the thirteenth-century Dominican friar Thomas Aquinas, a scholar, philosopher, theologian and jurist, but was equally happy delving into some of Oliver's pet subjects like shamanism and the lives of the Polynesians and Micronesians. Muriel's brain fizzed with interest and energy.[3]

She fell ill in October 1969 and was taken to a nursing home high on the hill behind St Leonards-on-Sea where she spent her ninety-second birthday on November 12. Five days later she died peacefully. Oliver didn't go to the funeral: 'I don't know why. I think I may have preferred to think of her as being alive.'

In the October 17, 1953, edition of the *Hastings & St Leonards Observer* Muriel Matters-Porter made one last plea for world peace. Prompted by a speech in parliament and the performances of her old nemesis, the prime minister Winston Churchill, she argued that Britain should use its renewed place in the world to strive for a Utopia of harmony. Her voice as a feminist and an orator rang clear in her soaring language:

> We see from this motherland (when a queen reigns) the
> greater scope; a whole humanity; one world, one people.
> 'Humanity is on the march again,' said Field Marshal Smuts.
> It is. Our instructive new song is 'Let's join the human race!'
> We answer the call of the maternal voice. Let's join the great
> army, not on king's horses (no trampling underfoot) but on
> foot we must go, the pilgrim way, universal.

We are being drawn together for this purpose – to go the organic way of life, in this time when the world is actually contracting to smaller dimensions. We are now girdled communicatively, enabling us to whisper our will to unite. We are now communicants of the great global communion, all sharing at the table of life the loaf of the living presence.

We give thanks by means of our national voice that 'all the world be healed', one universal brotherhood under one father-mother-hood.

NOTES ON SOURCES AND ACKNOWLEDGMENTS

The challenge of reconstructing a 'lost history' – a life ignored or forgotten – is the reality that pieces of the jigsaw puzzle have been scattered over the years, many of them lost and the people who were there to witness that life are long gone. A work of historical fiction can fill in the gaps but the nature of non-fiction means the boundaries of the genre can only be stretched so far. Some details are impossible to retrieve, if they ever existed, and some questions cannot be answered. In the end, it is best for the reader to make their own judgments.

Such is the case with the life of Muriel Matters. The papers and books kept in her rooms overlooking the English Channel at Hastings appear to have been lost or destroyed after her death, such was the ignorance of their value and her contribution to society. All we have about Muriel from a personal nature is a handful of letters and notes and a few speeches.

Instead, I have relied largely on contemporary newspapers and suffrage publications to provide the backbone of a timeline as reporters and editors, clearly fascinated by Muriel's exploits, reported her activities from one end of the country to the other as well as her Australian tours and early stage appearances.

Because of journalistic customs of the day, I have, in some instances, carefully and accurately turned the third person reporting style back into direct speech, to capture the language and power of Muriel's voice. And at major events such as the Grille protest, I have reconstructed what I believe to be an accurate reflection of events by considering the many versions produced by newspapers in the days afterwards. Every journalist had a slightly different view of the protest, physically and politically, with some wildly inaccurate accounts.

Authors are fortunate that searching archival material has been made simpler because of online archives although these remain imperfect, dependent largely on print quality which enables words to be recognised. Chasing rabbits down holes doesn't begin to describe the task at times, and much of the work remains searching by hand, either paper or microfiche records. One of the joys of such research are the side tracks down which you can wander, often for days before reminding yourself of the task at hand.

My reference materials have included the records of the Women's Freedom League kept by the Women's Library at the London School of Economics and the seemingly endless resources of the British Library where, after much searching, I managed to find bound copies of the *Christian Commonwealth*, the paper for which Muriel worked as a journalist between 1911 and 1913.

I have referred to numerous books and websites covering aspects of the history of the suffrage movement including the autobiographies of Emmeline and Sylvia Pankhurst, and biographies of suffrage leaders such as Charlotte Despard and Teresa Billington-Greig among others, as well as the work of Claire Eustance and her history of the WFL *Dare to be Free*.

I acknowledge Jocelyn Davis, Muriel's niece who, although having never met her aunt, was invaluable with family snippets, as was the gentle and spirited Oliver Waldren, the only person we have found who knew Muriel. Their contributions helped to bring her alive.

I thank my family for their indulgence, particularly my wife Paola and daughter Allegra whose proud teenage feminism was the inspiration for me searching to find a 'lost' suffragette whose story hadn't been told. I am also indebted to friends who agreed to read the manuscript and help me weed out mistakes and imperfect wording, including Andrea Dixon, Sue Morgan and Tracy Peacock among others, and to thank my publishers, Harper Collins, for supporting the project, and the delightful staff headed by Jude McGee, Brigitta Doyle, Kate Mayes, Matt Howard and my probing editor Amanda O'Connell.

I would also like to acknowledge the generosity of my mentor Richard Walsh and the amazing enthusiasm and care of Clare Drysdale, my British publisher who has been such a great support, not only with Muriel Matters but with also my previous two biographies on George Ingle-Finch and Sheila Chisholm. I am lucky to benefit not only from their professional skills but also to enjoy their friendship.

But most of all I would like to thank the irrepressible Frances Bedford MP who agreed to co-operate with the project and give me access to the collection of files in the back of her Adelaide electorate office. Frances has a dedicated team of enthusiasts who have also helped me and answered my questions, particularly Marie Maddocks. I hope the book adds something important to their society and ensure Muriel's amazing life and contribution are always remembered.

ENDNOTES

Chapter 1
1 Colonization Circular: Issues 1-19. January 1843.
2 www.theshipslist.com/ships/ Australia/seapark1852.shtml
3 *Dublin University Magazine*, 1839 (Volume 14).
4 www.sahistorians.org.au/175/ bm.doc/a-heritage-history-of-hindmarsh.doc
5 adelaidia.sa.gov.au/panoramas/ duryea-panorama
6 *Evening Journal*, December 14, 1880.
7 *South Australian Register*, March 15, 1886.
8 *Who's Who Australia*, 1935.
9 Woman's Suffrage League annual meeting, 1892.

Chapter 2
1 *South Australian Chronicle and Weekly Mail*, February 10, 1872.
2 *South Australian Register*, February 17, 1864.
3 Records of Frances Bedford MP.
4 Leonard Matters autobiography, 1932.
5 *The Express and Telegraph*, December 23, 1891.
6 *The Vote*, February 19, 1910. 'Concerning Muriel Matters'.
7 *The Courier*, December 26, 1863.
8 *The Star*, Ballarat, November 5, 1864.

9 Queen Victoria, letter to Sir Martin Theodore, Scottish poet, 1870.

Chapter 3
1 *Adelaide Observer*, December 22, 1894.
2 *Ibid.*
3 Letter to the Editor, *The Advertiser*, March 1, 1897.
4 An Autobiography, by Catherine Helen Spence, 1910.
5 *South Australian Register*, April 10, 1895.
6 Table Talk, Melbourne, June 23, 1910.
7 *Daily News*, Perth, April 1, 1910.
8 *Ibid.*
9 *The Register*, Adelaide, July 7, 1906.
10 *Following the Equator*, Chapter 19. Mark Twain, 1897.
11 *The Advertiser*, October 29, 1895.
12 The *South Australian Register*, October 30, 1895.
13 *The Express and Telegraph*, Adelaide, October 30, 1895.

Chapter 4
1 *Evening Journal*, Adelaide, November 30, 1897.
2 *The Express and Telegraph*, Adelaide, July 13, 1897.
3 *Evening Journal*, Adelaide, September 17, 1897.
4 *Quiz* and Lantern, Adelaide, April 9, 1896.

5   *Newcastle Morning Herald and Miners' Advocate*, May 1, 1896.
6   *Ibid.*
7   *South Australian Register, Adelaide Observer, Evening Journal*, April 23, 1896.
8   *The Australasian*, Melbourne, November 23, 1895.
9   *Sydney Morning Herald*, October 21, 1898.
10 *The Express and Telegraph*, Adelaide, October 24, 1898.
11 *Quiz and the Lantern*, Adelaide, September 7, 1899.
12 *The Advertiser*, Adelaide, September 5, 1899.
13 *Newcastle Morning Herald and Miners' Advocate*, May 22, 1895.
14 *The Bunyip*, South Australia, November 3, 1899.
15 *Ibid.*

Chapter 5
1   *Express and Telegraph*, Adelaide, April 12, 1900.
2   *Chronicle*, Adelaide, April 21, 1900.
3   *The Advertiser*, Adelaide, March 13, 1900.
4   *The Southern Sphere*, Melbourne, July 1, 1910.
5   *The Mercury*, Hobart, January 12, 1901.
6   *The Southern Sphere*, Melbourne, July 1, 1910.
7   *Quiz*, Adelaide, March 7, 1901.
8   *Quiz*, Adelaide, May 1, 1901.
9   *Critic*, Adelaide, March 15, 1902.
10 *Quiz*, Adelaide, May 30, 1901.
11 *Quiz*, Adelaide, April 4, 1901.
12 *The Register*, Adelaide, January 25, 1902.
13 *Critic*, Adelaide, March 2, 1901.

Chapter 6
1   *The Clarence and Richmond Examiner*, February 21, 1905.
2   *The Express and Telegraph*, Adelaide, August 30, 1902.

3   *Quiz*, Adelaide, May 23, 1901.
4   *The Register*, Adelaide, March 11, 1901.
5   *Quiz*, Adelaide, March 28, 1901.
6   *Critic*, Adelaide, March 16, 1901.
7   Records of Frances Bedford MP.
8   Interview with author.
9   Interview with Jocelyn Davis.
10 *The Register*, Adelaide, March 30, 1901.
11 *Daily News*, Perth, May 21, 1904.
12 *The West Australian*, May 23, 1904.
13 *Sunday Times*, Perth, May 28, 1905.
14 *The Southern Sphere*, Melbourne, July 1, 1910.

Chapter 7
1   *Gadfly*, Adelaide, April 16, 1906.
2   Letter, *Daily News*, November 9, 1905.
3   *Daily News*, Perth, November 30, 1905.
4   *Daily News*, Perth, November 6, 1906.
5   *Daily News*, Perth, April 4, 1907.
6   *The Age*, Melbourne, April 20, 1907.
7   *Daily News*, Perth, May 29, 1906.
8   My impressions as an agitator for social reform, by Muriel Matters, 1913.
9   *Weekly Times*, Melbourne, June 25, 1910.
10 My impressions as an agitator for social reform, by Muriel Matters, 1913.
11 *Weekly Times*, Melbourne, June 25, 1910.
12 My impressions as an agitator for social reform, by Muriel Matters, 1913.
13 *Daily Chronicle*, April 20, 1907.
14 My impressions as an agitator for social reform, by Muriel Matters, 1913.

Chapter 8
1   *Suffragette*, the autobiography of Emmeline Pankhurst, 1914.

2   *Ibid.*
3   *The Guardian*, October 16, 1905.
4   *Suffragette*, the autobiography of Emmeline Pankhurst, 1914.
5   *Ibid.*
6   *Ibid.*
7   *Charlotte Despard: A biography*, Margaret Mulvihill, 1989.
8   *The British Women's Suffrage Campaign 1866–1928*, by Harold L. Smith, 1998.
9   *Suffragette*, the autobiography of Emmeline Pankhurst, 1914.
10 *Literature of the Women's Suffrage Campaign in England*, edited by Carolyn Christensen Nelson, 2004.
11 *The Mercury*, October 26, 1907.
12 *The Suffragette Movement, an intimate account of persons and ideals*, Sylvia Pankhurst, 1931.

Chapter 9
1   *The Vote*, February 3, 1912.
2   *Manchester Courier and Lancashire General Advertiser*, November 25, 1907.
3   The Organ of the Women's Freedom League, 1915.
4   *The Observer*, Adelaide, January 11, 1908.
5   *The Gladfly*, Adelaide, January 2, 1908.
6   Concerning Muriel Matters, by Marion Holmes. *The Vote*, February 19, 1910.
7   *Women's Franchise*, March 19, 1908.
8   *Weekly Times*, Melbourne, June 25, 1910.
9   *Dundee Evening Telegraph*, April 9, 1908.
10 *Evening Post*, New Zealand, May 20, 1908.
11 *London Daily News*, April 10, 1908.
12 *Western Daily Press*, April 10, 1908.
13 *Manchester Courier and Lancashire General Advertiser*, April 23, 1908.
14 *Sheffield Evening Telegraph*, April 13, 1908.

Chapter 10
1   *The Age*, Melbourne, July 6, 1908.
2   *Manchester Courier and Lancashire General Advertiser*, April 22, 1908.
3   *Manchester Courier and Lancashire General Advertiser*, April 20, 1908.
4   *Manchester Courier and Lancashire General Advertiser*, April 24, 1908.
5   Votes for Women, WFL report, May 21, 1908.

Chapter 11
1   *Surrey Mirror*, May 19, 1908.
2   *Vanishing for the Vote: Suffrage, Citizenship and the battle for the Census*, By Jill Liddington, 2014.
3   *Women's Franchise*, June 4, 1908.
4   *Women's Franchise*, June 11, 1908.
5   *Ibid.*
6   *Women's Franchise*, June 18, 1908.
7   www.womanandhersphere.com. Suffrage stories: An army of banners.

Chapter 12
1   *Women's Franchise*, June 25, 1908.
2   *Ibid.*
3   *Sussex Agricultural Express*, July 18, 1908.
4   *The British–Australasian*, February 9, 1911.
5   *Bexhill-on-Sea Observer*, July 25, 1908.
6   *Women's Franchise*, July 23, 1908.
7   Violet Tillard unpublished obituary, by Muriel Matters, February 22, 1930.
8   *Kent & Sussex Courier*, July 3, 1908.
9   *Women's Franchise*, July 16, 1908.
10 *Bexhill-on-Sea Observer*, July 25, 1908.
11 *Ibid.*
12 *Eastbourne Gazette*, July 29, 1908.

Chapter 13
1   *Leamington Spa Courier*, July 31, 1908.
2   *Newcastle Herald*, Australia, May 1, 1891.

3   *The Times*, July 22, 1908.
4   *Truth*, Perth, August 15, 1908.
5   *Lichfield Mercury*, July 24, 1908.
6   *London Daily News*, September 2, 1908.

Chapter 14
1   *Sheffield Evening Telegraph*, January 17, 1908.
2   *Western Daily Press*, January 18, 1908.
3   *Ibid.*
4   www.parliament.uk/about/living-heritage/transformingsociety/electionsvoting/womenvote/overview/the-ladies-gallery
5   *The Non-violent Militant: Selected Writings of Teresa Billington-Greig*, Edited by Carol McPhee, Ann FitzGerald, 2001.
6   *London Daily News*, February 9, 1907.
7   *The Non-violent Militant: Selected Writings of Teresa Billington-Greig*, Edited by Carol McPhee, Ann FitzGerald,.
8   *Women's Franchise*, November 5, 1908.
9   *Essex Newsman*, October 10, 1908.
10   *The Suffragette Movement: An intimate account of persons and ideals*, by Sylvia Pankhurst, 1931.
11   *Gadfly*, 'Titbits from Aunt Tabitha', October 28, 1908.

Chapter 15
1   *Lancashire Evening Post*, December 7, 1908.
2   *Lancashire Evening Post*, October 29, 1908.
3   *The Evening Telegraph and Post*, Dundee, October 30, 1908.
4   *The Age*, December 16, 1908.
5   *Hansard*, House of Commons, October 28, 1908.
6   *Ibid.*
7   *The Age*, December 16, 1908.
8   *Ibid.*

9   *Ibid.*
10   *Ibid.*

Chapter 16
1   *Nottingham Evening Post*, October 29, 1908.
2   *Ibid.*
3   *Evening Journal*, Adelaide, June 14, 1910.
4   *Sheffield Evening Telegraph*, October 29, 1908.
5   *Evening Journal*, Adelaide, June 14, 1910.
6   Author interview with Jocelyn Davis.
7   *Illawarra Mercury*, March 19, 1909.
8   *Figaro*, Queensland, February 11, 1909.
9   *Western Mail*, Perth, November 7, 1908.
10   *The Register*, Adelaide, October 30, 1908.
11   *Yorkshire Evening Post*, November 14, 1908.

Chapter 17
1   *The Non-Violent Militant: Selected writings of Teresa Billington-Greig*, edited by Ann Fitzgerald and Carol McPhee, 2001.
2   *Hansard*, House of Commons,.
3   *Dundee Courier*, November 12, 1908.
4   *The West Australian*, Perth, November 7, 1908.
5   *Punch*, Melbourne, November 12, 1908.
6
7   *Truth*, Perth, January 23, 1909.
8   *Sheffield Independent*, December 7, 1908.
9   *Western Daily Press*, January 4, 1909.
10   *The Era*, March 27, 1909.
11   *Chelmsford Chronicle*, February 12, 1909.

Chapter 18
1   *Weekly Times*, June 25, 1910.
2   *Dundee Courier*, February 17, 1909.

3   *Hendon & Finchley Times*, February 19, 1909.
4   *Suffragettes: The Fight for Votes for Women*, by Joyce Marlow, 2000.
5   *Hendon & Finchley Times*, February 19, 1909.
6   *Dundee Courier*, February 17, 1909.
7   *Hull Daily*, February 17, 1909.

Chapter 19
1   *Suffragettes: The Fight for Votes for Women*, by Joyce Marlow, 2000.
2   *Derby Daily Telegraph*, February 18, 1909.
3   *Sevenoaks Chronicle and Kentish Advertiser*, March 12, 1909.
4   *Women's Franchise*, March, 1909.
5   *London Standard*, April 15, 1909.
6   *Leeds Mercury*, March 25, 1909.
7   *The Vote*, April 29, 1909.

Chapter 20
1   *Evening Express*, November 17, 1909.
2   *Evening Express*, Wales, October 20, 1909.
3   *The Cambrian*, August 6, 1909.
4   *Women's Franchise*, September 2, 1909.
5   *The Cardiff Times*, November 6, 1909.
6   *South Wales Weekly Advertiser*, August 20, 1909.
7   *The Cambrian*, August 6, 1909.
8   *The Cambrian*, September 3, 1909.
9   *ibid.*
10 *Evening Express*, September 2, 1909.
11 *Evening Express*, December 15, 1909.
12 *Evening Express*, August 25, 1909.
13 *Bendigo Independent*, August 26, 1909.
14 *The Herald*, Adelaide, October 2, 1909.
15 *The Advertiser*, Adelaide, March 4, 1910.
16 *Dublin Daily Express*, February 4, 1910.
17 *The Vote*, April 9, 1910.

Chapter 21
1   *The Vote*, October 1, 1910.
2   *Daily News*, Perth, May 17, 1910.
3   *Evening Journal*, Adelaide, June 14, 1910.
4   Author interview with Jocelyn Davis.
5   *The Vote*, October 1, 1910.
6   *The Advertiser*, Adelaide, June 6, 1910.
7   *Critic*, Adelaide, June 8, 1910.
8   *The Advertiser*, June 7, 1910.
9   *Daily Herald*, Adelaide, June 13, 1910.
10 *Daily Herald*, Adelaide, June 14, 1910.
11 *The Advertiser*, Adelaide, June 13, 1910.
12 *The Age*, Melbourne, June 20, 1910.
13 *The Advertiser*, June 13, 1910.
14 *Critic*, Adelaide, June 15, 1910.
15 *The Register*, June 13, 1910.
16 *The Mercury*, Hobart, September 5, 1910.
17
18 *The Vote*, October 15, 1910.
19 Table Talk, Melbourne, June 23, 1910.
20 *Punch*, Melbourne, June 23, 1910.
21 *Table Talk*, Melbourne, June 23, 1910.
22 *The Sunday Times*, Perth, August 10, 1910.
23 *The British–Australasian,* February 9, 1911.
24 *The Vote*, October 15, 1910.
25 *Hansard*, Australian Federal Parliament, 1910.

Chapter 22
1   *London Daily News*, January 11, 1911.
2   *The Vote*, January 28, 1911.
3   *Weekly Times*, Melbourne, January 27, 1912.
4   *The British–Australasian*, February 11, 1911.

5   *The Christian Commonwealth*, April 26, 1911 June 28, 1911.

6

7   *The Christian Commonwealth*, April 26, 1911.

8   *The Christian Commonwealth*, June 7, 1911.

9   *The Christian Commonwealth*, March 27, 1911.

10 *The Christian Commonwealth*, April 26, 1911.

11 *The Sun*, Kalgoorlie, April 30, 1911.

12 *The Sun*, Kalgoorlie, June 4, 1911.

13 Records of Frances Bedford MP.

Chapter 23

1   *Weekly Times*, Melbourne, January 27, 1912.

2   *Express and Telegraph*, June 22, 1912.

3   *Lichfield Mercury*, May 3, 1912.

4   *Bucks Herald*, May 25, 1912.

5   *Sunday Times*, Perth, August 25, 1912.

6   *Sunday Times*, Perth, May 25, 1910.

Chapter 24

1   *Australasians Who Count in London*, by Mrs Leonard Matters, 1913.

2   *Northampton Mercury*, February 28, 1913.

3   *Falkirk Herald*, June 21, 1913.

4   *Whitstable Times and Herne Bay Herald*, July 12, 1913.

5   *Western Times*, July 28, 1913.

6   *Dundee Courier*, July 28, 1913.

7   *Yorkshire Post*, January 28, 1913.

8   *Dundee Evening Telegraph*, April 2, 1913.

9   www.spartacus-educational.com/WpankhurstA.htm

10 *The Suffragette Movement: An intimate account of persons and ideals*, by Sylvia Pankhurst, 1931.

11 *Women's Dreadnought*, March 8, 1914.

Chapter 25

1   *The Sun*, Kalgoorlie, September 21, 1913.

2   Various records Ancestry.co.uk.

3   Records held by Frances Bedford MP.

4   *The Vote*, March 5, 1910.

5   *Daily News*, Perth, December 9, 1913.

6   *Daily News*, Perth, December 13, 1913.

7   *Daily Herald*, January 16, 1914.

8   *Surrey Mirror*, January 30, 1914.

9   *The Southern Sphere*, July 1, 1910.

10 *Western Times*, April 4, 1914.

11 *Hastings and St Leonards Observer*, February 7, 1914.

12 *Chester Chronicle*, March 7, 1914.

13 Berwickshire News and General Advertiser, March 17, 1914.

14 *Yorkshire Post* and *Leeds Intelligencer*, July 21, 1914.

15 *Bedfordshire Times and Independent*, May 15, 1914.

Chapter 26

1   *Critic*, Adelaide, November 18, 1914.

2   www.lieder.net/lieder/get_text.html?TextId=34664

3   *Grantham Journal*, August 15, 1914.

4   www.spartacus-educational.com/Wfirst.htm

5   *Surrey Mirror*, February 2, 1915.

6   The Woman Voter, Melbourne, July 1, 1915.

7   Records of Frances Bedford MP.

Chapter 27

1   *Coventry Herald*, December 3, 1915.

2   Individual work: Montessori and English Education Policy 1909–1939. Published 1994.

3   *Yorkshire Post*, June 22, 1914.

4   *A Gregarious Culture: Topical Writings of Miles Franklin*, edited by Jill Roe and Margaret Bettison. 2001.

Chapter 28

1   Files of Frances Bedford MP.

2   *Michael Collins Own Story,* by Hayden Talbot. 1923.

3   *The Suffragette Movement – an intimate account of persons and ideals, by Sylvia Pankhurst.* 1931.
4   *Hansard,* House of Commons, August 14, 1916.
5   *The Suffragette Movement – an intimate account of persons and ideals, by Sylvia Pankhurst.* 1931.
6   *Women's Dreadnought,* March 24, 1917.
7   Woman Voter, Melbourne, June 28, 1917.
8   *Hansard,* House of Commons, March 28, 1917.
9   *Ibid.*

Chapter 29
1   *The Scotsman,* August 16, 1917.
2   *Dundee Courier,* April 21, 1920.
3   Author interview with Jocelyn Davis.
4   *The West Australian,* July 4, 1922.
5   *Sunday Times,* Sydney, September 22, 1922.
6   *Daily News,* Perth, June 10, 1922.
7   *Daily News,* Perth, July 29, 1922.
8   Author interview with Jocelyn Davis.
9   *Women Humanitarians: A Biographical Dictionary of British Women Active between 1900 and 1950,* by Sybil Oldfield. 2001.
10 *The Military Writings of Leon Trotsky,* Volume 4: 1921-1923. 1969.
11 Violet Tillard unpublished obituary, by Muriel Matters, February 22, 1930.

Chapter 30
1   *Hastings and St Leonards Observer,* November 24, 1923.
2   *Hastings and St Leonards Observer,* December 1, 1923.
3   *Hastings and St Leonards Observer,* December 7, 1923.
4   *Dundee Courier,* June 3, 1924.
5   *Hastings and St Leonards Observer,* August 23, 1924.
6   *News,* Adelaide, October 21, 1924.
7   *Hastings and St Leonards Observer,* October 18, 1924.
8   *Ibid.*
9   *Hastings and St Leonards Observer,* October 20, 1924.
10 *Hastings and St Leonards Observer,* October 18, 1924.
11 *Hastings and St Leonards Observer,* November 8, 1924.
12 *Hastings and St Leonards Observer,* April 3, 1926.
13 www.bbc.co.uk/archive/suffragettes/8315.shtml

Chapter 31
1   Oliver Waldren interview with Frances Bedford MP, April, 2015.
2   Oliver Waldren interview with Author, July 2015.

Chapter 32
1   Muriel letter to Clarice Hatherleigh, April 24, 1956.
2   Muriel letter to Clarice Hatherleigh, August 16, 1959.
3   Oliver Waldren interview with Author, July 2015.

INDEX